Population and Labour Market Policies in China's Reform Process

This book investigates the population and labour management reforms implemented since the reform and opening-up of China in the early 1980s, giving insights into the economic and social implications of these reforms and future prospects for population governance.

The study examines three major components of China's population management strategy in terms of its history and implementation: the household registration (Hukou) system, family planning policy and the labour market system. Grounded in both qualitative and quantitative analysis, key metrics are introduced to better understand the Hukou system on the one hand while exploring the socio-economic issues arising from the policy, including the economic behaviour or residents, fertility, care of older people, entrepreneurship, institutional premiums and gender wage differentials. Based on these investigations, the author advances constructive suggestions to inform policymaking, aiming to deepen market-oriented reform of the economic system and improve social welfare in China.

The title will be a good reference for academics, students and policymakers interested in social policy, labour economics and, especially, China's population and labour policy and Chinese economy and society.

Sun Wenkai is Professor in the School of Economics at Renmin University of China and Associate Dean of the National Institute of Small and Medium-sized Enterprises (SME) at Renmin University of China. His main research areas include labour economics, development economics and SME development in China.

China Perspectives

The *China Perspectives* series focuses on translating and publishing works by leading Chinese scholars, writing about both global topics and China-related themes. It covers Humanities & Social Sciences, Education, Media and Psychology, as well as many interdisciplinary themes.

This is the first time any of these books have been published in English for international readers. The series aims to put forward a Chinese perspective, give insights into cutting-edge academic thinking in China, and inspire researchers globally.

To submit proposals, please contact the Taylor & Francis Publisher for China Publishing Programme, Lian Sun (Lian.Sun@informa.com)

Titles in sociology currently include:

Aging in the Context of Urbanization
Social Determinants for the Depression of the Chinese Older Population
Fan Yang

Organizational Transformation and Order Reconstruction in 'Village-Turned-Communities'
WU Ying

The Many Roads to Becoming Modern
A History of Collectivism in Rural Jiangsu Province
CHEN Jiajian

International Comparative Perspectives on the Treatment of 'Urban Diseases'
Reflections on the Low-Carbon Development of the Beijing-Tianjin-Hebei Region
Lu Xiaocheng

Population and Labour Market Policies in China's Reform Process
Sun Wenkai

For more information, please visit https://www.routledge.com/China-Perspectives/book-series/CPH

Population and Labour Market Policies in China's Reform Process

Sun Wenkai

Routledge
Taylor & Francis Group
LONDON AND NEW YORK

First published in English 2022
by Routledge
4 Park Square, Milton Park, Abingdon, Oxon OX14 4RN

and by Routledge
605 Third Avenue, New York, NY 10158

Routledge is an imprint of the Taylor & Francis Group, an informa business

British Library Cataloguing-in-Publication Data
A catalogue record for this book is available from the British Library

Library of Congress Cataloging-in-Publication Data
Names: Sun, Wenkai, 1982- author.
Title: Population and labour market policies in China's reform process / Sun Wenkai.
Other titles: Ren kou guan li zhong de zheng fu zheng ce jue ze. English
Description: Abingondon, Oxon ; New York, NY : Routledge, 2022. | Series: China perspectives | Includes bibliographical references and index.
Identifiers: LCCN 2021057175 (print) | LCCN 2021057176 (ebook) | ISBN 9781032263908 (hardback) | ISBN 9781032263915 (paperback) | ISBN 9781003288091 (ebook)
Subjects: LCSH: China--Population policy. | Labor policy--China. | China--Politics and government--1949-
Classification: LCC HB3654.A3 S85413 2022 (print) | LCC HB3654.A3 (ebook) | DDC 304.60951--dc23/eng/20220127
LC record available at https://lccn.loc.gov/2021057175
LC ebook record available at https://lccn.loc.gov/2021057176

ISBN: 978-1-032-26390-8 (hbk)
ISBN: 978-1-032-26391-5 (pbk)
ISBN: 978-1-003-28809-1 (ebk)

DOI: 10.4324/9781003288091

Typeset in Times New Roman
by MPS Limited, Dehradun

Contents

Figures

Tables

Preface

As far as improving the welfare of the people is concerned, population management and labour market policies are the policies most directly involved. In the decades of reform and opening-up, China has introduced a series of population management reform policies, covering the household registration (Hukou) system, family planning policy, labour market system and other aspects. Many of these regulations cannot meet the need of economic and social development anymore today, thus reforms are in pressing need. However, the whole society has yet to form a clear understanding of certain issues, while there still exists non-conformity to the rules of economy in the formulation of some regulations. These have created certain bottlenecks in improving economic efficiency and raising the urbanization rate, urban residents' disposable income and rural families' net income. Take Hukou system reform as an example: despite government efforts to weaken differentiated public services attached to Hukou, it is still some way from achieving true urban and rural integration; national networking of social security payment spanning different regions and urban and rural areas is not fully in place yet, which will hinder the free population flow nationwide; and the floating population still faces problems of unfair treatment and effective social integration in large cities. Besides, lack of multidimensional analysis of the overall impact of the family planning system has led to lack of a deep understanding of its short- and long-term economic and social impacts. It is, therefore, quite necessary to comprehensively examine various population and labour management policies in China, so that sound recommendations can be made for deepening the market-oriented reform of the economic system related to population management and improving the economic system per se and people's welfare.

The author of the book is a professor of economics at Renmin University of China, who has long studied labour economics and development economics, focusing on issues of economic development in China. Over the years, the author has accomplished multiple research achievements in Hukou system reform, family planning policy, labour market development and other fields. This book is an attempt to summarize the author's previous studies of various population control policies. The whole book is divided into three parts:

Discussion of Issues Related to the Hukou System, Discussion of Issues Related to Family Planning Policy and Discussion of Labour Market Policy. Each part is further divided into several chapters, which include both qualitative and quantitative analyses, covering the aspects of historical review of existing policies, evaluation of implementation effects and future prospects and recommendations.

Some of the chapters/sections of this book are simplified versions of papers that I have co-authored with my collaborators. Here, I would like to thank Sun Ang, Li Sanxi, Song Yang, Guo Xi, Wang Xiaoxia, Zhao Zhong and other co-authors for their contributions. I, especially, wish to thank my student Zheng Xinhuang for his excellent research assistance in the process of material preparation for this book. His work has helped me make the contents of each chapter more systematic. He also assisted in material sorting and contributed some text of the book. My thanks should also go to Wang Yijie, Wang Jiaxin, Li Hong, Fan Rong, Gu Yuqing and other students for their assistance in literature sorting.

I hope that this book will be of some help to scholars who study China's population and labour policy.

Sun Wenkai
Renmin University of China,
August 2017, Updated in November 2021

Part I

Discussion on Issues Related to the Hukou System

The household registration (Hukou) system is the most important population management system in China. Operationally, this system facilitates the government's management of the population. However, it is detrimental to both efficiency and equity by artificially creating labour market segmentation and income disparities. For this reason, it has been undergoing reform since the start of China's reform and opening up. Focusing on the study of the Hukou system, this part discusses related issues from five specific perspectives.

In Chapter 1, the author reviews the formulation, evolution and reform of China's Hukou system, examines its current situation and enumerates its existing problems.

Due to their different conditions, different localities have formulated different Hukou policies. In Chapter 2, the author establishes a set of metrics to measure the minimum requirements for obtaining Hukou and explains why there are significant differences between different cities in terms of Hukou system liberalization. Such differences are inherently driven by economic and demographic factors, with officials' personal traits also making an imprint on policies.

Divided into three sections, Chapter 3 examines in detail the microscopic impact of China's existing Hukou policy on residents' economic behaviour. The economic impact mainly falls into three aspects:

1. Consumption by the floating population. Based on CFPS tracking data, the author analyses the impact of Hukou changes on the household consumption behaviour of the floating population and finds that Hukou has different impacts on the consumption behaviour of migrant workers and the urban floating population.
2. Income inequality. Based on previous studies, our analysis suggests that the Hukou system still has a significant impact on income and is one of the major causes of urban and rural income inequality.
3. Demographic structure of large cities. The author demonstrates that a relatively stringent Hukou system will lead to a 'dumbbell-shaped' demographic structure in large cities.

DOI: 10.4324/9781003288091-1

In Chapter 4, the author argues that megacities should be the focus of Hukou system reform and that no cap should be set on current urban population sizes. Based on this view, the author makes some suggestions for reforming the Hukou system in large cities, and looks at the pros and cons of various reference metrics for measuring the performance of Hukou system reform.

There is a relationship of mutual influence and constraint between the development of cities and the evolution of China's Hukou system. In Chapter 5, the author expounds on the characteristics and future directions of China's urbanization process in the broad context of Hukou system reform, and proposes that the government should avoid assuming a 'caring father mentality' in pursuit of even development across regions in the process of promoting urban development. Instead, the author puts a case for intensified supply side reform to meet the needs of urban growth

1 Historical Evolution, Present Situation and Problems of the Hukou System

1.1 Historical Development of Central Government Policies

Following the founding of the People's Republic of China (often referred to as 'New China') in 1949, a Hukou system gradually took shape in the late 1950s. Since then, it has been the most important population management system in the country, affecting all aspects of social and economic life. At the macro level, the Hukou system has shaped the urbanization and population mobility landscape in China; at the micro-level, the Hukou system still has an impact on education, employment, income, marriage, consumption, social integration and other personal aspects of citizens. Overall, the negative impacts of the Hukou system outweigh its positive impacts. As such, reforming the Hukou system has also become a persistent political and economic topic since the 1980s.

Seen from the history of policy development, changes in the Hukou system were gradually formed and developed, with the central government being the basic driving force behind it. Up to the start of this century, the central government's Hukou policy documents were basically implemented across the country. A change happened with the onset of this century. Under the guidance of the central government's policy documents, local governments have begun to formulate local Hukou policies according to local conditions by varying degrees. This has led to quite significant variations in the level of Hukou system liberalization from locality to locality. In recent years, a new round of Hukou system reform has been gathered pace under the central government's overall coordination. As it stands, China's Hukou system reform can be basically summarized aid down a plan for the 1954 as a process of 'centralisation—decentralisation—re-centralisation'. In general, the central government's policy documents still play a fundamental role in the development of the Hukou system. Table 1.1 summarizes the major policy documents on the development of the Hukou system in China over the years.

DOI: 10.4324/9781003288091-2

Table 1.1 Evolution of Central Government Policy on Hukou

Year	*Regulations*	*Summary*
1950	Measures for the Administration of Special Populations	Measures to deal with counter-revolutionaries.
1951	Interim Regulations on the Administration of Urban Hukou	Stipulated the control measures for birth, death, inbound migration, outbound migration, 'social changes' (social identity) and other matters; the first regulations on Hukou management after the founding of the People's Republic of China; basically unified the household registration system in cities across the country.
1953	Registration Measures for Nationwide Censuses	Laid down a plan for the 1954 census;
	Resolution of the CPC Central Committee on the State Monopoly on the Purchase and Marketing of Grain	The state monopolized the purchase and marketing of grain, cotton, etc.
1955	Measures for Grain Rationing in Towns	Urban residents were required to present grain coupons when purchasing grain;
	Instruction on the Establishment of a Regular Household Registration System	Unified household registration work in urban and rural areas across the country, and stipulated that a household registration system should be established in cities, market towns and villages throughout the country, and household registration statistics should be conducted once every year.
1957	Instruction and Notice on Stopping the Aimless Outflow of Population from Rural Areas	Provided for the repatriation of rural residents who had moved aimlessly to cities.
1958	Regulations of the People's Republic of China on Household Registration	Classified urban and rural residents into two types of Hukou for the first time: 'agricultural Hukou' and 'non-agricultural Hukou', thus laying down the basic framework of China's current Hukou management system.
1959	Notice on Immediately Stopping Recruiting New Workers and Regularizing Temporary Staff	All enterprises and institutions shall immediately stop recruiting new workers and continue to stabilize temporary workers.
1962	Opinions on Strengthening Hukou Management Work	Migrations from rural to urban areas shall be strictly controlled; for migrations from urban to rural areas, settling shall be granted in all cases and no control shall be

(*Continued*)

Table 1.1 (Continued)

Year	*Regulations*	*Summary*
		imposed; normal migrations between cities shall be allowed, but migrations from small cities to large cities, especially migrations to the five major cities of Beijing, Shanghai, Tianjin, Wuhan and Guangzhou shall be properly controlled.
1964	Regulations of the Ministry of Public Security on the Handling of Hukou Transfers (Draft)	Imposed strict restrictions on migrations from rural areas to cities and market towns, and from market towns to cities.
1977	Regulations of the Ministry of Public Security on the Handling of Hukou Transfers	Strengthened the strict management of Hukou transfers.
1979	Report of the State Council on the Approval and Transmission of the Opinions of the Ministry of Public Security and the Ministry of Grain on Strictly Controlling the Conversion of Agricultural Populations into Non-agricultural Populations	Required public security organs at all levels to effectively strengthen control over the movement of agricultural populations into cities and towns, and required grain departments to put a stop to the practice of unauthorized conversion of agricultural populations in units under collective ownership into non-agricultural populations.
1981	Circular of the State Council on Strictly Controlling the Entry of Rural Labour Force into Cities and the Conversion of Agricultural Populations into Non-agricultural Populations	Required the strengthening of Hukou and grain management, ordered grain departments to strictly control the conversion of agricultural populations into non-agricultural populations in accordance with relevant policies and regulations and stipulated that no commodity grain should be supplied to those who did not meet the requirements.
1984	Circular on the Issue of Farmers Settling in Market Towns	For farmers who apply to work, do business or provide services in market towns, public security departments shall grant permanent residence to them and their dependents, and register them as households with self-reliant grain supply, provided that they have fixed residences in market towns, the ability to run businesses or stable employment in township enterprises or institutions.

(*Continued*)

Table 1.1 (Continued)

Year	*Regulations*	*Summary*
1985	Interim Provisions on Temporary Resident Populations in Cities and Towns, Regulations of the People's Republic of China on Resident Identity Cards	Established a resident identity card system. Identity cards emphasize the identification of individual citizens; they are easy to carry; they are different from household registers that prove the identities of members of a family and their relationship with each other; they represent one of the major changes in our Hukou system.
1995	Measures for Application for Temporary Residence Permits (Ministry of Public Security)	Established measures for the administration of temporary residence permits for the floating population.
1997	Circular of the State Council on the Approval and Transmission of the Ministry of Public Security's Pilot Scheme for Reform of the Hukou Management System in Small Towns and Opinions on Improving the Hukou Management System in Rural Areas	Stipulated that 'rural residents who work or live in small towns and meet certain requirements may apply for permanent residence in small towns'.
1998	Circular of the State Council on the Approval and Transmission of the Opinions of the Ministry of Public Security on Resolving Several Outstanding Issues in the Current Hukou Management Work	Newborn babies living with their fathers, people living apart from their spouses, elderly dependent parents, as well as citizens who invest and start businesses or buy commercial housing in cities and their immediate family members shall be granted Hukou for settling in cities, provided that they have a legitimate and fixed dwelling or a legitimate and stable occupation or source of income in cities, have lived in the cities for a certain period and meet the relevant provisions of local governments.
2001	Opinions on Advancing Reform of the Hukou Management System in Small Towns	People who apply for permanent residence in small towns are no longer subject to quotas.
2012	Notice of the General Office of the State Council on Actively and Steadily Advancing Reform of the Hukou Management System	Guide the orderly transfer of non-agricultural industries and rural populations to small and medium-sized cities and designated towns, gradually meet the settling needs of eligible rural populations, and gradually achieve equality access to basic public services between urban and rural areas.

(*Continued*)

Table 1.1 (Continued)

Year	*Regulations*	*Summary*
2013	Decision of the CPC Central Committee on Some Major Issues Concerning Comprehensively Deepening Reform	Innovate population management, speed up Hukou system reform, fully liberalize restrictions on settling in designated towns and small cities, liberalize restrictions on settling in medium-sized cities in an orderly manner, reasonably determine the requirements for settling in large cities and strictly control the population size of megacities.
2014	Opinions on Deepening Reform of the Hukou System	Called for thoroughly implementing the Hukou system reform requirements of the 18th National Congress of the CPC and the Third Plenary Session of the 18th CPC Central Committee and the Central Work Conference on Urbanisation, encouraged efforts to turn permanent residents with the ability to get stable employment and live in small towns into townspeople, fully put the residence permit system into practice and steadily extend urban basic public services to the entire permanent resident population.
2015	Opinions on Key Work of Deepening Economic System Reform in 2015	Called for stepping up the implementation of Hukou system reform and Hukou liberalization policies, improving supporting measures, and establishing a unified urban and rural Hukou system.
2015	Interim Regulations on Residence Permit	Citizens who have left their permanent residence places and lived in another city for more than half a year may apply for a residence permit in accordance with the provisions of the Regulations if they meet any of the following requirements: have a legal and stable job, have a legal and stable domicile or have attended school on a continuous basis.
2016	Opinions of the State Council on Deepening New-type Urbanisation	Called for speeding up the implementation of Hukou system

(*Continued*)

Table 1.1 (Continued)

Year	*Regulations*	*Summary*
		reform policies, fully putting the residence permit system into practice, extend urban basic public services to the entire permanent resident population and accelerate the establishment of an incentive mechanism for tuning rural migrants into townspeople.
2016	Notice of the General Office of the State Council on Issuing the Plan for Promoting the Settling of 100 Million Residents Without Local Household Registration in Cities	Make overall planning and synergetic push, and fully relax the requirements for agricultural residents to transfer and settle in cities except for a few mega cities. During the 13th Five-Year Period, speed up the removal of barriers to Hukou transfer between urban and rural areas, further improve the supporting policy system and call for an increase of over 1% in the average annual urbanization rate of residents with household registration in the country during the 13th Five-Year Plan period, with an average of more than 13 million people having their Hukou transferred to cities annually; and raising the above rate to 45% and narrowing the urbanization rate gap between residents with household registration and the permanent resident population by more than 2% from the 2013 level at the end of 2020.

1.1.1 Preparatory Stage of Plan-Based Population Management

The early days of the People's Republic of China were basically a period of free population mobility, with stringent restrictions on the freedom of movement only limited to special groups such as political opponents. After the Movements Against the 'Three Evils' and the 'Five Evils' and the Socialist Transformation of Capitalist Industry and Commerce, the state was able to exercise fairly good plan-based control over investment and other corporate decisions. However, the difficulty of enforcing plan-based control over population mobility also made it difficult to implement economic plans. For this reason, this period was also the stage of preparation for plan-based population management. Due to relatively large-scale population movements, central government policies during this period gradually showed signs of an inclination to curb population mobility. This was evidenced in the introduction of a food coupon system to regulate the food supply. *The Instructions and Notice on Stopping the Aimless Outflow of Population from Rural Areas* issued in 1957 even provided for the direct repatriation of rural residents who had moved to cities. During this period, preparations were basically made to undertake household registration and population management, as represented by the relevant population registration regulations enacted in 1951, 1953 and 1955. Though people were legally free to move at the time, it was during this very preparatory period that the Hukou system was gradually linked with other sectoral benefits and subsequently came to play the most important role in controlling population mobility in China.

1.1.2 Period of Strict Population Mobility Control through the Hukou System

The period from 1958 to 1984 can be seen as a period of strict urban Hukou control, during which it was difficult for rural residents to obtain urban Hukou. For the first time, the *Regulations of the People's Republic of China on Household Registration* issued in 1958 classified rural and urban residents into two types of Hukou: 'agricultural Hukou' and 'non-agricultural Hukou', thus laying down the basic framework of China's current Hukou management system where urban and rural populations are managed separately. Subsequent policies made it even more difficult for rural people to obtain urban Hukou, while putting the floating population under tighter control. For example, the *Opinions on Strengthening Hukou Management* issued in 1962 strictly restricted the movement of rural residents to cities, and the *Regulations of the Ministry of Public Security on the Handling of Hukou Transfers (Draft)* issued in 1964 stipulated two 'strict restrictions'. As recently as 1979, *the Report of the State Council on the Approval and Forwarding of the Opinions of the Ministry of Public Security and the Ministry of Grain on Strictly Controlling the Conversion of Agricultural Populations into Non-agricultural Populations* still required public security organs at all levels to effectively strengthen control over the movement of agricultural populations into cities and towns, and demanded grain departments to put a stop to the practice of unauthorized conversion of the agricultural populations in units under collective ownership into non-agricultural populations. This made it more difficult for residents with rural Hukou to obtain urban Hukou. In addition to grain provision control, employment was another means of control imposed on the citybound migration of the rural population. It was very difficult for rural residents to get employment in cities. This period, which saw strict control over urban Hukou and numerous differentiated welfare policies attached to urban and rural Hukous, practically laid the foundation for the dual Hukou system in the ensuing decades, with lasting adverse effects—until now, rural residents have yet to gain equal status with city dwellers.

1.1.3 'Period of Semi-openness' with Gradual Hukou Relaxation in Small Towns

Thanks to the reform and opening-up drive and the progress of the market economy, there was a gradual inflow of rural labourers who ventured to work and live in cities and towns. In the process, the shortcomings of past policies of strict Hukou control were further exposed and laid bare. To address the problem, the *Circular on the Issue of Farmers Settling in Market Towns* promulgated in 1984 allowed farmers to obtain Hukou in small towns, stipulating that 'For farmers who apply to work, do business or provide services in market towns, public security departments shall grant permanent residence to them and their dependents and register them as households with self-reliant grain supply, provided that they have fixed domiciles in market towns, the ability to run businesses, have stable employment in township enterprises or institutions'. From 1984 to 2001, the central government stepped up efforts to promote an open policy for rural people to settle down in small towns, but strict restrictions remained for settling in large and medium-sized cities. Therefore, this period can only be called a "period of semi-openness" of the Hukou system'. During this period, there was basically no strict control over the flow of rural populations into cities, and the movement of population between urban and rural areas and between cities was elementarily realized. In 1985, the concept of temporary residence was put forward in the *Interim Provisions on Temporary Resident Populations in Cities and Towns.* A decade later, measures for the administration of temporary residence permits were formally introduced, which were soon widely adopted by major cities to manage migrant populations. However, as 'outsiders', peasants still faced restrictions in terms of housing, employment, social benefits, education and other aspects. To adapt to the special individuality of the floating population, the *Regulations of the People's Republic of China on Resident Identity Cards* were promulgated in 1985, replacing household registers (a family relationship document) with identity cards (personal identification) to facilitate population mobility and management. Meanwhile, local governments also introduced multiple measures to attract investment and talents, and implemented more liberal and preferential residence and migration policies for business investors and skilled migrants, but only on a small scale. The *Circular of the State Council on the Approval and Forwarding of the Opinions of the Ministry of Public Security on Resolving Several Outstanding Issues in Current Hukou Management Work* issued in 1998 opened the door for immediate family members, investors and homebuyers to settle in cities. On the whole, however, the state still pursued a Hukou policy of fully liberalizing restrictions on settling in small towns and strictly controlling settlement in large cities.

1.1.4 Period of Differentiated Push of Hukou Reform between Regions

During the period from 2001 to 2012, the central government did not issue any major policy document on Hukou reform. However, with the advancement of the market economy and the formation of a bigger floating population, there were intensified population movements between localities. During this period, various localities pursued differentiated Hukou reforms according to their local conditions. In some large cities with net population inflows such as Beijing, Hukou control remained tight, and the reform process even rolled back at times: for example, in the earlier years, people could obtain Hukou by living with their immediate family members as dependents or buying homes; in recent years, however, non-locals face more stringent home buying restrictions, effectively closing one channel for them to obtain urban Hukou. But for most localities, especially small and medium-sized cities, it has become easier for rural people to obtain urban Hukou. This is particularly true in localities with net population outflows, where Hukou reform is carried out with great vigour. For example, Chongqing began aggressive Hukou reform in 2010. As early as the beginning of this century, some provinces piloted the unification of urban and rural Hukou as resident Hukou. Though the benefits attached to one's Hukou still depended on one's place of residence, at least equal treatment was realized in the name. During this period, different levels of Hukou liberalization between localities formed a firewall that allowed local governments to implement other policies within their localities, such as the Hukou-based allocation of educational resources and housing resources, thus shielding them from the influence of migrant populations residing in their localities.

1.1.5 Stage of Vigorous Reform Push since 2012

In 2012, the central government issued the *Notice of the General Office of the State Council on Actively and Steadily Advancing Reform of the Hukou Management System*, calling for guiding an orderly transfer of non-agricultural industries and rural populations to small and medium-sized cities and designated towns, gradually meeting eligible rural populations' need for settling in cities and towns and achieving equal access to basic public services between urban and rural areas step by step. *The Decision of the CPC Central Committee on Some Major Issues Concerning Comprehensively Deepening Reform* issued in 2013 put forward such requirements as innovating population management, speeding up Hukou system reform, fully liberalizing restrictions on settling in designated towns and small cities, orderly liberalizing restrictions on settling in medium-sized cities, reasonably determining the requirements for settling in large cities and strictly controlling the population size of megacities. In July 2014, the State Council issued the *Opinions on Further Advancing Reform of the Hukou System*, specifically calling for widely promoting the residence permit system in large cities and gradually removing the benefits attached to Hukou, so that permanent urban residents without Hukou could also enjoy urban public benefits to a certain extent. In 2016, two schemes were introduced in succession. Among them, the *Opinions of the State Council on Deepening New-type Urbanisation* further called for speeding up the implementation of Hukou system reform policies, fully putting the residence permit system into practice, extend urban basic public services to the entire permanent resident population and accelerate the establishment of an incentive mechanism for tuning rural migrants into townspeople. It is evident that while the idea of tiered Hukou management was persistently implemented for megacities, large cities, medium-sized cities and small cities during this period, substantial breakthroughs were nevertheless made in the reform of benefits attached to Hukou. On October 11, 2016, the State Council issued the *Plan for Promoting the Settling of 100 Million Residents Without Local Household Registration in Cities*, calling for an increase of over 1% in the average annual urbanization rate of residents with household registration in the country during the 13th Five-Year Plan period, with an average of more than 13 million people having their Hukou transferred to cities annually; and raising the above rate to 45% and narrowing the urbanization rate gap between residents with household registration and the permanent resident population by more than 2% from the 2013 level at the end of 2020. These policies make it easier than ever to obtain Hukou in all cities but megacities. Even megacities are proactively promoting a points-based system of granting Hukou to applicants and opening up access to various social benefits through residence permits. In a word, Hukou now becomes much less a barrier of migration for the floating population.

1.2 Overview of Current Situation of the Hukou System

1.2.1 Hukou Policies in Different Regions

In the past 30 years, Hukou system reform in China has basically followed a model of guidance by the central government and specific implementation by local governments. Consequently, different localities enjoy much autonomy in the Hukou system reform. Due to different economic, social and demographic environments, Hukou liberalizations vary significantly from city to city.

At the local level, common Hukou systems can be divided into two types: the access system and the points-based system which has emerged in recent years. The access system generally has special provisions for different social groups, which are often classified into general workers, talents introduced from outside, personnel returning to China after study abroad, people living with family members, investors and home buyers, and so on. Corresponding requirements to get urban Hukou are formulated for each of these groups. Over certain periods, some regions also implemented a Blue Print Hukou policy. Granting holders some rights, Blue Print Hukou is something falling between a temporary residence permit and the official Hukou.

A classification of Hukou settlement requirement dimensions under the access system can be found in the summary made by Wu Kaiya and Zhang Li (2010), as shown in Table 1.2. With regard to requirement dimensions, some policies are constantly adjusted with the economic environment. For example, the requirements for investors and homebuyers to settle in cities are often liberalized during economic downturns. By contrast, cities restrict non-locals from buying homes during economic booms. Overall, large cities have generally tightened Hukou control on those who come to live with their family members. However, the Hukou policy for talents with high academic qualifications has remained relatively stable.

The other Hukou settlement system is a points-based system, which has been in implementation in recent years. In 2014, the State Council issued the *Opinions on Further Deepening Reform of the Hukou System* and called for 'large cities and megacities with an urban population of 5 million or more to establish and improve a points-based Hukou settlement system based on their comprehensive carrying capacities and economic and social development needs, taking possession of legitimate and stable occupation, ownership of legitimate and regular domicile, duration of participation in urban social insurance and length of continuous residence in the local city as the main assessment indicators for granting Hukou to qualified people'. The requirements for people to settle in large cities with an urban population of 1 million to 5 million are as follows: having a legitimate and stable occupation in the city for a certain period, having a legitimate and regular domicile and having participated in urban social insurance as required by the state for a certain period (but it shall not exceed five years at the maximum). However, large cities with an urban population of 3 million to 5 million may set out their own provisions on the scope of legitimate and stable occupations and the scope and requirements of legitimate and regular domiciles. These cities may also establish a points-based Hukou settlement system based on their specific conditions. Table 1.3 summarizes the points calculation rules of the points-based system in some major cities in China. It is evident that there are considerable differences in the points calculation rules between different cities.

1.2.2 Hukou Reform Progress in Different Regions

In 2016, 31 provinces and municipalities in China issued opinions on deepening provincial-level Hukou system reform. These opinions show that local governments have generally implemented the following measures for Hukou system reform:

1. All provinces have proposed to establish a unified urban and rural Hukou system. As a matter of fact, the practice of unifying urban and rural Hukous as 'resident Hukou' was implemented by some provinces

Table 1.2 Relevant Hukou Settlement Control Dimensions under the Access System

Actual Investment			*Tax Payment*			*Home Buying*			*High-end Employment (Talents)*			*Ordinary Employment*					
Total amount of actual investment	Amount of average investment per household	Additional restrictive requirement on investment-based Hukou settlement	Amount of actual tax payment	Amount of average tax payment per household	Additional restrictive requirement on Hukou settlement based on tax payment	Total amount of home purchase (floor space)	Amount of home purchase per person per household	Additional restrictive requirement on Hukou settlement based on home purchase	Minimum academic qualification requirement	Normative requirement on employment	Additional restrictive requirement on Hukou settlement based on high-end employment	Minimum requirement on educational background	Minimum skills or qualification requirement	Normative requirement on employment	Requirement on length of residence	Housing requirement	Additional restrictive requirement on Hukou settlement based on ordinary employment
Family Reunion										*Special Contributions*			*Others*				
Marriage				*Care of Family Members*				*Hukou Settlement with Father or Mother*		*Winning of Major Award or Outstanding Performance*			*System Transformation*		*Other Special Circumstances*		
Number of years of marriage	Age requirement	Educational background & qualifications	Additional restrictive requirement on marriage-based Hukou settlement	Age requirement for those who settle in with immediate family members	Age requirement for immediate family members with whom applicants are to settle in	Essential requirements	Additional requirement for Hukou settlement through care of family members	Type of Hukou of father or mother in local city	Age requirement for children who settle in with parents	Award class	Merit class	Other restrictions on award winning or determination of outstanding performance	Township turned into neighbourhood	Agricultural land turned into urban construction land	Hukou settlement requiring special consideration		

Table 1.3 Current Rules of Points Calculation in Major Chinese Cities

City	*Rules of Points Calculation*	*Notes*
Beijing	Age + educational background + honors & commendations + tax payment + stable employment + regular domicile + innovation & entrepreneurship + law-abiding record	
Tianjin	Basic points (age, educational level, skills level, social insurance, regular domicile) + guidance points (stable employment + settled area) + extra points (tax payment, marriage status, honors, working years, ex-servicemen) + negative points (law violations & dishonesty)	
Shenyang	Educational background (professional qualifications) + age + years of continuous application for *residence permit* + participation in social insurance	Points for educational level and vocational skills are not cumulative. The highest score is 100 points.
Shanghai	Basic indicators (age, educational level, technical competency/ skills, social insurance) + indicators for bonus points (highly demanded job, tax payment, employment promotion, work area, graduating student, honours, marriage status) + indicators for (false materials, administrative detention, general criminal crimes,) + one-vote veto indicators	Points for educational level and vocational skills points are not cumulative. The highest score is 100 points. Applicants are entitled to local public services if they score points above the minimum requirement, but are not directly granted Hukou.
Nanjing	Basic indicators (length of continuous local residence, regular domicile, social insurance payment) + indicators for bonus points (age, educational level, skills, Hukou settlement area, tax payment, social service, honours, employment promotion) + indicators for minus points (poor credit record, law violations, crimes) + negative points (law violations & dishonesty)	

(*Continued*)

Table 1.3 (Continued)

City	*Rules of Points Calculation*	*Notes*
Ningbo	Educational level + skills/ occupation + honors + social service + skills innovation + position served	
Qingdao	Basic points (age, educational level, skills, social insurance status, regular domicile) + guidance points (highly demanded job) + extra points (honours + tax payment + social service) + negative points (law violations & dishonesty)	
Haikou	Basic indicators (age, stable employment, regular domicile, length of social insurance coverage) + bonus items (honours) + minus items (false materials, law violations dishonesty) + one-vote veto	
Guiyang	Basic points (age, regular domicile, marriage status, educational level, skills, social insurance, stable employment) + bonus points (honours, social service, urgently needed talent, tax payment) + minus points (law violations & crimes, family planning policy breach)	
Guangzhou	Educational level + skills/ occupation + social service + tax payment	For anyone who wants to settle in Guangzhou
Guangzhou	Basic points (age, educational level/skills, social insurance, regular domicile) + guidance points (settled area, highly demanded job) + extra points (honors, social service, tax payment)	For migrant workers and residents who do not reside in the ten downtown districts of Guangzhou
Shenzhen	Basic requirements (age, physical health, residence permit) + personal qualities (educational level, vocational skills, honors) + regular domicile + social insurance coverage + social service, points-reduction indicators (family planning policy breach, law violations & dishonesty)	For migrant workers

(*Continued*)

Table 1.3 (Continued)

City	*Rules of Points Calculation*	*Notes*
Shenzhen	Personal qualities (educational level/skills, honors) + tax payment + insurance participation status + regular domicile + age + bonus points (social service) + minus points (dishonesty, law violations, family planning policy breach)	Talents attracted from outside

in the past century, but there was no Hukou unification at the national level. In recent years, reform in this area has intensified, basically achieving the unification of Hukou for urban and rural residents. Efforts have also been made to establish educational, healthcare, family planning, employment, social security, housing, land and demographic systems compatible with the unified urban and rural Hukou system.

2. All provinces have proposed to establish a residence permit system. With the residence permit as the carrier, a basic public service provision mechanism has been generally established and improved, which is linked with the length of residence and other requirements. All new local Hukou reform plans stipulate that those citizens who leave their place of permanent residence and live in cities with districts at or above the prefecture level for more than six months may apply for a residence permit in their current place of residence. Eligible residence permit holders may apply for Hukou at their place of residence. Residence permit holders are entitled to the same rights as locals, such as labour employment, basic public education, basic healthcare services, family planning services, public cultural services and license and certificate handling services. Those residence permit holders who meet the minimum requirements for duration of continuous residence and length of participation in social insurance will gradually enjoy the same rights as locals in respect of secondary vocational education, employment support, housing security, pension services, social welfare and social aid. In the meantime, their children will also be gradually eligible to take the senior high school entrance examination and the national college entrance examination in cities where they live with their parents. In fact, Shanghai came up with the residence permit system as early as 2002. But the system was only vigorously promoted by various regions in China in 2016 after the central government introduced new rules on residence permit. In the promotion of residence permit, the benefits attached to Hukou are separated, so that even those who have not obtained local Hukou can still share some public services. However, the

benefits attached to the residence permit and the benefits attached to urban Hukou vary from city to city.

3. Taking 2020 as the deadline, most provinces have set specific targets for Hukou system reform. Various provinces have generally adopted the following indicators: urbanization rate of permanent resident population, urbanization rate of Hukou population, difference in urbanization rate between permanent resident population and Hukou population, number of agricultural transfer population, number of people settled with Hukou and so on. For example, Henan Province has called for efforts to have approximately 11 million agricultural transfer population and other permanent residents settled in cities and towns and achieve a 56% urbanization rate of the permanent resident population in the whole province by 2020. Hebei Province has set the target to have 6 million urban villagers, 4 million agricultural transfer population and other permanent residents settled in towns and cities and achieve a 45% urbanization rate of its entire Hukou population by 2020. For Heilongjiang Province, the target urbanization rate for its Hukou population is 55% by 2020.
4. Provinces have also classified their cities into designated towns and small cities, medium-sized cities, large cities and megacities, and put forward respective Hukou liberalization reform requirements for them. These include full Hukou liberalization in designated towns and small cities, orderly liberalization of Hukou restrictions in medium-sized cities, reasonable determination of Hukou requirements in large cities and strict population size control in megacities. In small cities, people may apply for Hukou if they have a legitimate and regular domicile (including rented ones). But in medium-sized cities, people must have a legitimate and stable occupation and a legitimate and regular domicile (including rented ones), and have participated in urban social insurance for a certain number of years as stipulated by the state. In addition to the regular domicile and stable employment requirements, cities demand a longer period of social insurance payment on non-locals to apply for Hukou. For their part, most megacities adopt the points-based Hukou settlement system, with more stringent requirements.
5. Most provinces have put forward institutional safeguards for Hukou system reform, mainly including safeguards for improving the rural property rights system and fiscal safeguards for strengthening basic public services. For example, regarding rural property rights system improvement, Jilin Province has proposed to basically complete the confirmation, registration and certification of rural land contractual management rights by the end of 2017. Starting from 2015, Jilin has been making efforts to establish and improve a market-based service system for the transfer of rural land contractual management rights (rural property rights trading) in four years, while promoting the standardized operation of rural property rights trading. Jiangsu

Province has called for speeding up the establishment of a rural property rights transfer market. It aims to build a linked rural property rights market trading system at the provincial, municipal, county and township levels in the whole province and comprehensively set up rural property rights transfer markets in counties (cities, districts) and towns by the end of 2017. As for strengthening fiscal safeguards for basic public services, Guizhou Province has proposed to formulate through study relevant policies linking financial transfer payment with agricultural transfer population before June 2016, further increase financial transfer payment to regions receiving population inflow and promote the realization of full coverage of urban basic public services over the permanent resident population in the whole province. Inner Mongolia has suggested that it will take into full account the gross size of its Hukou population and resident permit holders population, investment in basic public services and other factors, improve the calculation method of balanced transfer payment, adjust the conversion ratio of public services expenditure on the agricultural and animal husbandry transfer population, scientifically define the basic public service powers of people's governments at all levels and establish and improve a mechanism of work division and collaboration for people's governments at all levels.

1.3 Existing Problems in Current Hukou System Reform

1.3.1 Government Reform Efforts Are Inadequate in Large Cities

Based on our collected local Hukou policy documents and our analysis of the wording and content of existing local reform plans already introduced by some provinces, autonomous regions and municipalities under the Central Government, we have found that most provinces, especially those with net population outflows, have made great efforts to reform their Hukou systems. However, certain Hukou restrictions still exist in large cities. In its *Opinions on Further Deepening Reform of the Hukou System*, the State Council also laid down the principle for city-specific Hukou reform, which provides policy support for Hukou reform in megacities. We have compiled the Hukou liberalization index for more than 200 prefecture-level cities in China for the 2010–2016 period and found that most cities have substantially liberalized their Hukou restrictions in recent years. However, there is no substantial change in Beijing, Shanghai, Guangzhou or Shenzhen.

1.3.2 Many Public Welfare Benefits Are Still Tied to Hukou

China's current Hukou system goes far beyond the demographic function. It is attached with too many benefits and rights. Surveys show that more than 20 personal rights are currently tied to Hukou, involving political rights, employment rights, educational rights, social security, family planning and various other aspects, as well as replacement policy and standard for ex-servicemen, personal injury compensation in traffic accidents and so on. In almost all provinces, these welfare benefits differ between urban Hukou and rural Hukou and between the floating population and locals.

The public services and welfare benefits tied to Hukou are mainly manifested in the economically developed eastern regions and medium-sized and large cities in the country. Since the Ministry of Public Security issued the *Opinions on Advancing Reform of the Hukou Management System in Small Towns* in 2001, Hukou control in small towns has been substantially liberalized. In some small towns, citizens can easily settle in local towns where they live if they have a job with a steady income or their own housing, or have certain vocational skills. Despite such incentive measures taken by the government, however, the number of people who choose to settle in small and medium-sized cities is still small, mainly because these cities are relatively weak in providing employment opportunities, public services and social welfare. In medium-sized and large cities in economically developed regions, large numbers of migrant workers and non-locals are still not entitled to the same public services (mainly including housing subsidies, children's education, social security and so on) which locals enjoy. While the residence permit does provide certain welfare functions of Hukou, it can still not completely replace Hukou.

1.3.3 A Unified Urban and Rural Hukou Has Not Solved Hukou-Based Welfare Disparities

On 24 July 2014, the State Council issued the *Opinions on Further Deepening the Reform of the Hukou System*, calling for establishing a unified Hukou system for urban and rural areas and abolishing the distinction between agricultural Hukou and non-agricultural Hukou, as well as Blue Print Hukou and other derivative types of Hukou. Does this mean that China's Hukou system has disappeared ever since, or that holders of different types of Hukou are entitled to equal public services if they live in the same area? In fact, this is not the case. Hukou in China has two dimensions, namely the nature of Hukou (i.e. agricultural Hukou vs non-agricultural Hukou) and the location of Hukou. Even if the differences in the nature of Hukou are eliminated, the differences in the location of Hukou still lead to different Hukou attributes for different people. These attributes directly affect every citizen's employment opportunities, as well as the various public services which people can access in the workplace. In fact, even before the above *Opinions* were issued, many provinces had already abolished the distinction between urban Hukou and rural Hukou and changed it to a unified Hukou. However, urban and rural welfare disparities still more or less exist.

1.3.4 Overall Coordination by the Central Government Remains Inadequate

Currently, the central government has not made enough coordination efforts in the areas of healthcare, social security and provision for the elderly. Basically, it still relies on local governments to formulate their own policies. For one thing, medical insurance is locally based. For example, once hospitalized, farmers in a county in Jilin Province can get 70% of their medical costs reimbursed by the country hospital through medical insurance. But if they seek in-patient medical treatment in another country or outside Jilin, the proportion of reimbursement will be significantly lower. This will obviously have a negative impact on the cross-regional flow of some migrant workers. In addition, because the payment base for pension and other types of insurance vary from region to region, it is more difficult to make payment transfers between regions. Despite regional breakthroughs in Hukou reform through the points-based system, the widespread existence of restrictions on length of local employment (such as five years), as well as the duration requirement for eligibility to claim pensions and other welfare benefits often make it very difficult for relatively mobile people to get the same treatment as urban Hukou holders do. These two examples illustrate that the different welfare benefits attached to Hukou in different regions makes it difficult to solve the fundamental issue of nationwide population migration.

1.3.5 The Points-Based Hukou System Only Has a Very Limited Role

This is because the points-based Hukou settlement system in large cities is essentially to attract the so-called 'Three-Highs' people to settle in ('Three-Highs' people refer to people who have high incomes, are highly educated and have high assets), while opportunities are still few for most of the floating population who are unskilled and have relatively low incomes. Statistics show that 70% of the people who settled in Guangzhou in 2014 through the points-based Hukou system were under 35 years old, and 90.6% had junior college (higher vocational) education or above, with approximately 70% of them holding a Bachelor's or Master's degree. On average, they had paid social and medical insurance for more than 84 months, with the longest at 147 months. In its points-based residence permit system, Shanghai takes educational level and wealth level as the main points-gaining indicators, which make many people lose the opportunity to increase their points and access more public services.

The limitations of the points-based Hukou settlement policy are also reflected in the too high standard for getting points in large cities and in a serious imbalance between supply and demand. For example, 1.6 million of the 3.12 million permanent residents in Zhongshan City, Guangdong Province were a floating population in 2013. However, only 3,600 points-

Table 1.4 Salient Features of Existing Points-Based Hukou Settlement Systems (Taking Shanghai as an Example)

Feature	*Specific Manifestations*
People with high assets and high income are more popular	Residence permit holders who invest and start a business in Shanghai and have an average tax payment of RMB100,000 or more, or employ ten or more people with local Hukou on average each year in the past 3 consecutive years will get 10 points for paying every RMB100,000 of taxes paid or for employing ten people with local Hukou, with up to 100 points to be awarded. Residence permit holders who pay social insurance for their employees in Shanghai at a base which is equal to or higher than 80%–100% times, 1–2 times and more than 2 times employees' average social pay of the previous year in the past 3 consecutive years will get 25, 50 and 100 points respectively.
Highly educated people are more popular	Residence permit holders who have obtained a junior college degree, an undergraduate degree, an undergraduate degree and Bachelor's degree, a Master's degree and a doctoral degree will get 50, 60, 90, 100 and 110 points respectively.
Highly skilled people are more popular	Residence permit holders who have obtained National Vocational Skills Competency Grade V, Grade IV, Grade III, Grade II and Grade I can respectively receive 15, 30, 60, 100 and 140 points; residence permit holders who have obtained Intermediate Professional and Technical Post Qualification and Senior Professional and Technical Post Qualification will respectively get 100 points and 140 points.

based Hukou quotas were allocated to the floating population that year, while the total public school enrollment quotas allocated to migrant workers' children were merely 8,800. Despite increases in the quotas from 2012 (which had 3,000 Hukou quotas and 8,000 school quotas to the floating population), they were far from enough to meet the demand of the 1.6 million floating population. Consequently, the points-based Hukou and schooling policy is regarded as 'lacking sincerity' (Table 1.4).

1.3.6 Inadequate Rural Land Ownership Confirmation Dents Farmers' Willingness to Settle in Cities

Currently, cities are relatively more attractive overall. However, as urban welfare benefits are constantly made open to people with a rural Hukou and rural areas possess other advantages that towns and cities do not have, farmers' willingness to settle in cities has been hindered. A rural Hukou corresponds to 'Three Rights', namely the right to contract land, the right to own homestead and the right to allocate returns on rural collective assets. None of these rights is possessed by urban residents. If farmers abandon their rural Hukou and settle in cities, there is a possibility that they will lose these 'Three Rights'. Taking arable land contracting as an example, rural arable land is now collectively owned by villages and contracted by rural households in the villages. However, the right of land management is open to transfer, which means that farmers no longer need to turn in some of their retained profits as before. In fact, they can get certain government subsidies from the land. If even farmers go and work in cities, they still can get education and other types of welfare treatment for their children in the cities. Therefore, residents with a rural Hukou in fact enjoy double benefits. In this context, farmers' willingness to settle in cities is limited. Even something called 'reverse urbanization' has happened when urban residents want to go the other way around and settle down in rural areas. Surveys of farmers' willingness to settle in cities conducted in different provinces and cities show that only about 40% of migrant workers are truly willing to settle in cities. If the 'Three Rights' in rural areas can be confirmed and allowed to be transferred freely, farmers will even be less willing to settle in cities. However, the current government policy does not allow the transfer of the 'Three Rights'.

2 Hukou Liberalization Metrics and Influencing Factors

2.1 Literature Review

2.1.1 Quantitative Evaluation of Minimum Hukou Settlement Requirements

There is relatively limited research progress in the quantitative analysis of minimum or threshold requirements for people to get Hukou and settle in cities. Except for some theoretical models and simulation work with specified parameters, most existing quantitative analyses and research on the Hukou system are focused on certain specific dimensions of Hukou system reform. Such research either sets a certain dimension of Hukou system reform as a dummy variable and then develops Difference-in-differences and other models to examine the macro and micro effects of the variable (Sun Wenkai et al., 2011), or directly adopts individual Hukou status in the micro data to reflect the overall situation of Hukou settlement and further study the possible impact of Hukou system reform (Sun Wenkai and Wang Yijie, 2016).

In an analysis of the overall difficulty of Hukou settlement in cities, Wu Kaiya and Zhang Li (2010) conducted cluster analysis on 45 sample cities by introducing investment, employment, family reunion, special contribution and other factors and established a Hukou settlement threshold index to reflect the comprehensive characteristics of Hukou settlement requirements in different cities. A recent article on the quantification of Hukou liberalization came from a study on population movement by the National Health and Planning Commission. In the article, Liu Jinwei (2016) set up several Level-1 indicators and corresponding Level-2 indicators, as well as specific Hukou settlement criteria evaluation indicators from the aspects of living with spouses, home purchase, investment, tax payment and employment. They quantitatively measured the degree of Hukou liberalization in 63 cities in China.

2.1.2 Analysis of Factors Influencing Hukou System Reform

It is generally believed that Hukou system reform is externally driven by the government. Consequently, there is relatively little research on the driving

DOI: 10.4324/9781003288091-3

factors of Hukou system reform per se. Most existing studies are qualitative discussions and can be divided into two types: analysis of hindering factors and analysis of driving factors.

2.1.2.1 Hindering Factors

Current academic analyses of hindrance to Hukou system reform mainly focus on economic development, public services, taxation system, political system and historical tradition.

2.1.2.1.1 ECONOMIC DEVELOPMENT

Based on a review of progress in Hukou system reform, Wang Meiyan and Cai Fang (2008) pointed out that China established the Hukou system to ensure the implementation of its strategy to prioritize the development of heavy industries. After the reform and opening-up started, the state implemented a strategy of letting the eastern regions of the country develop first. An important source of the scissors difference in the coastal regions lies in such economic benefits as low wage costs which are brought by the rural labour force, while the responsibility for providing healthcare and education services is left to the governments of the places where the migrant workers come from. Deng Kebin and Ding Juhong (2010) pointed out that one important reason why large cities insist on Hukou control is that it can accelerate the per capita income growth of urban centres and make Hukou owners vested interests. The vested interests lack the internal motivation to carry out Hukou system reform, which leads to higher Hukou restrictions in economically developed regions. Qu Xiaobo and Cheng Jie (2013) estimated that the value of Hukou is highly related to the population situation and the degree of economic agglomeration. In cities that are economically developed and have a big floating population, Hukou is worth much more. This in turn leads to far greater regional disparities of Hukou reform cost than regional disparities of economic development, which restricts the motivation of local governments to push forward with Hukou system reform. In his research, Liu Jinwei (2016) pointed out that disparities of economic development, fiscal spending and population mobility all affect the degree of Hukou liberalization in different regions. As Hukou system reform means the elimination of the scissors difference-induced policy dividend brought by the old economic strategy and the increase of labour cost, large cities do not have much incentive to pursue Hukou system reform.

2.1.2.1.2 PUBLIC SERVICES AND FISCAL INVESTMENT

In their research, Xia Jijun (2004) pointed out that large cities have relatively more welfare policies in respect of education, healthcare, employment, housing, social security and so on. As local governments are often worried that Hukou liberalization may increase their financial burdens and lower the welfare level of local residents, they are inclined to set up certain mobility barriers and protect the interests of local residents by limiting the inflow of non-locals. At the same time, the central government has taken corresponding measures to limit population flows to stimulate the enthusiasm of local governments to supply public goods.

In 2011, a research team at the Development Research Center of the State Council estimated the specific cost of migrant workers' integration into the city. When inputs into social security, public services, housing security investment and other areas are included, the public expenditure cost for a typical migrant worker (including his or her corresponding dependents) to get the same treatment as locals was about RMB80,000. The huge reform cost has slowed down Hukou system reform. Zhang Li and Wu Kaiya (2013) used urban basic public service cost to estimate the settlement cost of non-local residents, and found a positive correlation between the Hukou settlement cost and the Hukou settlement threshold: Shanghai, Shenzhen and Beijing which are the Top 3 cities in terms of basic public service cost also rank in the top three spots in terms of Hukou threshold. High fiscal pressure often prompts local governments to adopt more stringent Hukou policies.

2.1.2.1.3 TAX COMPETITION AND FISCAL AND TAXATION SYSTEMS

When the population is highly mobile, there will be tax competition among regions to get good tax bases. As a result of such Nash tax competition, regions often lower their tax rates and their total tax revenues fall as a result. Therefore, the central government has incentives to control population mobility cost in order to maximize the gross tax revenue and avoid the prisoner's dilemma caused by local governments competing to reduce population mobility cost and attract tax bases. This shows that the lack of basic social security coordination at the central government level is a major hindrance to Hukou system reform. Zhang Li and Wu Kaiya (2013) pointed out that tax revenues are now mainly in the hands of the central government, while local governments are chiefly responsible for investing in livelihood for the people. If free Hukou is practised under the current arrangement of administrative and financial powers, local governments will have neither the power nor the resources to coordinate for a fiscal balance between the areas where the population flows in and the areas where the population flows out. As a result, local governments will have a strong incentive to choose not to carry out the reform. Hou Li (2014) also pointed out that lack of financial transfer makes it difficult to effectively push forward with Hukou system reform.

2.1.2.1.4 GOVERNMENT BEHAVIOUR AND THE POLITICAL SYSTEM

By establishing an urban Hukou threshold index, Wu Kaiya and Zhang Li (2010) quantitatively compared the Hukou settlement requirements in various cities, and concluded that deepening Hukou system reform would involve a wider pattern of political, economic and social operations well beyond administrative powers and the interaction of reforms in various fields. When local interests are generally legalized and local discretionary power is getting stronger, the only way to improve the fiscal revenue and distribution relationship and more effectively reform the Hukou system is to make breakthrough changes in defining the functions of the government and improving external constraint and incentive mechanisms. Qu Xiaobo and Cheng Jie (2013) pointed out that local governments are also constrained by the existing political system in promoting Hukou system reform. Factors like local competition patterns and mechanisms of promotion for officials are all strong incentive factors for local governments to get involved in economic affairs and promote growth. However, Hukou system reform is essentially about distribution, not growth, or to be more precise, the re-distribution of the results of growth. Therefore, under the current system where there are prominent contradictions between 'growth' and 'distribution', it is difficult for local government-promoted Hukou system reform to make big headways.

2.1.2.1.5 HISTORICAL TRADITION

Dutton (1992) reckoned that China's dual urban and rural Hukou system is an inheritance of the Bao-Jia System implemented during the Qing Dynasty before 1949. Lu Yilong (2002) believed that New China's Hukou system was established with a view to re-establishing social order, with full reference to the experiences and lessons of population control in feudal dynasties. Yuan Gang (2008) argued that China's Hukou system was formed in the Spring and Autumn Period and took full shape the Qin and Han dynasties. The system closely linked Hukou, land and tax together to achieve the goal of social control by strictly controlling population flow, thus laying down the historical foundation of China's dual urban-rural society today.

2.1.2.2 Driving Factors

Existing literature on the driving forces of Hukou system reform mainly covers two aspects: economic development strategy adjustment and urban development.

2.1.2.2.1 Economic Development Strategy

With the reform of the household contract system, large numbers of surplus labourers were released in rural areas, and higher pay from non-agricultural activities attracted labour transfers, and more and more rural labourers went to work in cities. However, due to the lack of urban Hukou, there is a big gap between rural labourers and urban residents in terms of pay and social security benefits. With economic growth, there is a strong call from rural labourers for Hukou system reform. Based on their research, Xia Jijun (2004) believed that the inflow of population can bring a new tax base for the population-receiving region, increase the regional tax revenueeffective demand of these people, spur economic and optimize the allocation of factors in the region. Moreover, when land can be traded freely, an increased population will send land rents and land prices higher, which will benefit local landowners. Zou Yinan (2015) pointed out that as China's economic development strategy shifts focus from encouraging exports to stimulating domestic demand after the 2008 financial crisis, there is an objective call for relaxing Hukou restrictions and promoting the integration of 270 million migrant workers into urban life, which will stimulate the effective demand of these people, spur economic growth and optimize the economic structure.

2.1.2.2.2 Urban Development

In the early days after the founding of New China, the government implemented a strict Hukou system to control city sizes, which resulted in serious urban and rural segmentation and hampered the urbanization process (Wang Xiaolu, 2002). Based on the data from 205 cities in China, Au and Henderson (2006) found that strong government control resulted in small sizes for 51%–62% of the cities. They went on to conclude that China's current urbanization progress lags behind the industrialization level of the country. To address the difficult issues of inadequate urban agglomeration and failure to achieve an optimal size for most cities that face China's economic development, it is imperative to vigorously push forward with Hukou system reform and relax Hukou control in cities. In their theoretical work, Chen Zhao and Lu Ming (2008) showed that in China's urbanization and urban development process, there are three levels of interaction from 'segmentation' to 'integration' between urban and rural areas and within cities. In the long run, an inevitable requirement for eventually removing social segmentation within cities and further promoting harmonious urbanization and sustainable economic development is to eliminate discriminations in the labour market, and achieve 'social integration', equal public services and 'power integration' for people with different types of Hukou. Liu Xiaofeng et al. (2010) further internalized the Hukou policy formulation and selection process and proved that when urbanization reaches a certain stage and urban migration attains a certain level, public service discriminations against migrants may aggravate the income gap and social conflict between labourers with different types of Hukou in cities, thus resulting in the non-productive consumption of social resources and negatively impacting capital gains in the urban sector. The amplification of such negative impacts will promote Hukou policy changes. Qu Xiaobo and Cheng Jie (2013) further pointed out that as something called 'incomplete urbanization' (i.e. the gap and mismatch between the overall urbanization level and the urbanization level of the people with urban Hukou) currently exists in China, there is an objective need to reform the Hukou system.

With the deepening of Hukou system reform and the continuous emergence of hindering factors, research focus should shift from the analysis of single indicators of the Hukou system to the quantitative analysis of the overall situation. Moreover, after ten years of Hukou system reform by varying degrees in different regions and cities of different sizes, grasping the driving factors behind Hukou changes is now vitally important for understanding the development and reform of the Hukou system.

Despite existing Hukou research literature, there is still inadequate comprehensive analysis of Hukou system reform. Moreover, most existing quantitative research studies still remain at the cross-sectional data analysis level, and no panel data have been established for quantitative indicators of Hukou system reform in different cities. All these are not helpful for understanding the promotion of Hukou system reform between regions, conducting in-depth quantitative analysis of the influencing factors of Hukou reform, or explaining the development trend. Moreover, it is also difficult to solve potential endogenous statistical problems of mutual causality.

2.2 Quantitative Analysis of Minimum Hukou Settlement Requirements

According to the current policies and regulations of the central government and local governments, Hukou systems in cities above a certain size can be generally divided into two types: the access system and the points-based system that has emerged in recent years. The access system generally has special provisions for different types of people. Under the access system, channels for people to settle in cities can be roughly generalized into investment, employment, family reunion, home purchase, talent introduction and employment, among others. Following the release of the State Council's *Opinions on Deepening Reform of the Hukou System* in 2014 and the introduction of the new regulations on residence permit in 2015, applying for urban Hukou through residence permit under the points-based system has become another important way for non-locals to settle in cities. For this reason, residence permit-related systems are also taken as a channel of Hukou settlement in the quantification research of this book.

Relatively speaking, there are rather strict requirements for people to settle in cities through ways like changing agricultural Hukou to non-agricultural Hukou, living with parents, living with children, transfer to civilian work by ex-servicemen, conversion of township into neighbourhood, winning of major awards or rendering of meritorious service. Moreover, the number of people who meet such requirements is relatively small. Therefore, they are not included in the scope of quantitative research here. In this book, six Level-1 indicators and 28 corresponding Level-2 indicators are established, and specific rules are set forth for each Level-2 indicator. These quantitative evaluation indicators form multi-dimensional variables and serial indicators to evaluate Hukou thresholds in cities. The indicators system is shown in Table 2.1.

In the current study, the author further divides employment channels in the evaluation system. According to 'recruitment from campus' and 'recruitment from society', employment channels for people to settle in cities are divided into employment of graduating students, and employment of non-graduating students/talent introduction for separate research. Among the 28 evaluation indicators, age, marriage length requirement, home floorspace, amount of investment and amount of tax payment are specific numerical variables, while educational requirement, minimum educational level and minimum professional title are variables ranked by level of requirement. For all the other variables, a '0–1' dummy variable is constructed by whether the answer to a specific indicator is 'Yes' or 'No'. In the current study, the author selects 21 large cities with a regular urban population of more than 5 million for analysis. After the various indicator values are obtained, the analytical hierarchy process (AHP) with expert-designated weights and the equal weight method is adopted to estimate the standard Hukou liberalization value for each of the 21 cities in the 2014–2016 period. The results are shown in Table 2.2.

2.3 Analysis of Factors Influencing Minimum Hukou Settlement Requirements

To further quantitatively analyse factors that influence Hukou liberalization, this study selects four major dimensional factors, namely government's ability to provide public services, the standard of living that reflects city attractiveness, urban population and traits of city officials, as explanatory variables. These major indicators are further divided into indicators at lower levels, as shown in Table 2.3.

In this study, the calculation results of the analytic hierarchy process are used as the explained variable in the regression to measure the level of Hukou liberalization in the various megacities. In the meantime, economic indicators, quality-of-life indicators, population indicators, officials-related indicators and other data are adopted for regression analysis using the panel data method. The panel data fixed effect model is as follows:

$$Y_{it} = \beta * X_{it-1} + \delta_i + \mu_t + \epsilon_{it}$$

Wherein, Y_{it} represents the Hukou liberalization index under research, X_{it-1} represents control variables, including economic indicators, quality-of-life indicators, population indicators and officials-related indicators, δ_i represents the unobservable fixed effect of a city, μ_t expresses the time effect and ϵ_{it} stands for random disturbance items. In this model, some

Table 2.1 Summary List of Quantitative Indicators for the Hukou System

	Level-1 Indicators	*Level-2 Indicators*	*Evaluation Indicators for Level-2 Indicators*
	Living with spouses (B1)	Restrictive conditions on living with spouses	Age requirement (C1)
			Marriage length requirement (C2)
		Conditions attached to investment	Whether there is any regular domicile requirement (C3)
			Whether there is any family planning requirement (C4)
			Any (C5)
	Home purchase (B2)	Total floorspace of home purchased	Floorspace (C6)
		Conditions attached to home purchase	Whether there is any social insurance payment length (C7)
			Whether there is any home purchase amount requirement (C8)
			Whether there is any educational qualification requirement (C9)
			Whether there is any home property ownership duration requirement (C10)
Minimum requirements for settling in cities (A)	Investment and business startup (B3)	Amount of investment	Amount of investment (C11)
		Conditions attached to investment	Whether there is any social insurance payment requirement (C12)
			Whether there is any requirement on hiring locals (C13)

(*Continued*)

Table 2.1 (Continued)

	Level-1 Indicators	*Level-2 Indicators*	*Evaluation Indicators for Level-2 Indicators*
			Whether there is any operating length requirement (C14)
			Annual tax payment amount requirement (C15)
	Employment of graduating student (B4)	Minimum education requirement	Educational requirement (C16)
		Conditions attached to employment	Whether there is any age requirement (C17)
			Whether there is any social insurance requirement (C18)
			Whether there is any contract requirement (C19)
			Whether there is any regular domicile requirement (C20)
	Employment of non-graduating student/talent introduction (B5)	Educational level and professional title requirement	Minimum educational level (C21)
			Minimum professional title (C22)
		Conditions attached to talent introduction	Whether there is any age requirement (C23)
			Whether there is any contract requirement (C24)
	Residence permit system (B6)	Status of promotion	Whether it has been promoted (C25)
		Application requirements	Residence duration requirement (C26)
			Whether there are attached requirements (C27)
			Whether application can be made for Hukou settlement (C28)

Table 2.2 Calculation Results of Hukou Liberalization in Selected Large Cities in China

City	*Analytic Hierarchy Process*		*Equal Weight Method*	
	Standardized Value	*Ranking*	*Standardized Value*	*Ranking*
Beijing	0.8278	1	0.70029	1
Guangzhou	0.7873	2	0.64483	2
Shanghai	0.6537	3	0.53828	3
Shenzhen	0.6090	4	0.53391	4
Wuhan	0.5813	5	0.44483	8
Suzhou	0.5372	6	0.52080	6
Tianjin	0.5301	7	0.44167	9
Dongguan	0.4759	8	0.52414	5
Xi'an	0.4450	9	0.45241	7
Qingdao	0.4437	10	0.36552	10
Foshan	0.3887	11	0.33103	14
Chengdu	0.3848	12	0.34023	12
Ningbo	0.3732	13	0.24770	18
Nanjing	0.3392	14	0.31103	15
Shenyang	0.2971	15	0.32782	14
Harbin	0.2967	16	0.34109	11
Hangzhou	0.2892	17	0.26402	17
Chongqing	0.2758	18	0.23138	19
Shijiazhuang	0.2624	19	0.27069	16
Changsha	0.1466	20	0.19103	20
Wenzhou	0.0901	21	0.12356	21

unobservable fixed effects are controlled, so the parameter estimation results are more unbiased and consistent than the regression results obtained using only one-year cross-sectional data.

With consideration of possible endogenous problems (i.e. changes in Hukou liberalization may affect economic development, regional pay level, population mobility and even the promotion of officials) and the time lag from policy formulation to promulgation, this study adopts the various indicators of the year before Hukou policy is introduced as explanatory variables and takes logarithms to reduce the impact of extreme values. With the results of the analytic hierarchy process as explanatory variables, we adopt fixed effect, random effect and mixed cross-section methods to perform regression analysis. The results are shown in Table 2.4.

At the economic indicators level, we can see that with the deepening of reform and opening up, regional disparities of economic development can largely explain the differences in urban Hukou thresholds. The higher the level of economic development, the more fiscal expenditure and the more welfare benefits the government provides for residents in respect of education, healthcare, employment, housing, social security and other aspects, the more local residents as 'vested interests' will worry about the migrant

Table 2.3 The Indicators System for Factors Influencing Minimum Hukou Settlement Requirements

Level-1 Indicators	*Level-2 Indicators*	*Level-3 Indicators*
Factors influencing minimum Hukou settlement requirements in cities	Government's ability to provide public services	GDP (RMB100 million)
		Public financial expenditure (RMB100 million)
		Investment in urban real estate development and construction (RMB100 million)
	Urban residents' standard of living	In-service workers' average pay (RMB)
		Urban disposable income (RMB)
		Housing price level (RMB/m^2)
	Urban population	Total Hukou population size (10,000)
		Mechanical growth rate of population (‰)
		Population density (persons/m^2)
	Traits of city officials in charge	Age
		Source
		Native place

population's squeezing on their resources and other negative externalities, thus putting pressure on the government to a certain degree. This invisible pressure forces cities to set higher requirements for non-locals to get urban Hukou. The higher the Hukou reform cost is, the greater the obstacles to Hukou reform will be. However, it is worth mentioning that investment in real estate construction is found to have a slightly weak negative impact. If real estate investment is used to expand city size, adjust livelihood interests and increase the supply of public goods, it can alleviate the pressure of population inflows to a certain extent and slightly lower the Hukou threshold.

At the living indicators level, high housing prices in megacities make it difficult for the floating population to bear the cost and 'find a regular domicile to live in', and form a strong push for these groups to leave cities. To a certain extent, this might weaken their willingness to move to cities and slightly reduce the urban Hukou threshold. However, we find that housing price seems to have no significant impact or even have a slightly negative impact on the urban Hukou threshold. For one thing, this may be because high housing prices effectively keep the floating population at bay, thus

Table 2.4 Regression Results of Three-year Panel Data of 21 Cities Based on Analytic Hierarchy Process

Indicator/Evaluation Method	*Fixed Effect Model*	*Random Effect Model*	*Mixed Regression Model*
Per capita GDP	0.00851*** (2.77)	0.01026*** (2.68)	0.01361** (1.98)
Financial expenditure	0.01680*** (6.12)	0.01685*** (5.93)	0.01256** (2.49)
Investment in real estate development	−0.00317 (−1.30)	−0.00265* (−1.73)	−0.00106 (−1.44)
Workers'average pay	0.07532*** (3.14)	0.05672*** (2.60)	0.04941* (1.40)
Housing price	−0.00986 (−1.01)	−0.00421 (−1.38)	−0.00696 (−1.12)
Urban disposable income	0.00566*** (3.14)	0.00312*** (3.47)	0.00341** (2.23)
Population growth rate	0.00405** (2.33)	0.00365 (1.49)	0.00431* (1.78)
Population age	0.00020*** (3.06)	0.00012* (1.73)	0.00012** (2.37)
Age of officials	−0.00459* (−1.89)	−0.00349 (−1.40)	−0.00407* (1.90)
Whether officials are locals	−0.00928** (−2.10)	−0.00797*** (−3.39)	−0.01457* (1.93)
Whether officials are assigned by the central government	−0.00934* (−1.69)	−0.00821*** (−4.68)	−0.00632** (2.55)
R^2	0.5108	0.4420	0.4560
N	66	66	66

Note: Figures in brackets are t statistics. ***, ** and * represent the significant levels of 1%, 5% and 10%, respectively.

reducing demand for urban Hukou. However, high levels of pay and income in megacities nevertheless have strong appeals to the floating population. In megacities, economic growth, technological progress, effect of scale and other factors can increase the average marginal output of workers in various economic entities, thus bringing higher pay in return. Large enterprises and big corporations are inclined to set up their headquarters in developed regions, and they often can also provide higher salaries than their peers in other regions. With relatively more economic opportunities and high pay and income, megacities attract large numbers of migrant workers, thus raising the Hukou threshold.

At the population indicators level, we observe no significant regression coefficient (relevant results are not reported) after the total Hukou population is put into the model as an explanatory variable. However, a significant impact can indeed be seen after population density, which takes the area factor into account, is put into the model. At the same time, the influence coefficient of the mechanical growth rate of population, which measures the net population inflow pressure, is also rather significant. In order to ease the aggravated people-land contradiction caused by the massive flow of migrant workers into cities, cities with higher net population migration pressure and higher population densities can only prevent the excessive inflow of people from outside by raising the Hukou threshold and not opening to the floating population public services that consume local resources, when these cities are unable to effectively control the increase of their permanent resident population.

At the officials-related indicators level, the regression results of this study show that locally born and elder officials dispatched by the central government are more inclined to make bolder reforms: on the one hand, locally born officials have a stronger sense of responsibility for advancing local development, as well as a better understanding of local situations. On the other hand, an older age means richer experience, and dispatching by the central government often means more political support, thus enabling officials to better solve the problems they encounter in the reform process.

After this study, we have adopted the same method to calculate the degree of Hukou liberalization in more than 200 prefecture-level Chinese cities. Thanks to the more vigorous unified efforts by the central government, Hukou liberalization in China has substantially improved in recent years. Currently, Hukou liberalization remains at a relatively low level only in Tier-1 cities like Beijing, Shanghai, Guangzhou and Shenzhen or in special cities such as Wenzhou, all other cities have basically liberalized their Hukou restrictions. Optimistically speaking, China's Hukou system will gradually return to the demographic function in the near future, and Hukou's distortion of resources allocation will disappear step by step.

3 Hukou System Reform and Residents' Economic Behaviour

3.1 Impact of Hukou Changes on Household Consumption of the Floating Population

3.1.1 Background

The importance of understanding Chinese households' consumption behaviour is self-evident. Currently, there are many explanations for the low consumption in China, but there are relatively few studies focusing on specific consumer groups. China's Hukou system divides the whole population into an urban population and a rural population. In recent years, the number of migrant workers who hold a rural Hukou and work in cities has increased significantly. According to the national floating population monitoring report released by the National Bureau of Statistics, China's floating population totalled 273 million in 2014, accounting for a considerable proportion of the national labour force. Existing statistical data show that the economic behaviour of the floating population and their families is different from that of both traditional farmers who work in rural areas and residents with an urban Hukou. The floating population has the lowest household consumption rate among these three groups, and the rate is still falling (Table 3.1). This is an important reason for the overall low consumption rate in China (Zhang Xun et al., 2014). The consumption income data of the floating population monitored by the National Bureau of Statistics in recent years has revealed a further decline in consumption rate. In terms of consumption composition, there are significant differences between the floating population and urban residents: the consumption mode of the floating population is relatively monolithic, with subsistence consumption still occupying an important position in their overall expenditure (the Research Team of the Development Research Center of the State Council, 2010).

In addition to migrant workers who have attracted high public attention, the floating population also includes the city-to-city floating population, namely migrants who move from one city to work in another city. While they have a non-agricultural Hukou, these people hold no Hukou in the cities where they work. For example, many non-locals working in Beijing have an

DOI: 10.4324/9781003288091-4

Table 3.1 Consumption Rates of Urban Residents, the Floating Population and Rural Residents Working in Rural Areas

	2002	*2007*	*2009*
Residents with rural Hukou who work in rural areas	74.10%	77.86%	77.49%
Residents with urban Hukou	77.40%	68.24%	63.74%
The floating population	74.02%	66.71%	56.90%

Source: *China Statistics Yearbook* and calculations based on the China Household Income Panel Studies Database (CHIPS).

urban Hukou in their hometowns, but they hold no local urban Hukou in Beijing. This still makes it difficult for them to get the social welfare and other public services in Beijing, which in turn makes their household consumption behaviour different from that of local residents. At the same time, considering both the urban and rural floating population and the city-to-city floating population, this author believes that obtaining an urban Hukou alone is not enough for the floating population. The only way to completely break the institutional barriers that separate them from local residents is for the floating population to get an urban Hukou in the cities where they work. For this reason, the Hukou changes subsequently mentioned in this book are all about the floating population obtaining a local urban Hukou.

Does the Hukou system limit the consumption expenditure of the floating population? Can obtaining a local urban Hukou increase the household consumption of the floating population? Similar ideas have been discussed in some academic literature (Cai Fang, 2011; Chen Binkai et al., 2010; Chen et al., 2015; Song et al., 2010), but they did not pay attention to the acquisition effects of 'local Hukou'. The impact of the Hukou system on the consumption behaviour of the floating population still requires further exploration, including research on the improvement of research methodology and a detailed analysis of the time frames under research (long-term impacts and short-term impacts). This study will use a relatively new and large-scale micro database and focus on the floating population whose local urban Hukou attributes have changed, and adopt a method combining propensity score matching and difference-in-differences to construct counterfactuals and estimate the impact of Hukou changes on the household consumption behaviour of the floating population. In addition, after analyzing the short-term consumption effect of turning the floating population into townspeople, this study will go on to discuss its likely long-term impact.

3.1.2 Data Description and Research Methodology

3.1.2.1 Definition of Variables

The micro data used in this study are from China Family Panel Studies (CFPS). CFPS provides four types of household expenditure data, namely living expenditure, transfer expenditure, security expenditure and housing loan expenditure. In this study, living expenditure is mainly selected, which includes food expenditure, clothing expenditure, transportation and communication expenditure, daily household expenses/household appliances/ service expenditure, residential expenditure, healthcare expenditure, entertainment and leisure expenditure, education expenditure and other expenses. However, the contents of each specific living expenditure item in the three-year questionnaire (i.e. 2010, 2012 and 2014) were not consistent, with differences between 2012 and 2014 being the smallest and the differences between 2010 and the subsequent two periods being the biggest. To ensure data comparability between different years, this study takes the consumption statistical criteria of 2010 as the basis, and retains all the consumption items in the questionnaire. Finally, the four types of household consumption expenditure are divided by net household income to get the four defined household consumption rates[1], which are the main variables in this study.

3.1.2.2 Definition of Treatment Group and Control Group

This study divides urban[2] residents into two types: local[3] residents and the floating population. Local residents refer to the population holding a local urban Hukou. The floating population is further divided into two types: migrant workers who may be local migrant workers (holding a local rural Hukou), or migrant workers (holding a rural Hukou in another place) and the city-to-city floating population. These migrants already have a non-agricultural Hukou, but do not have a Hukou of the city they flow into. As shown in Table 3.2, most of the floating population in cities are migrant workers, and migrant workers have the highest Consumption Rates 1 and 2 among the three groups. The consumption rate of the city-to-city floating population depends on the specific definition of the consumption rate. Under the definitions of Consumption Rates 1, 2 and 4, the city-to-city floating population has the lowest consumption rate. However, it has the highest consumption rate under the definition of Consumption Rate 3.

By their nature, the CFPS data enable us to observe changes in respondents' Hukou status and economic behaviour. This study focuses on the changes in the household consumption behaviour of the urban floating population (i.e. migrant workers and the city-to-city floating population) after their Hukou has been changed. Both rural migrant workers with a rural Hukou and the city-to-city floating population holding an urban Hukou face the same restrictions on access to social security and social services, which make it impossible for them to fully release their consumption potential. Therefore, Hukou changes in this study refer to obtaining a local urban Hukou, not just an urban Hukou. This is also a major difference between this study and other existing studies.

Table 3.3 presents the Hukou changes of the urban floating population from 2020 to 2012. It shows that most of the urban floating population kept their

Table 3.2 Population Distribution in the Total Samples in 2010

	Classification	*Size*		*Consumption Rate 1*	*Consumption Rate 2*	*Consumption Rate 3*	*Consumption Rate 4*
Urban residents	Local residents	2,218	58.15%	0.781	0.769	0.582	0.571
	Migrant workers	1,399	36.68%	0.815	0.797	0.588	0.571
	City-to-city floating population	197	5.17%	0.731	0.688	0.595	0.554
	Total	3,814	100%	0.791	0.775	0.585	0.570
Rural residents	Local residents	4,280	91.08%	0.935	0.926	0.632	0.623
	City-to-village floating population	341	7.26%	0.778	0.771	0.517	0.510
	Village-to-village floating population	78	1.66%	0.884	0.865	0.657	0.635
	Total	4,699	100%	0.923	0.913	0.624	0.615

Note: In order to fully describe the distribution of the total samples, rural residents are also included in the table. The distribution of the different groups is not completely consistent between different years. What is reported here is the situation in 2010. Consumption Rates 1, 2, 3 and 4 are respectively the consumption rates based on the original data, data excluding house rents, data excluding medical and education expenditures and data excluding housing, medical and education expenditures.

Table 3.3 Hukou Changes of the Floating Population from 2010 to 2012

Nature of Hukou	*Non-agricultural Hukou to Agricultural Hukou*	*No Hukou Change*	*Agricultural Hukou to Non-agricultural Hukou*	*Total*
Local migrant workers	0	1,079	153	1,232
Non-local migrant workers	0	140	27	167
City-to-city floating population	4	193	0	197
Hukou location	*Local Hukou to non-local Hukou*	*No Hukou change*	*Non-local Hukou to local Hukou*	*Total*
Local migrant workers	8	1,224	0	1,232
Non-local migrant workers	0	114	53	167
City-to-city floating population	0	85	112	197

Hukou unchanged. In this study, the group with no change in both the nature and location of their Hukou is taken as the control group, and the corresponding treat group includes local migrant workers who changed from rural Hukou to urban Hukou, non-local migrant workers who changed from non-local rural Hukou to local urban Hukou, and the city-to-city floating population who changed from non-local Hukou to local Hukou. In this study, a small number of special cases are excluded where members of the city-to-city floating population changed from urban Hukou to rural Hukou, local migrant workers changed from local Hukou to non-local Hukou and non-local migrant workers who only changed the nature or location of their Hukou).

After the samples were classified according to the method above, 1,255 control group samples and 281 treat group samples were obtained. The specific analysis is shown in Table 3.4. Among them, 153 local migrant

Table 3.4 Distribution of the Treat Group and the Control Group from 2010 to 2012

	Control Group	*Treat Group*	*Total*
Local migrant workers	1,071	153	1,224
Non-local migrant workers	103	16	119
City-to-city floating population	81	112	193
Total	1,255	281	1,536

workers changed from local rural Hukou to local urban Hukou and separate calculations show that 16 non-local migrant workers changed from non-local rural Hukou to local urban Hukou and 112 members of the city-to-city floating population changed from non-local urban Hukou to local urban Hukou. It can be seen that the city-to-city floating population made the most Hukou changes, which is consistent with the fact that in real Hukou reform practice, the city-to-city floating population is more likely to get a local Hukou than migrant workers. The sample size of the treat group of migrant workers was too small for separate analysis, and there was a relatively high similarity between non-local migrant workers and local migrant workers. Therefore, we will no longer distinguish between local migrant workers and non-local migrant workers in the subsequent analysis, but take them as a unified group of migrant workers for analysis.

Table 3.5 shows changes in consumption between the treat group and the control group in different years. It can be found that the household consumption expenditure of all four groups increased year by year, and the consumption rate followed the same changing trend. The consumption rate in both the short term (2012) and the long term (2014) was greater than that of the base year (2010). Despite their similarity in consumption patterns, the four groups nevertheless had quite different household characteristics. Among the migrant workers, the treatment group that obtained urban Hukou persistently had higher household income and net assets than those without urban Hukou. Similar characteristics were also found in respect of the age, educational level and health status of heads of household ('HoHs'). Moreover, children made up a relatively high proportion of the households, while the proportion of elderly family members was relatively low. Different from the case of the migrant workers, the treat group of the city-to-city floating population that obtained local Hukou actually had a lower average household income and net assets than those that did not obtain local Hukou. In the treat group, HoHs' educational and health levels were also relatively low. However, as in the case of the migrant workers, children also made up a relatively high proportion of the households of the treat group, while the proportion of elderly family members was relatively low.

This implies a certain selectivity among those households of the floating population that chose to change Hukou. To a certain extent, this problem can be solved by the approach combining matching and difference-in-differences methods adopted below. In addition, considering the different characteristics of their treat groups and control groups, the migrant workers and the city-to-city floating population will be analysed separately below (Table 3.6).

3.1.2.3 Methodology

Tracking data have been rarely used in past studies on the Hukou system's impact on the consumption behaviour of the floating population. However, the use of cross-sectional data alone may cause the neglect of the

Table 3.5 Changes in Household Consumption Behaviour of Four Types of Floating Population

	Variable	*2010*			*2012*			*2014*		
		Sample Size	*Mean*	*Standard Deviation*	*Sample Size*	*Mean*	*Standard Deviation*	*Sample Size*	*Mean*	*Standard Deviation*
Treatgroup of migrant workers	Household Living Expenditure 1 (RMB)	169	27,233	17,989	169	32,986	20,211	124	40,354	24,340
	Household Living Expenditure 2 (RMB)	169	26,566	17,509	169	32,692	20,145	124	39,593	23,658
	Household Living Expenditure 3 (RMB)	169	20,002	13,672	169	26,771	16,397	124	32,482	20,217
	Household Living Expenditure 4 (RMB)	169	19,336	13,045	169	26,477	16,305	124	31,721	19,547
	Household Consumption Rate 1	169	0.809	0.565	169	0.837	0.610	116	0.827	0.536
	Household Consumption Rate 2	169	0.794	0.557	169	0.829	0.606	116	0.809	0.524
	Household Consumption Rate 3	169	0.574	0.389	169	0.673	0.502	116	0.651	0.397
	Household Consumption Rate 4	169	0.559	0.380	169	0.665	0.498	116	0.632	0.382
Control group of migrant workers	Household Living Expenditure 1 (RMB)	1,174	6,381	5,044	1,174	7,688	5,692	875	8,979	6,234
	Household Living Expenditure 2 (RMB)	1,174	6,194	4,760	1,174	7,592	5,588	875	8,720	5,802
	Household Living Expenditure 3 (RMB)	1,174	4,760	4,064	1,174	6,132	4,946	875	7,079	5,237

(*Continued*)

Table 3.5 (Continued)

	Variable	*2010*			*2012*			*2014*		
		Sample Size	*Mean*	*Standard Deviation*	*Sample Size*	*Mean*	*Standard Deviation*	*Sample Size*	*Mean*	*Standard Deviation*
	Household Living Expenditure 4 (RMB)	1,174	4,573	3,730	1,174	6,036	4,848	875	6,820	4,738
	Household Consumption Rate 1	1,174	0.819	0.525	1,174	0.841	0.648	776	0.854	0.579
	Household Consumption Rate 2	1,174	0.802	0.515	1,174	0.833	0.642	776	0.838	0.566
	Household Consumption Rate 3	1,174	0.590	0.361	1,174	0.656	0.514	776	0.650	0.429
	Household Consumption Rate 4	1,174	0.573	0.348	1,174	0.648	0.507	776	0.636	0.416
Treat group of city-to-city floating population	Household Living Expenditure 1 (RMB)	112	28,797	16,394	112	33,903	18,769	83	42,137	22,800
	Household Living Expenditure 2 (RMB)	112	27,330	15,715	112	33,570	18,374	83	41,658	22,672
	Household Living Expenditure 3 (RMB)	112	23,985	14,785	112	27,328	16,105	83	35,021	18,371
	Household Living Expenditure 4 (RMB)	112	22,518	14,150	112	26,994	15,599	83	34,543	18,108
	Household Consumption Rate 1	112	0.765	0.456	112	0.865	0.639	81	0.779	0.456
	Household Consumption Rate 2	112	0.725	0.436	112	0.857	0.635	81	0.768	0.451
	Household Consumption Rate 3	112	0.622	0.357	112	0.687	0.507	81	0.638	0.341

	Household Consumption Rate 4	112	0.583	0.332	112	0.680	0.504	81	0.627	0.333
Control group of city-to-city floating population	Household Living Expenditure 1 (RMB)	81	16,084	10,089	81	16,551	8,649	58	22,795	10,928
	Household Living Expenditure 2 (RMB)	81	14,937	9,318	81	16,095	8,133	58	21,845	10,175
	Household Living Expenditure 3 (RMB)	81	13,542	9,120	81	13,888	7,889	58	19,641	10,259
	Household Living Expenditure 4 (RMB)	81	12,395	8,335	81	13,432	7,563	58	18,691	9,451
	Household Consumption Rate 1	81	0.654	0.378	81	0.820	0.611	56	0.730	0.441
	Household Consumption Rate 2	81	0.605	0.331	81	0.805	0.613	56	0.704	0.425
	Household Consumption Rate 3	81	0.545	0.315	81	0.659	0.491	56	0.616	0.335
	Household Consumption Rate 4	81	0.501	0.292	81	0.644	0.492	56	0.590	0.317

Note: The per capita consumption expenditure of households was adjusted according to the provincial rural consumer price index or urban consumer price index, with the index of 2010 taken as 100. Compared with the 2010–2012 panel data, the missing sample size in 2014 was due to the reorganization and change of some households (as reflected in the change of household numbers), making reasonable comparison with the situation in the base year impossible. So, the data were excluded. In 2014, the sample size of the household consumption rate was less than that of household consumption expenditure, because the net household incomes reported by some households were missing. Similar situations existed in 2010 and 2012. Because no subsequent analysis can be made if the consumption rate is missing, the relevant samples are directly excluded.

Table 3.6 Descriptive Statistics of the Characteristic Variables of the Four Types of Floating Population

	Variable	*Sample Size of Treat Group*	*Mean*	*Standard Deviation*	*Sample Size of Control Group*	*Mean*	*Standard Deviation*
Migrant workers	Logarithm of household net income	169	10.46	0.698	1,174	10.21	0.718
	Logarithm of total household assets	166	11.82	3.364	1,160	11.51	3.187
	Head of household's age	169	54.16	13.51	1,174	47.39	11.45
	Head of household's length of education	169	7.899	4.909	1,174	6.509	4.103
	Head of household's health status (1 = Healthy; 5 = unhealthy)	169	1.799	1.009	1,174	1.746	0.934
	Head of household's gender (1 = Male; 0 = Female)	169	0.657	0.476	1,174	0.705	0.456
	Head of household's marital status (1 = married; 0 = others)	169	0.870	0.337	1,174	0.928	0.258
	Head of household's ethnic group (1 = Han Chinese; 0 = others)	169	0.976	0.152	1,171	0.964	0.186
	Head of household's Party membership (1 = Yes; 0 = No)	169	0.225	0.419	1,174	0.0537	0.225
	Family size	169	3.503	1.566	1,174	3.902	1.504
	Proportion of elderly members at or over 60 in family	169	0.0896	0.137	1,174	0.145	0.169
	Proportion of children under 15 in family	169	0.251	0.340	1,174	0.0999	0.232

	Rate of endowment insurance coverage over adult family members	169	0.560	0.369	1,174	0.615	0.313
	Rate of medical insurance coverage over whole family	169	0.422	0.428	1,174	0.197	0.340
City-to-city floating population	Logarithm of household net income	112	10.55	0.746	81	11.05	0.880
	Logarithm of total household assets	109	11.79	2.904	80	12.52	3.649
	Head of household's age	112	47.62	13.83	81	45.98	15.10
	Head of household's length of education	112	10.71	4.001	81	11.77	3.287
	Head of household's health status (1 = Healthy; 5 = unhealthy)	112	1.607	0.764	81	1.679	0.804
	Head of household's gender (1 = Male; 0 = Female)	112	0.634	0.484	81	0.556	0.500
	Head of household's marital status (1 = married; 0 = others)	112	0.804	0.399	81	0.840	0.369
	Head of household's ethnic group (1 = Han Chinese; 0 = others)	112	0.946	0.226	81	0.975	0.156
	Head of household's Party membership (1 = Yes; 0 = No)	112	0.232	0.424	81	0.123	0.331
	Family size	112	2.795	1.572	81	2.864	0.959
	Proportion of elderly members at or over 60 in family	112	0.0898	0.151	81	0.107	0.159

(*Continued*)

Table 3.6 (Continued)

Variable	*Sample Size of Treat Group*	*Mean*	*Standard Deviation*	*Sample Size of Control Group*	*Mean*	*Standard Deviation*
Proportion of children under 15 in family	112	0.196	0.342	81	0.150	0.311
Rate of endowment insurance coverage over adult family members	112	0.573	0.373	81	0.565	0.345
Rate of medical insurance coverage over whole family	112	0.469	0.444	81	0.451	0.436

Note: For the sake of brevity and given that only the characteristic variables of the base year are used in subsequent matching, this table only reports on the situation in 2010.

unobservable heterogeneity of the floating population and urban residents, which limits the reliability and extrapolation of the research conclusions. In this study, we use tracking panel data, as well as rich personal, household and other information. By adopting an approach that combines the propensity score matching and difference-in-differences methods, it is possible to relatively effectively solve the endogenous problems caused by missing variables and selectivity. Propensity score matching can weaken the selectivity bias and get the comparable samples of the treat group and the control group in the common support domain. The difference-in-differences method can help to overcome the influence of unobservable variables, especially the influence of time-invariant factors and time-synchronous factors.

In specific data computations, the biggest difference between the approach combining the propensity score matching and difference-in-differences methods and the general propensity score matching model lies in the result variable. In the former case, the result variable is no longer cross-sectional data, but the changing value of data in the continuous temporal dimension. Heinrich et al. (2010) summarize the computation process and pointed out that this approach is more effective than the simple propensity score matching model. In this study, the differences in household consumption rate between the treat group and the control group of the two types of the floating population in their respective time series are found first, which can eliminate the possible influence of unobservable and time-invariant factors. Then, the difference value is used as the explained variable, and a series of characteristic variables are used to make matching and estimate the average treatment effect.

3.1.3 Empirical Results

This section mainly reports on the impact of Hukou changes on the household consumption rate of the floating population as estimated by the combined propensity score matching and difference-in-differences approach. Before reporting the main results, we have found from test that there is no significant difference in the mean value of each covariate between the control group and the treat group, and the overall joint test also accepts the conclusion that there is no significant difference in these covariates.

Based on the above test, this study estimates the impact of Hukou changes on the household consumption rate of the floating population. Due to their big differences, migrant workers and the city-to-city floating population are analysed separately. Table 3.7 shows the impact of Hukou changes on migrant workers. Most results show a significant fall in the consumption rate of those migrant workers who changed Hukou. Taking Consumption Rate 4 as an example, the household consumption rate fall ranged from 9.8% to 13.1%. Table 3.8 reports on the impact of Hukou changes on the city-to-city floating population. It shows that for all consumption rate definitions and

Table 3.7 Impact of HoH Attribute Changes on the Household Consumption Rate of the Floating Population—Migrant Workers

	Matching Method	*Treat Group*	*Control Group*	*Average Treatment Effect*	*Standard Deviation*	*Common Support Sample Size*	
		Two-year Changes	*Two-year Changes*			*Treat Group*	*Control Group*
Consumption Rate 1	One-to-one matching: k = 1	0.032	0.201	−0.169	0.102	165	1,157
	k Nearest neighbour matching: k = 5	0.032	0.246	−0.214**	0.084	165	1,157
	Radius matching: δ = 0.01	0.014	0.219	−0.205**	0.084	149	1,157
	Kernel matching: k;norm;bw;0.01	0.032	0.218	−0.186**	0.086	165	1,157
Consumption Rate 2	One-to-one matching: k = 1	0.039	0.213	−0.174*	0.101	165	1,157
	k Nearest neighbour matching: k = 5	0.039	0.251	−0.212**	0.083	165	1,157
	Radius matching: δ = 0.01	0.021	0.224	−0.202**	0.083	149	1,157
	Kernel matching: k;norm;bw;0.01	0.039	0.223	−0.184**	0.084	165	1,157
Consumption Rate 3	One-to-one matching: k = 1	0.103	0.206	−0.103	0.079	165	1,157
	k Nearest neighbour matching: k = 5	0.103	0.237	−0.134**	0.061	165	1,157
	Radius matching: δ = 0.01	0.107	0.228	−0.121*	0.063	149	1,157
	Kernel matching: k;norm;bw;0.01	0.103	0.203	−0.099*	0.059	165	1,157

Consumption Rate 4	One-to-one matching: k = 1	0.110	0.215	−0.105	0.077	165	1,157
	k Nearest neighbour matching: k = 5	0.110	0.241	−0.131**	0.061	165	1,157
	Radius matching: δ = 0.01	0.114	0.231	−0.116*	0.062	149	1,157
	Kernel matching: k;norm;bw;0.01	0.110	0.209	−0.098*	0.058	165	1,157

Note: The first two columns in the table are the average changes in the household consumption rate of the corresponding groups (treat group or control group) in the two years. The average treatment effect is the quadratic difference of the changes in household consumption rate between the two years. The common support sample size refers to the number of samples that meet the common support hypothesis. The same definitions are adopted in the tables below. *** $p < 0.01$, ** $p < 0.05$ and * $p < 0.1$.

Table 3.8 Impact of HoH Attribute Changes on the Household Consumption Rate of the Floating Population—City-to-City Floating Population

	Matching Method	*Treat Group*	*Control Group*	*Average Treatment Effect*	*Standard Deviation*	*Common Support Sample Size*	
		Two-year Changes	*Two-year Changes*			*Treat Group*	*Control Group*
Consumption Rate 1	One-to-one matching: k = 1	0.134	0.194	−0.059	0.132	102	80
	k Nearest neighbour matching: k = 5	0.134	0.171	−0.036	0.123	102	80
	Radius matching: δ = 0.01	0.151	0.197	−0.047	0.133	94	80
	Kernel matching: k;norm;bw;0.01	0.134	0.202	−0.068	0.125	102	80
Consumption Rate 2	One-to-one matching: k = 1	0.169	0.238	−0.069	0.124	102	80
	k Nearest neighbour matching: k = 5	0.169	0.210	−0.041	0.118	102	80
	Radius matching: δ = 0.01	0.188	0.245	−0.057	0.127	94	80
	Kernel matching: k;norm;bw;0.01	0.169	0.255	−0.086	0.121	102	80
Consumption Rate 3	One-to-one matching: k = 1	0.087	0.109	−0.023	0.101	102	80
	k Nearest neighbour matching: k = 5	0.087	0.098	−0.012	0.095	102	80
	Radius matching: δ = 0.01	0.099	0.101	−0.001	0.103	94	80
	Kernel matching: k;norm;bw;0.01	0.087	0.111	−0.024	0.098	102	80
Consumption Rate 4	One-to-one matching: k = 1	0.131	0.088	0.042	0.138	100	80
	k Nearest neighbour matching: k = 5	0.121	0.128	−0.007	0.093	102	80
	Radius matching: δ = 0.01	0.137	0.141	−0.005	0.101	94	80
	Kernel matching: k;norm;bw;0.01	0.121	0.155	−0.035	0.095	102	80

matching methods, the change of Hukou has no impact on the consumption rate of the city-to-city floating population.

3.1.4 Discussion on Mechanisms and Long-Term Effects

According to the above estimates, the impact of obtaining local urban Hukou on migrant workers and the city-to-city floating population was not consistent. For migrant workers, obtaining a local urban Hukou significantly lowered their household consumption rate, while for the city-to-city floating population, it does not affect their family consumption rate. This section will mainly discuss the possible reasons for this conclusion. Due to limited data, not all the possible reasons can be tested in this study. Instead, the discussion will focus on the impact of Hukou changes on household consumption expenditure and household income. In addition, the panel data of CFPS 2010–2012 selected above also chiefly reflect the short-term effect of Hukou changes. In this section, an attempt will be made to use the panel data of CFPS 2010–2014 to estimate the long-term consumption effect of Hukou changes. The purpose is to provide a comprehensive explanation of the impact of Hukou changes on the household consumption of the floating population.

3.1.4.1 Changes in Household Consumption Expenditure

This section will examine the impact of Hukou changes on the absolute amount of household consumption expenditure. To eliminate the influence of inflation, household consumption expenditure is adjusted according to the provincial rural consumer price or urban consumer price index, with the index for 2020 taken as 100. To save space, only the results of Household Consumption Expenditure 4 are reported in the main text here. The results are as shown in Table 3.9. It can be seen that there was a notable increase in migrant workers' consumption expenditure after they obtained a local urban Hukou. For the city-to-city floating population, Hukou changes had no significant impact on their household consumption expenditure.

3.1.4.2 Changes in Household Income

The household consumption rate is jointly determined by household consumption and household income. After the analysis in the above section on the impact of obtaining local urban Hukou on the household consumption rate and total consumption expenditure of the floating population, this section focuses on its impact on household income, to further understand changes in the consumption rate. To eliminate the influence of inflation, household income is adjusted according to the provincial rural consumer index or urban consumer price index, with the index for 2010 taken as 100. The results are shown in Table 3.10. It can be seen that there was a

Table 3.9 Impact of HoH Attribute Changes on Household Consumption of the Floating Population (Under Definition 4)

	Matching Method	*Treat Group*	*Control Group*	*Average Treatment Effect*	*Standard Deviation*	*Common Support Sample Size*	
		Two-year Changes	*Two-year Changes*			*Treat Group*	*Control Group*
Migrant workers: Consumption Expenditure 4	One-to-one matching: k = 1	7,339	3,575	3,763**	1,881	161	1,157
	k Nearest neighbour matching: k = 5	7,339	4,238	3,100**	1,506	161	1,157
	Radius matching: δ = 0.01	8,338	5,155	3,182**	1,403	149	1,157
	Kernel matching: k;norm;bw;0.01	7,339	4,692	2,647*	1,498	161	1,157
City-to-city floating population: Consumption Expenditure 4	One-to-one matching: k = 1	4,490	8,336	−3,845	2,817	103	80
	k Nearest neighbour matching: k = 5	4,490	7,634	−3,143	3,168	103	80
	Radius matching: δ = 0.01	5,277	7,560	−2,283	3,069	92	80
	Kernel matching: k;norm;bw;0.01	4,490	7,500	−3,009	3,338	103	80

Table 3.10 Impact of HoH Attribute Changes on Household Income of the Floating Population

	Matching Method	*Treat Group*	*Control Group*	*Average Treatment Effect*	*Standard Deviation*	*Common Support Sample Size*	
		Two-year Changes	*Two-year Changes*			*Treat Group*	*Control Group*
Migrant workers	One-to-one matching: k = 1	15,881	6,593	9,287	7,117	165	1,157
	k Nearest neighbour matching: k = 5	15,881	2,005	12,875**	6,226	165	1,157
	Radius matching: δ = 0.01	18,129	6,194	11,934*	6,440	149	1,157
	Kernel matching: k;norm;bw;0.01	15,881	4,169	11,712**	5,828	165	1,157
City-to-city floating population	One-to-one matching: k = 1	14,937	13,348	1,588	15,600	103	80
	k Nearest neighbour matching: k = 5	14,937	12,832	2,104	15,421	103	80
	Radius matching: δ = 0.01	18,976	15,203	3,773	14,780	92	80
	Kernel matching: k;norm;bw;0.01	14,937	11,421	3,515	16,594	103	80

significant increase in the household income of those migrant workers who had changed Hukou, while the household income of those urban migrants who also had changed Hukou did not change significantly. Along with the estimated changes in consumption rate, consumption expenditure and income, we can roughly reach the following conclusion: Hukou changes increase both household income and consumption expenditure, but due to its inertia, consumption expenditure does not increase as fast as income. Consequently, the consumption rate falls.

3.1.4.3 Long-Term Consumption Effect

All the analyses above are based on the panel data of CFPS 2010–2012, which can be regarded as the short-term effect of Hukou changes. This section will use the panel data of CFPS 2010–2014 to estimate the consumption effect of Hukou changes over a longer-term. Though CFPS guarantees tracking surveys for all households in the base year, the sample size for 2014 as analysed in this study is nevertheless smaller. This is mainly because for household behaviour analysis, data on those households which were reorganized or changed (as reflected in the change of household number) must be excluded, as household reorganization or change makes reasonable comparison with the base year situation impossible. Besides, to ensure that the estimated results indeed show the long-term effect, households with Hukou changes from 2012 to 2014 are also excluded. Therefore, the treat group consisted of the floating population who obtained a local urban Hukou from 2010 to 2012 and kept their Hukou unchanged in 2014, while the control group was the floating population who kept their Hukou unchanged in 2010, 2012 and 2014. To save space, only the results of Consumption Rate 4 and corresponding consumption expenditure are reported here.

The analysis results about the migrant workers are shown in Table 3.11, showing that Hukou changes had no significant impact on the consumption rate of migrant workers in the long run. The long-term effect of Hukou acquisition on consumption expenditure and household income were consistent with the short-term effect, while Household Consumption Expenditure 4 rose significantly. As household income also increased significantly, the consumption rate remained unchanged.

The analysis results about the city-to-city floating population are shown in Table 3.12. For the floating population who obtained a local urban Hukou, there was no significant change in their consumption rate, consumption expenditure or household income in the long run, which was consistent with the short-term impact of Hukou acquisition.

3.1.5 Summary of Impact of Hukou Changes on Consumption

This study does not directly compare the households of the floating population with those of the urban population. Rather, it looks for comparable

Table 3.11 Long-Term Impact of HoH Attribute Changes on Household Consumption Behaviour of the Floating Population—Migrant Workers

	Matching Method	*Treat Group*	*Control Group*	*Average Treatment Effect*	*Standard Deviation*	*Common Support Sample Size*	
		Two-year Changes	*Two-year Changes*			*Treat Group*	*Control Group*
Consumption Rate 4	One-to-one matching: k = 1	0.087	0.207	−0.120	0.087	93	715
	k Nearest neighbour matching: k=5	0.087	0.190	−0.103	0.074	93	715
	Radius matching: δ = 0.01	0.039	0.137	−0.098	0.076	75	715
	Kernel matching: k;norm;bw;0.01	0.087	0.145	−0.059	0.081	93	715
Consumption Expenditure 4	One-to-one matching: k = 1	13,605	10,546	3,059	2,694	93	715
	k Nearest neighbour matching: k = 5	13,605	9,723	3,881*	2,391	93	715
	Radius matching: δ = 0.01	15,324	9,948	5,375**	2,649	75	715
	Kernel matching: k;norm;bw;0.01	13,605	9,464	4,140**	1,974	93	715
Income	One-to-one matching: k = 1	17,904	6,891	11,012*	6,851	93	715
	k Nearest neighbour matching: k = 5	17,904	9,245	8,659	5,464	93	715
	Radius matching: δ = 0.01	21,639	8,683	12,956***	5,095	75	715
	Kernel matching: k;norm;bw;0.01	17,904	9,831	8,073	6,153	93	715

Table 3.12 Long-Term Impact of HoH Attribute Changes on Household Consumption Behaviour of the Floating Population—City-to-City Floating Population

	Matching Method	*Treat Group*	*Control Group*	*Average Treatment Effect*	*Standard Deviation*	*Common Support Sample Size*	
		Two-year Changes	*Two-year Changes*			*Treat Group*	*Control Group*
Consumption Rate 4	One-to-one matching: k = 1	0.097	0.316	−0.219	0.134	50	36
	k Nearest neighbour matching: k = 5	0.097	0.143	−0.046	0.102	50	36
	Radius matching: δ = 0.01	0.109	0.213	−0.104	0.120	17	36
	Kernel matching: k;norm;bw;0.01	0.097	0.259	−0.163	0.118	50	36
Consumption Expenditure 4	One-to-one matching: k = 1	17,468	26,006	−8,538	7,173	49	36
	k Nearest neighbour matching: k = 5	17,468	24,453	−6,984	5,907	49	36
	Radius matching: δ = 0.01	17,042	27,954	−10,912	6,807	17	36
	Kernel matching: k;norm;bw;0.01	17,468	27,647	−10,179	6,380	49	36
Income	One-to-one matching: k = 1	36,188	30,027	6,161	20,953	50	36
	k Nearest neighbour matching: k = 5	36,188	30,147	6,041	19,835	50	36
	Radius matching: δ = 0.01	11,634	44,496	−32,862	20,968	17	36
	Kernel matching: k;norm;bw;0.01	36,188	34,330	1,858	25,973	50	36

control groups and treat groups within the floating population. By comparing households of the floating population that obtained a local urban Hukou with those who kept their Hukou unchanged in the short-term (2010–2012) or long-term (2010–2014), this study analyses the impact of Hukou changes on the household consumption behaviour of the floating population. In addition, in order to overcome the problems of individual selectivity and missing variable bias, this study adopts an approach combining the propensity score matching and difference-in-differences methods to construct counterfactuals, and estimate the impact of Hukou changes in a quasi-experimental environment.

From the estimates, it is found that Hukou had different impacts on migrant workers and the city-to-city floating population. For migrant workers, obtaining a local urban Hukou could significantly lower their household consumption rate, mainly because their household income increased markedly after they got a local urban Hukou. Therefore, while their gross household consumption expenditure increased significantly, their overall consumption rate was still declining. In the long run (2010–2014), however, though obtaining a local urban Hukou increased consumption and income, it could longer significantly lower the household consumption rate. This shows that in the medium and long term, obtaining a local urban Hukou helps to increase residents' income and absolute consumption, but one should not pin too much hope on it for raising the consumption rate. Of course, from another perspective, it can be said that Hukou changes do increase the consumption rate, because the consumption rate actually falls when income rises. For the city-to-city floating population, whether in the long or short term, obtaining a local Hukou basically does not change household consumption behaviour, and there is no significant change in consumption rate, total consumption expenditure or itemized expenditure. The conclusion of this study provides a new basis for re-understanding the impact of Hukou changes on micro and macro consumption.

3.2 Hukou System, Income and Inequality

Since the 1990s, the urban and rural income gap in China has basically remained at a ratio of 3:1, with no effective narrowing. Behind this, the Hukou system has played a key role. Wan Haiyuan and Li Shi (2013) conducted relevant research using survey data from the 2007–2008 period. To overcome the problems of self-selection and sample deviation of individual Hukou types, they took the endogeneity issue into account and focused on those groups with changed their Hukou attributes. They adopted the PSM-DID method to measure the income enhancement effect brought by Hukou to the floating population, and went on to evaluate the impact of Hukou discriminations on the urban and rural income gap. Their research results show that Hukou-based occupation selection discriminations alone could reduce individual rural households' income by 3.5% in the short term.

In developed cities, this gap widened to 7.9%. These findings are similar to our income test results using the CFPS data as reported above. Over a longer time frame, such discriminatory effect is very likely to increase. Hukou itself is taken as a screening and selection mechanism. Obtaining an urban Hukou is equivalent to giving a signal that keeps farmers or migrant workers who have obtained an urban Hukou away from job discrimination. After the Hukou discrimination factor is excluded, the overall income gap will fall significantly. On average, the Gini coefficient will drop from 0.499 to 0.488, showing that Hukou discriminations have a significant impact on the income gap in China. Rural residents and migrant workers are always in a vulnerable and marginalized position (Table 3.13).

3.3 Hukou System and Demographic Structure of Large Cities

Currently, the two camps of opinion on urban development have reached the following consensus: first, urbanization is a general trend that goes along with economic development. In particular, large cities will inevitably exist and expand because of their agglomeration effect; and second, there should be no multiple factors within a country to separate different groups of people and cause discrimination and other kinds of unfair treatment to them. Otherwise, it will result in efficiency loss. But in China, there is still deliberate suppression of the development of large cities. In Beijing where a quota system is implemented, it has become more difficult for non-locals to get Hukou in recent years. In Shanghai and other large cities which adopt a points-based Hukou settlement system, the proportion of the floating population is also increasing. Migrant workers who have a rural Hukou but work in cities are the group most affected by the Hukou system. Other affected groups include a small number of people who hold the urban Hukou of a small city but work in large cities, as well as college graduates who choose to find employment in large cities.

Some statistical data show that starting from 2011, fairly large-scale home returns have successively happened to migrant workers in many provinces. In 2015, the total number of migrant workers in China was still growing, but there were just 77.45 million migrant workers flowing across provinces, 1.22 million or 1.5% fewer than in the previous year. These cross-province migrant workers accounted for 45.9% of the total number of migrant workers in the country, down 0.9% from the previous year. In terms of the pace of growth, local migrant workers started to outpace those migrant workers who sought jobs in other cities, while the total increment of migrant workers mainly came from local migrant workers.

A direct explanation for this is that in the process of seeking jobs elsewhere, a considerable number of older migrant workers have chosen to stay in their home provinces, thus becoming local migrant workers. The result is that while the total number of migrant workers does not fall, there are nevertheless regional distribution changes. Some older migrant workers with

Table 3.13 Impact of Hukou Discrimination on the Urban and Rural Income Gap (2008)

City	*Gini Coefficient*			*Theil Index*		
	Before Elimination of Hukou Impact	*After Elimination of Hukou Impact*	*Coefficient Change Ratio (%)*	*Before Elimination of Hukou Impact*	*After Elimination of Hukou Impact*	*Index Change Ratio (%)*
Nationwide	0.499	0.488	2.124	0.446	0.429	3.922
Developed cities	0.372	0.367	1.267	0.239	0.233	2.316
Medium-developed cities	0.411	0.406	1.269	0.295	0.290	1.586
Developing cities	0.421	0.417	0.871	0.349	0.344	1.552

Note: This table adds household-related discriminatory income to individuals with a rural Hukou and thus obtains the income disparity index after the impact of Hukou is eliminated. Basically, similar results are obtained using an income disparity index method when household-related discriminatory income is deducted for individuals with an urban Hukou.

a certain income base opt to leave large cities and return to regions close to their hometowns for work.

A further question is why older migrant workers return to their hometowns for work. There have been some discussions on this issue. One explanation is that the cost of living, especially housing cost in coastal areas is increasing gradually. Even if income in coastal areas is high, its actual purchasing power is not high after the expenses of clothing, food, housing, transportation and other daily necessities are considered. The second explanation is that working far from home is not good for those elderly migrant workers who need care from others. Once they reach a certain age, they need to return home and reunite with their relatives. Of course, as backward regions are fast catching up, it is not too difficult for migrant workers to return home and get jobs there. For example, after Foxconn moved its plants from Shenzhen to Henan and Chongqing, locals found it easier to find jobs than before. Of course, all these explanations are reasonable in some sense, but the core issue is still the Hukou system.

If migrant workers still cannot get an urban Hukou, especially a Hukou of megacities after working there for many years, it will not be possible for them to get various local social security benefits when they grow old. Medical insurance is a particular concern. The current rural medical insurance system is one of designated medical treatment and in-patient reimbursement linked to the hospitals in the place where people's native Hukou is located. Local county-level hospitals offer a high proportion of reimbursement, but the reimbursement rate is much lower if one gets medical treatment in another county. As a result, elderly migrant workers who work away from their hometowns are inclined to return to their home when they need more medical services. Similarly, minimum living allowance, affordable housing and other social welfare regimes which are critical for livelihood still exclude migrant workers who have no local Hukou. Migrant works who have lived in cities for more than ten years are still regarded as non-locals. This is more obvious in large cities. Various rights and benefits are still attached to Hukou. As these rights and benefits are not offered to non-locals based on their place of residence. As a result, returning home is almost the only choice for migrant workers after they grow old. The Hukou system and its lingering impact make most adults and their family members who come from rural areas but work in cities not regard themselves as 'townspeople'. There are still big obstacles for them to get integrated into cities. Consequently, those migrant workers in the 'middle tier' and the 'sandwiched layer' who have worked away from home for many years, accumulated certain savings but are still some way from shouldering the high living cost in cities will choose to leave large cities and return to their hometowns.

In the meantime, the proportion of college graduates who stay in large cities is also declining. For example, there were 7.95 million college graduates in China in 2017. But more and more graduates now choose to go to Tier-2 cities or central and western regions for employment. A student employment counsel at a famous University in Beijing made the following observation,

> 60% or 70% of our students chose to stay in Beijing a few years ago. Now, the figure has fallen to just 50%. Many students are willing to go to other cities due to difficult Hukou problems and high pressure in Beijing. Most of the times, they make such decisions on their initiative.

The two phenomena mentioned above force us to think about the internal relationship between the Hukou system and the demographic structure of large cities and the future trends of change.

Compared with its impact on other aspects, the Hukou system does not have a clear impact on urban population distribution. To a certain extent, it does result in distorted demographic structures in large cities. In a theoretical study, my col*Labour*ators and I demonstrated that a stricter Hukou system in large cities would lead to a 'dumbbell-shaped' urban demographic structure. In other words, there are fewer people in the middle layer in the cities. The reason is that the difficulty in getting Hukou in large cities makes people in the middle layer more inclined to return to cities of the next tier or their hometowns to get a local Hukou and corresponding welfare benefits, and enjoy a relatively high social position. People of the highest quality can obtain Hukou in large cities and stay there.

As they face discrimination wherever they go, people of the lowest quality tier would rather prefer to stay in large cities in order to get relatively high incomes. When discussing the existence and promotion of skills complementarity in big cities, Eeckhout et al. (2014) gave the distribution of groups with different skill levels in cities. As shown in Figure 3.1, the solid line represents the distribution structure of people with different skill levels after the Hukou policy was introduced, while the dashed line shows the situation when the Hukou policy is not introduced. It can be seen that the Hukou policy significantly suppressed the middle class, resulting in a 'dumbbell-shaped' distribution curve of people with different knowledge and skill levels. In other words, people of the highest quality tier and people of the lowest quality tier carry bigger weights in cities.

We use a micro database to analyse the Hukou system's impact on the demographic structure. Adopting Grade Point Average and English test score as indicators of student quality, we have found that students with the highest and the lowest qualities both chose to stay in Beijing, while most of the students in the middle layer went back to their provincial capitals to find jobs. This evidence demonstrates that large cities with higher Hukou thresholds are likely to have a 'dumbbell-shaped' demographic structure.

A healthy city should be the one that is shared by all kinds of talents, with a suitable demographic structure. By contrast, a 'dumbbell-shaped' demographic structure reinforces social stratification, which is not conducive to social integration.

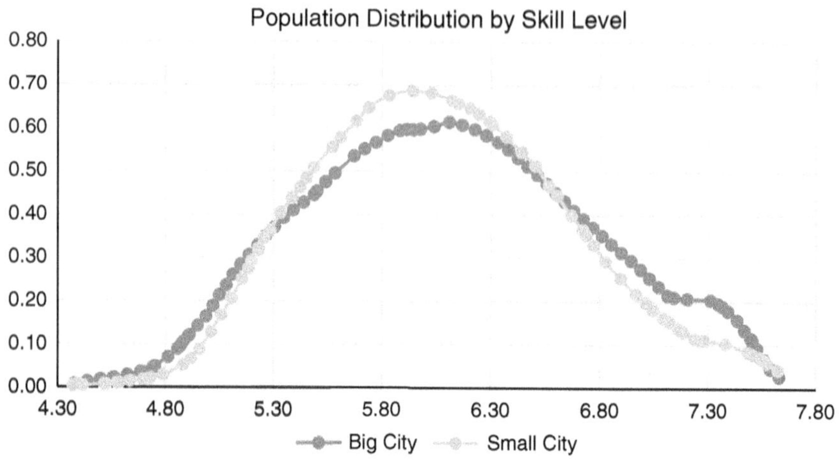

Figure 3.1 Population Distribution by Skill Level.

Note: The horizontal axis represents the skill reflected by actual income, and the vertical axis is the probability density function.

A strict Hukou system has multiple negative effects. On the contrary, Hukou liberalization will improve on these aspects. In recent years, Chongqing has carried out relatively large-scale Hukou system reforms. One prominent feature is that a lot of public rental houses have been built for the 'middle layer', which solves not only the Hukou problem, but also the corresponding housing problem. As a result, Chongqing has attained a natural urban demographic structure, unlike the prominently 'dumbbell-shaped' demographic structure in Beijing or Shenzhen. At the same time, the Hukou system reform in Chongqing has boosted the local economy, reduced income inequality and accelerated social integration. In all aspects, especially in terms of the measures adopted for the 'middle layer', Chongqing has set an example for Hukou system reform in other large cities in eastern China.

Notes

1 There are still outliers in the obtained consumption rates, and the maximum value of some consumption rates is a two-digit figure. For this reason, the 5% Winsorize extreme value handling method is used to deal with the calculated consumption rates. We tried 1% and 10% treatments, respectively, and the conclusions were consistent.

2 The urban-rural classification in this study is based on the urban-rural classification of the National Bureau of Statistics of China.

3 CFPS inquires whether a respondent's Hukou location is his or her village/neighbourhood committee, other township/town/neighbourhood in local township/town/neighbourhood, other township/town/neighbourhood in local county/

county-level city/district, other county/county-level city/district in local province, and other province/autonomous region/municipality directly under the Central Government. In this study, the scope of 'Local' is limited to the first three cases. If one's Hukou location is in another county/county-level city/district in the local province, or another province/autonomous region/municipality directly under the Central Government, it will not be counted as 'Local'.

4 Thoughts on Promoting Hukou Reform in Large Cities

4.1 Megacities Are in More Need of Hukou System Reform

4.1.1 Hukou System Reform Is Not Vigorously Promoted in Large Cities

China began to gradually tighten its Hukou system from 1950 to 1958, and maintained strict Hukou control until 1984. After the State Council issued the *Circular on the Issue of Farmers Settling in Market Towns* in 1984, farmers were allowed to settle down in market towns and get the same rights and perform the same obligations as town residents, as long as they could provide grain rations on their own. In 1998, the *Circular of the State Council on the Approval and Transmission of the Opinions of the Ministry of Public Security on Resolving Several Outstanding Issues in the Current Hukou Management Work* was issued, which further relaxed the Hukou system. According to this Circular,

> newborn babies living with their fathers, people living apart from their spouses, elderly dependent parents, as well as citizens who invest and start businesses or buy commercial housing in cities and their immediate family members shall be granted Hukou for settling in cities, provided that they have a legitimate and fixed dwelling or a legitimate and stable occupation or source of income in cities, have lived in the cities for a certain period of time and meet the relevant provisions of local governments.

In its *Opinions on Further Deepening Reform of the Hukou System* in 2014, the State Council stipulated that

> It is necessary to further adjust the Hukou transfer policy, unify the urban and rural Hukou systems, fully implement the residence permit system, speed up the establishment and sharing of a national population basic information database, and steadily promote compulsory education, employment service, basic pension, basic healthcare, housing

DOI: 10.4324/9781003288091-5

> security and other basic urban public services to cover all permanent residents. Efforts should be made to establish, by 2020, a new people-centred, scientific, efficient, regulated, and orderly Hukou system that is suitable for building a moderately prosperous society in an all-round way, which can also effectively support social management and public services and safeguard citizens' rights in accordance with the law.

The draft 13th Five-Year Plan Outline has specified measures to accelerate the transformation of migrant workers into urban citizens. The target of having around 100 million agricultural transfer population and other permanent residents settle in cities and towns is expected to be realized in the next five years.

As far as the general policy evolution trend is concerned, there has been an emerging tendency towards the large-scale liberalization of the Hukou system. However, strict Hukou control has remained in place in megacities until today, with no substantive progress since 1998. Currently, the biggest change was the implementation of the residence permit system which started in 2015. According to my survey, the degree of Hukou substitution by the residence permit varies from city to city. For example, the residence permit can replace 90% of Hukou's corresponding functions in Kunming. The percentage is 63.8% in Wuhan, but much lower in Beijing, Shanghai, Guangzhou and Shenzhen.

4.1.2 The Negative Impact of the Hukou System Still Exists

In large cities and especially in megacities, the level of income is higher than in other cities and much higher in rural areas. While the floating population continues to increase, a large proportion of the resident population still cannot get local Hukou in cities. The Hukou system still has a great impact on people's work and life. Research work summarized above shows that under the same personal qualifications in the same city, people who have a local urban Hukou can get a higher income than people who hold a rural Hukou. This is one of the important sources of income inequality in Chinese society. Because different types of Hukou correspond to different levels of social security, people who have a rural Hukou but work in cities have a significantly lower consumption rate than those who hold a local urban Hukou in the same city. This is also an important reason for the low consumption rate in China. Due to the long existence of different types of Hukou-induced personal identity and status, many migrant workers and their families tend to see themselves as 'rural people', thus having difficulty in getting integrated into the urban society. This is an important cause of social segmentation.

The negative impact of the Hukou system is especially evident in large cities. In our computations using open micro data, we have found that municipalities directly under the Central Government offer higher incomes than other cities, while an urban Hukou in the municipalities has higher premium than a rural Hukou. This means that Hukou carries a greater economic value in megacities. Conversely, one can get more potential benefits from Hukou liberalization.

4.1.3 There Are Directional Errors in the Current Hukou System

Starting from the *Opinions on Several Prominent Issues in Current Hukou Management* issued in 1998, China has basically laid down the general direction and principles for liberalizing the Hukou system, namely strictly controlling the size of big cities, and rationally developing small cities and medium-sized cities. In its 13th Five-Year Plan, China did propose to further relax Hukou control, while also calling for

> developing small towns and small and medium-sized cities in the central and western regions, and accommodating more migrant workers for employment and entrepreneurship in places close to them, so that they can earn money and take care of their families at the same time.

In recent years, most provinces and autonomous regions in China have carried out different levels of reforms according to their specific situations. However, they have basically followed the intent that was set forth in 1998, namely making the biggest Hukou system reform in small towns, intermediate Hukou reform in small and medium-sized cities and the least Hukou system reform in provincial capital cities and megacities. During this period, Hukou system reform in large cities has actually gone backwards. In the earlier years, for example, it was possible for people to settle in Beijing and other big cities by living with relatives and buying homes. Later, restrictions were imposed again.

The current Hukou liberalization strategy has a directional problem, mainly because the idea of strictly controlling Hukou in large cities while liberalizing Hukou control in small and medium-sized cities runs against the law of the market. The current situation is that larger cities have stronger agglomeration effects and higher personal productivity, thus attracting a bigger floating population. Survey data from the National Bureau of Statistics show that among the migrant workers who went out for work in 2015, about 11.9 million entered cities at or above the prefecture level, accounting for 66.3% of the total migrant workers; and 80% of the migrant workers moved across provinces and flowed into medium-sized and big cities at or above the prefecture level, while 54.6% of within-province migrant workers entered medium-sized and large cities at or above the prefecture level. At the conference to release the *National New Urbanisation Report 2015*, Xu Lin, Director of the Planning Department of the National Development and Reform Commission, pointed out that large cities attracted most of China's migrant workers, while less than 10% of migrant workers flowed into small towns below the county seat level. All these show that large cities account for a larger proportion of the floating population in China. Though the floating population can get higher incomes in large cities than in small and medium-sized cities, there are still discriminatory policies against them, making it impossible for them to get fair treatment and difficult to integrate into cities, which in turn leads to significantly different economic behaviours between the floating populations and urban residents. In essence, Hukou restrictions on the floating population in big cities are exploitation of vulnerable groups who are in a disadvantaged economic or social position, or are taxation in disguised form. For example, migrant workers themselves are groups with relatively low incomes in cities. Their children may have attended school in cities for a long time, but they can only go to special schools for migrant workers' children and must pay tuition fees. Free compulsory education is simply beyond their reach.

Given that income and consumption in large cities are much higher than in small towns, there is no doubt that liberalizing Hukou control in large cities will bring about much greater economic effects. In other words, Hukou liberalization generates both economic and social benefits, especially in big cities. Cities have an agglomeration effect, which can produce a bigger market, a more suitable environment for entrepreneurship and a more effective labour-market match. Even public services such as old-age care are more intensive and efficient in large cities. All these can be regarded as positive externalities of population inflow. From an economic perspective, all actions that can generate positive externalities should be subsidized. However, current Hukou control, which has been in place for a long time, is very much a kind of exploitative taxation in disguised form on the floating population. In large cities, subsidies can solve public welfare and housing problems. Existing policies focus more on the negative impacts of population inflow on large cities, while the positive impacts are ignored as vested interest. In fact, large cities can reduce negative impacts like congestion and pollution through more effective urban management and bring them down to a level even lower than in small and medium-sized cities. Currently, Hukou system reforms in different regions have basically followed the thinking of fully liberalizing Hukou control in small and medium-sized cities while imposing due Hukou restrictions in large cities. To address the situation, it is imperative for the central government to point out the corresponding problems and correct the deviations in the overall direction.

4.1.4 Hukou System Liberalization Should Be Further Integrated with Market-Oriented Means of Urban Management

In the current reform, Hukou control has been tightened from small towns to big cities. As big cities have the largest floating population, if ongoing Hukou reform avoids tackling the crucial issues, its effect on controlling the floating population will be compromised. Meanwhile, the current Hukou situation has widened the income gap, reduced consumption and resulted in social segmentation. It is a deprivation of the vulnerable groups. Given that it has caused efficiency loss and failed to achieve the goal of population control, we suggest that large cities should relax their Hukou restrictions as soon as possible, so as to achieve greater economic and social benefits. The institutional transformation of Hukou liberalization can promote the healthy transformation of the Chinese economy and society.

Of course, as large cities have good income acquisition means and favourable public resources, full Hukou liberalization will bring them a series of problems due to the sudden increase of the floating population. Population pressure, especially the shortage of healthcare, education and other public resources, is a primary reason why big cities stick to their Hukou restrictions. To understand this problem, the first thing to remember is that Hukou restrictions in large cities mainly focus on the use of public resources, while the impact on the flow of the income-seeking population is not significant. In fact, a large proportion of the population who have moved to cities for higher incomes have already lived in large cities for a long time. Hukou liberalization will only give them equal access to public resources, without increasing population pressure. Secondly, for the large number of people who are likely to enter cities purely for the sake of public resources, market-oriented means may be appropriately adopted to regulate it. Congestion is a negative externality. Through taxation, supply liberalization, price hikes and other market-oriented means, the government can effectively manage the traffic, housing and pollution problems caused by excessive population inflows. Meanwhile, the central government should make public resources equally accessible as much as possible and promote the trans-regional transfer of social security coverage and other resources. This will boost regional equity and rational population flows.

Regardless of the practical difficulties and the current situation, our research findings show that large cities are the places of most exploitation for migrant workers. At the same time, large cities are also the regions that are likely to get the biggest economic and social benefits from the relaxation of Hukou constraints. Policymakers should fully understand the economic and social effects of Hukou system reform. Instead of avoiding the crucial issues, they should confront the most difficult issues head-on and strive to solve the problem of Hukou restrictions in large cities.

4.2 The Government Should Not Set Population Targets for Large Cities

In their 13th five-year plan outlines, megacities including Beijing, Shanghai, Guangzhou and Shenzhen have all set specific population control targets for 2020. Beijing proposed to control its permanent resident population within 23 million, while the target is 25 million for Shanghai, 15.5 million for Guangzhoun or source of income in cities, and 14.8 million for Shenzhen. It is generally believed that setting a red line on population is the practical need to solve the big city disease. In recent years, some people have attributed many of the problems like traffic congestion, pollution, high housing prices and resource shortage in large cities to the existence of too many people, and then come up with the idea of urban population control. Many large cities have set population planning goals, usually by imposing population caps, and taken various measures to achieve these goals. Such a practice of limiting demand cannot solve the problem. On the contrary, it will reduce the vitality and efficiency of cities and the sense of happiness of the people. However, these problems can indeed be solved through the regulation of the market price mechanism, as well as various government measures to increase supply, adjust structure and make proper industrial layout. The reasons are as follows:

Firstly, many problems currently existing in cities are not caused by excessive population, but resulted from inadequate planning and management. Data analysis shows that localities with higher population densities in developed countries in fact have smaller per capita carbon emissions, because people work near where they live. They do not need to drive too far away to work, and public transport services are also close at hand. But if consumption and education resources are concentrated in city centres and there are relatively few residential areas there, people will have to live far away from the city centres. As a result, they need to go a long way to do shopping, and drive their children to school. Analysis has also found that traffic congestion becomes less serious during the summer vacation (when people don't have to drive their children to school), and the per capita inhalable particles drop by 20 micrograms per cubic metre. In other words, the government can solve congestion and pollution problems by providing high-quality public services and reducing the living distance. In addition, compared with Tokyo, the built-up areas in Beijing and Shanghai are relatively small, and their metro network coverage and density are far from enough. This is also an important reason why Beijing and Shanghai have a smaller population than Tokyo, but they give people a feeling of greater congestion.

Secondly, there are both theoretical and practical problems with the administrative restrictions over population. Theoretically, there is almost no way to estimate how many people a city should accommodate. This is because the carrying capacity of a city is not a static concept, but it is growing dynamically with urban industrial structure, technological progress and other factors. For example, many people think that water resources are a factor restricting the population of Beijing. However, the total population of Beijing has almost doubled since 2001, while total water consumption in the city has actually declined. Why? The economies of scale have led to a decrease in water consumption per capita. Economic restructuring reduces the proportion of the industry, which is a major water consumer. Moreover, water can be transported from elsewhere, and any scheme is feasible, as long as it brings more benefit than its cost. In Los Angeles, California, 80% of the water used there is transported from outside. We simply cannot decide how many people Beijing can accommodate by how much water resources it has. From the practical point of view, when we limit the population of a city, we must decide who can and who cannot stay in the city. This means that we have to divide people into different types, which inevitably involves the issue of fairness. In fact, this is equivalent to letting those who are under control bear the cost of urban population growth, while those who continue to live in cities can enjoy the benefits of the scales of economy in cities.

Thirdly, some restrictive policies of the government, such as Hukou control, will lead to falling labour productivity in cities. The use of Hukou and lack of public service coverage to restrict the entry of the low-end population often result in a shortage of low-end labourers in big cities. In fact, high-end labourers and low-end labourers are complementary to each other in large cities. For example, when Bill Gates goes to a city, his nannies will also follow him. The supply shortage of low-end labourers will lead to rising low-end labour cost, which ultimately results in a productivity decline of high-end labourers. In other words, if nannies are restricted from entering big cities, it will be more costly for people to hire nannies. If people can't afford to hire nannies, they will have to look after their children and do housework on their own. This means less work time for people, and their productivity will fall. China's Hukou system is highly linked with the social security and pension systems. Workers with no local Hukou will spend less in large cities when they consider future income falls and other factors, which will lead to falling wages for service people in the cities. The more money which non-locals in a city remit to their hometowns, the lower the wage level in the local services industry will be. All these show that Hukou and other population restriction policies can easily distort the development of industries.

Fourthly, the market adjusts everyone's choice through the price mechanism, and the government may play a role in promoting urban development by reducing negative externalities and increasing positive ones. In the short term, when the resources and environmental constraints of a city are given, there will be a price mechanism to regulate people's choices. When supply is fixed, growing demand will lead to price increases, which means a constant rise in people's cost to enter large cities. This in turn will slow down population growth in big cities. In the long run, rising prices imply a continuously expanding profit space for suppliers, which will lead them to increase supply until the marginal returns fall to zero. Then, supply and demand will reach a long-term equilibrium point. On this basis, what the government can do is to change externalities. While increasing positive externalities and reducing negative ones, the government also dynamically expands the capacity of cities to accommodate people. For example, the government may increase supply through technical management means. Shanghai used to rely on the electricity generated by local thermal power plants, which caused power shortages in summer. However, after West-to-East power transmission technology was adopted, the situation has changed substantially. Today, the local thermal power plants in Shanghai already face overproduction. After some local thermal power plants are laid idle, emissions from them have also fallen. In this process, the electric power restrictions on the population are greatly reduced. This shows that the government can in fact help cities to grow bigger and become more efficient.

Fifthly, the development trend that big cities get bigger and bigger and small cities getting smaller and smaller is conducive to improving overall public welfare. International experiences and existing theoretical studies both show that the largest city in a country often has a population twice that of the second-largest city, and city size will fall along with city rank. It is inefficient to 'balance' all regions in terms of population size through population control. On the one hand, as mentioned above, keeping low skilled workers out of the cities is no good for highly skilled workers. On the other hand, some payment transfer policies that are intended to promote the balanced development of cities will lead to a mismatch of resources. For example, China has built many industrial parks in the western region after 2003, and many of them are now empty. This implies that the more transfer payment the government makes, the higher the opportunity cost for labourers to flow into large cities. The wages of these workers in large cities will also rise accordingly, which means an increase in labour cost. However, those industry parks without comparative advantages will inevitably face the problem of rising debts in their long-term operations.

In a word, the government should consider more about relying on the market to make urban management decisions. For its part, the government should only focus its work to meet market demand and solve the problem of insufficient positive externalities or too many negative externalities. There is no sufficient reason for the government to set a population size target in the process of controlling the large cities.

4.3 Wrong Indicators Are Unhelpful for Hukou System Reform

Since 2014, under the guidance of the central government's policies, Hukou system reform has been progressing fast across China. In the process, the term 'urbanization rate of registered residents' or 'urbanization rate of Hukou population' has also frequently entered public view. Currently, it has become the main reference indicator of Hukou system reform. In 2016, the State Council issued the *Notice on Issuing the Plan for Promoting the Settling of 100 Million Residents Without Local Household Registration in Cities*, explicitly calling for raising the urbanization rate of the Hukou population by more than 1% annually on average during the 13th Five-Year Plan Period and the national urbanization rate of Hukou population to 45%, and narrowing the urbanization rate gap between the Hukou population and the resident population in various regions by more than 2% from the 2013 level by 2020.

For years, the urbanization rate of Hukou population in China has been far lower than that of resident population. In 2016, the urbanization rate of Hukou population was 41.2%, while that of resident population reached 57.35%. This means that at least 16% of China's total population living in towns and cities had no normal access to corresponding local public welfare benefits. Moreover, the urbanization rate of Hukou population also increases slower than that of resident population. For example, from 2010 to 2016, the urbanization rate of resident population rose from 49.68% to 57.35%, with an average annual increase of 1.28%. However, the urbanization rate of Hukou population increased from 34.17% to 41.2%, with an average annual rise of 1.17%. This means a continuous expansion of the number of urban residents who cannot enjoy local public welfare benefits.

It is worth mentioning that the figures above still underestimate the degree of Hukou-related public service inequality, because the internal structure of the Hukou population is not taken into account. For example, residents who have an urban Hukou in one city but actually work and live in another city also face restrictions on public service access. It is clear that the urbanization rate of Hukou population is not a good index for guiding urban system reform. To understand how to choose more appropriate policy objectives in practice, we will focus on discussing the following concepts.

Besides the urbanization rates above, the third indicator to measure the urbanization rate of population is the urbanization rate of urban resident population. By definition, the urbanization rate of Hukou population is the proportion of people who hold a local urban Hukou among the total local Hukou population of a place, while the urbanization rate of resident population refers to the proportion of people who hold a local urban Hukou among the total local resident population of a place. The difference between the two lies in the different population bases used. The urbanization rate of Hukou population is based on the total population with a local Hukou in a place, while the urbanization rate of resident population is the local resident population. Nationwide, the difference between the two reflects the proportion of the population who cannot fully enjoy urban public welfare benefits in towns and cities. But in fact, the proportion of people who cannot enjoy public welfare benefits in the cities and towns where they live is bigger than this, because there are many people who have an urban Hukou but work and liver in other towns and cities. These people have no full access to the public welfare benefits in their place of employment. Especially in big cities like Beijing, Shanghai, Guangzhou and Shenzhen, there are many working people from other rural areas and towns of the country. The third indicator, namely the Hukou rate of urban resident population, refers to the proportion of urban Hukou holders among the resident population in a city or town. The unique feature of this indicator is that its base is the resident population in a city or town. All the three indicators above have certain practical significance. Currently, the urbanization rate of Hukou population is a reference indicator that government departments use to measure actual progress in the implementation of Hukou system reform policies. There are two reasons for it. The first reason is that by looking at the proportion of the population with an urban Hukou, one can roughly judge the proportion of people who live an urban life. The second reason, which is also more important, is that this indicator is highly operational, since it can be directly estimated using the Hukou data of the Ministry of Public Security, thus making it easier to estimate and evaluate the policy effect. These two aspects are the advantages of this indicator, but the existence of a large floating population in towns and cities makes it not so practical. For developed cities like Beijing, Shanghai and Guangzhou, this indicator often overestimates Hukou reform progress, because these cities have a relatively small number of rural Hukou holders among their overall Hukou population and their urbanization rates of local Hukou population thus calculated may be very high. But at the same time, the large floating population living in the cities is ignored. A high urbanization rate of Hukou population conceals most non-local people's need to get a local urban Hukou. In other words, in developed areas that attract the inflow of the floating population, using the urbanization of Hukou population as a reference indicator for Hukou system reform is often not conducive to genuine Hukou system reform. In some cities in the central and western regions which are places of population outflows, this indicator will underestimate their progress in Hukou system reform, because many local rural Hukou holders there have already flowed into developed regions, thus leading to a higher urbanization rate of the remaining local Hukou population.

To a certain extent, the urbanization rate of resident population can make up for the deficiencies caused by using the urbanization rate of Hukou population as a reference indicator for policymaking. It also has better economic significance. However, the resident population suffers certain statistical inaccuracies. Conceptually, the resident population consists of people who have lived in a place for more than six months in a year and are integrated into the place economically and in everyday life. If all these people can get a local urban Hukou or enjoy equal public services, then the urbanization rate of resident population can well reflect the progress of Hukou system reform. This statistical indicator carries a good economic significance, but it also has some operational problems. First and foremost, the six-month time limit may be arbitrarily defined in practical census work. But the biggest problem is that the statistics department often fails to fully fulfil its responsibilities in conducting resident population surveys. The resident population statistics they get often contain some omissions. All these factors cause inaccuracies in the use of the urbanization rate of residents as a reference indicator for policymaking.

Compared with the urbanization rate of resident population, the urbanization rate of urban resident population is a better indicator, which can avoid the influence of different urbanization levels in different places. Different levels of economic development are accompanied by different levels of urbanization. If all provinces are required to meet the 45% target as set forth in the *Notice of the General Office of the State Council on Issuing the Plan for Promoting the Settling of 100 Million Residents Without Local Household Registration in Cities*, economically underdeveloped regions may face very big pressure and find it very difficult to have so many rural residents settle in cities within a short time of time. In such a situation, only examining the proportion of Hukou holders in the local urban resident population can avoid the problems caused by different stages and levels of urbanization. If the resident population in towns and cities can basically get a local urban Hukou, it will mean that Hukou system reform has been carried out very well, because migrant workers and other non-local groups in the urban resident population can also access some local welfare benefits. Economically underdeveloped regions often have a relatively big agricultural population, which is included in the calculation of the urbanization rate of Hukou population. The relatively high proportion of such agricultural populations is a problem arising from the economic development rather than the Hukou system. Because of this, using the urbanization rate of Hukou population thus computed as a reference indicator for policymaking may cause the risk of rush urbanization. In principle, the urbanization rate of urban resident population provides a better indicator in such cases. But again, collecting statistics on the urban resident population is a task prone to significant errors.

The above explanations show that all the three indicators have their respective advantages and disadvantages in reflecting the progress of Hukou system reform. An ideal situation is that the statistics department can fairly accurately count the resident population and then use the urbanization rate of urban resident population as a reference indicator for policymaking. However, because non-locals cannot get corresponding welfare benefits, they lack the motivation to register with the statistics department. It is also difficult to collect statistics on the resident population. This itself is an inherent contradiction. We can only hope that the Hukou system can be further relaxed so that all people living locally can get a local Hukou or gain equal access to public welfare benefits. This is the goal of Hukou system reform. At the same time, it also facilitates the conducting of demographic census, so that other economic and demographic policies can be effectively realized.

5 Urban Development in the Context of Hukou System Reform

5.1 The Issue of Urbanization Efficiency in China and Its Countermeasures

5.1.1 The Nature of City and Urbanization in China

From the historical development trend, we can see that city size is restricted by the development of productivity. Cities are relatively densely populated areas that are not dependent on their own crop cultivation to meet food demand. The emergence of cities depends on the increase of productivity. Only when the agricultural population can provide enough food to meet the needs of the urban and rural population can cities come into being. Consequently, though humans with relatively high intelligence appeared some 40,000 years ago, the emergence of cities was a relatively recent thing. In 3500 BC–4000 BC, the world's largest city only had a population of about 25,000. Over the past few 100 years, urbanization has grown slowly, and megacities have only appeared sporadically. Scholarly research shows that Beijing had a population of 600,000 in 1500 AD but it was already the largest city in the world at that time. It was not overtaken by London until 1830. In the Edo Period (1700 AD), Tokyo had around 500,000 people. In 1700, London and Paris also had a population of approximately 500,000 each.

The 20th century was a period of fastest urbanization in the world. The population not only continuously converged to cities, but also tended to concentrate in large cities. For example, Buenos Aires, the capital of Argentina, had a population of 12 million in 1914, making it the second-largest city in America, only after New York, accounting for 20% of the total Argentinean population. In 1995, Mexico City had a population of 18 million. According to population statistics from the United Nations Economic and Social Programme, there were no less than 20 cities with a population of 10 million in the world by 2005. From 1900 to 1950, the global urbanization rate increased from 13% to 29%. The figure rose to 50% in 2005. According to the *World Urbanisation Outlook 2005*, urbanization is still expanding. By 2030, 60% of the global population is expected to live in

DOI: 10.4324/9781003288091-6

cities. The urban population will continue to expand, then hitting a total of 4.9 billion.

At the same time, urbanization also promotes the development of the productive force. The development experiences of many countries convincingly show that urbanization boosts economic growth. This has also been quantitatively demonstrated by academic research.

China's economic growth over the past years has largely come from an average annual increase of more than 1% in urbanization. Currently, China has just passed the 50% urbanization mark, and a considerable proportion of the urban residents included in the statistics actually do not enjoy as many welfare benefits as locals have. This is very much a case of semi-urbanization. This typical characteristic shows that urbanization in China has been a slow process. According to international comparisons, China's average urban population growth (at 3.5% per year) is lower than that (at 5%–6%) in other countries during the same period of economic growth. China's corresponding urbanization level for 2009 (at 46%) was also lower than that (at 55%) of countries with similar real per capita income. In other words, urban development in China lags behind the needs of economic development. In addition, scholars at home and abroad generally believe that despite a large number of cities in China, their scale effect is not sufficient. This means that Chinese cities are relatively small and have yet to reach their optimal economic scale. Therefore, there is still room for Chinese cities to expand in size and improve their per capita productivity and per capita income. The small average size of Chinese cities is mostly attributable to control on population mobility, or discriminatory policies against the floating population. While most Chinese cities are small, some large cities, especially Beijing, the national capital, and Shanghai, a financial hub, are among the largest cities in the world. Most provincial capitals are also the largest cities in their respective provinces. These large cities are often too big.

It is precisely because urbanization and economic growth can promote each other that urbanization is now considered as the biggest driving force for China's further economic growth. This view was also mentioned in the work report delivered to the 18th National Congress of the Communist Party of China, reflecting the importance which the government attaches to urbanization. However, the contradiction between economy and environment has had a profound impact on the development direction of China's small, medium-sized and large cities. On the one hand, large cities generally have higher per capita income and productivity, thus deserving vigorous development in the economic sense. On the other hand, large cities often face the problems of overcrowding, serious pollution and resources shortage, making it necessary to implement some policies to restrict their further expansion. Since 1995, the national policy of limiting the size of large cities and rationally developing small and medium-sized cities seems to have remained unchanged. This is evident from the tightening of the Hukou system across the country. Beijing's policy of restricting commercial housing sales to non-locals also reflects this thinking. At the annual "Two Sessions" of 2013, while stressing the importance of urbanization, some state leaders specifically called for developing small and medium-sized cities and limiting the size of large cities. Rational analysis and evaluation of these policies is of great significance for clarifying China's future economic growth model and spatial distribution pattern. Generally speaking, the most important thing about evaluating whether the size of a city is big or small and whether it should be expanded or limited is to see whether its size is an optimal one for economic growth. In addition, other problems like pollution should also be considered.

5.1.2 Theoretical Basis for Urbanization-Induced Efficiency Improvement and Current Urban Efficiency in China

Urbanization often boosts productivity: most manufacturing and service products can be produced more efficiently in urban areas, because enterprises there can more easily learn advanced technological and management experiences from advanced companies, and get skilled workers, transportation services and other intermediate inputs. As early as the days when Western economic founder Adam Smith lived, it was observed that bigger cities and regions with higher population densities had higher per capita productivity and wages, which has been confirmed by more and more empirical research. Various studies have found that city size expansion can reduce the distance between consumers, intermediate factor suppliers and producers, thus lowering transaction cost. It can also help to achieve large-scale and efficient production. Urban development can promote the specialized division of labour, and boost productivity through knowledge spillover between enterprises and knowledge complementarity among industries.

In short, knowledge spillover, specialized division of labour and effects of scale are the sources of higher output in cities, all of which can significantly improve per capita productivity. Quantitative analyses have further shown that the elasticity between productivity and employed population density is about 4%–10%. In other words, when population density increases by 1%, per capita productivity will rise by 0.04%–0.1%. Based on state-wise data from the United States, a famous study by American scholars found that employment density doubled with a 6% increase of per capita productivity. Employment density variations can explain more than half of the variation of state-level output. Though the formation of any city of a certain size is more of a market-driven process, government investment in public goods such as infrastructure and legal system building, along with a certain degree of urban planning, is an essential element of urban development. These are the experiences of urban development in developed countries.

Overall, the relationship between urbanization and economic development in China cannot be separated from the above experience. Some of

China's special national conditions may cause slightly different characteristics in the scale effect of urbanization from those in developed countries.

Firstly, for historical reasons, China has gradually relaxed restrictions on labour flow and urban Hukou. Out of concerns about slums and other problems which the blind expansion of urban population can cause, the government has introduced many urban development plans. Imposing various restrictions, these plans have slowed down overall urban development in the country. The requirements for people to get an urban Hukou are not based on factors of economic needs such as residence and working years, but on government policies. This may lead to deviations in economic effects. Overall, cities may become small, falling short of their optimal size.

Secondly, there is imbalanced development between cities. Large cities like Beijing and provincial capitals have accumulated considerable political, economic and cultural resources, which give them growing appeals to outside workers. By contrast, cities of low tiers have relatively fewer resources and appeal less to people. The result may be that large cities exceed their optimal economic size, while small cities are short of it. In 2010, the smallest city at or above county level in China had a population of less than 20,000, while the largest county-level city was inhabited by over 15 million people. Their spatial areas also varied greatly. Similarly, there were gaps of up to several hundredfolds in terms of per capita GDP, per capita fiscal expenditure and per capita financial lending.

Thirdly, labour flows are restricted. State-owned enterprises still make up a big proportion of the Chinese economy, while the education sector, which employs a large proportion of the work force, basically operates within the state system. In cities, state-owned organizations offer secure jobs for their employees, which restricts the flow of labourers within and cross industries and results in limited capabilities of mutual learning between industries. In addition, knowledge spillover effects in China are limited, which affect the specialized division of labour. Moreover, government-led competition between regions may also lead to inadequate specialization within regional cities.

The results of a recent study conducted by this author using Chinese urban data reinforce the above conjecture. Generally speaking, the larger the city size, the higher the per capita income, but the economic effect of city size is rather small and labour specialization is inadequate. The advantages of industry size are not well manifested. In China, there is high consistency between urban development and administrative rank. In provincial capitals which have a high administrative rank, per capita investment in fixed assets is often more than four times that in county-level cities. This is mainly because provincial capital cities are more likely to get capital and financial resources, which in turn attract enterprises and the floating population and lead to faster population growth or even overcrowding in large cities. By contrast, small and medium-sized cities are too small.

5.1.3 Discussion on Typical Problems in the Urbanization Process and Steps of Future Urbanization in China

Some of the urban development characteristics in China are in line with the international experience. For example, urbanization promotes economic growth, and cities with bigger populations have higher per capita income. However, there are also some aspects of urban development in China that run contrary to the world experience, as reflected in the inverted U-shaped (i.e. increasing first and then decreasing) relationship between urban population density and per capita income, and lack of enhanced specialized division of labour due to urban expansion. Besides, China also has some unique urban development characteristics of its own: city size is highly related to the administrative rank of cities, many large cities have developed in the inland regions, and some pollution is caused. Those characteristics which are in common with the world experience do not need much explanation, while most of China's unique urban development characteristics are caused by the system and policies of the country. The only way for us to provide guidance on how to develop cities in the future is to understand the causes of China's unique urbanization and their economic consequences.

The current level and pattern of urbanization in China are mainly the result of institutional or policy factors. First, the Hukou system and other historical problems have prevented migrant workers and their family members from getting the same treatment as townspeople, which makes it difficult to achieve true urbanization and thus suppress the overall level of urbanization. Second, by making it difficult for no-locals to get local Hukou, the Hukou system has prevented the formation of a theoretically rational population distribution under which economically developed coastal regions and large cities should accommodate more people, while underdeveloped inland regions should have a large population flowing into coastal cities. Third, the policy of strictly restricting large cities and encouraging the development of small towns has resulted in China's most urban population being mainly distributed in small towns with an average size of about 10,000 people, which limits the effect of economic scale for cities. Fourth, the current fiscal system means that townships, counties and small and medium-sized cities only have limited financial resources, which makes it difficult for them to develop infrastructure while restricting their capacity to expand. By contrast, thanks to their good infrastructure, provincial capitals and other large cities can absorb more enterprises and people. Because the fiscal system is still under the control of the government to some extent, provincial capitals and other large cities can easily get financial resources support, which enables them to expand in size. Finally, as employment system reform is slow, state-owned and public institutions still make up a considerable part of the employment market, and their rigid employee mobility system hinders the specialized division of labour and knowledge spillover.

The economic and social effects thus caused are obvious. First, the low urbanization rate and the lack of the economies of scale in population distribution have restricted the improvement of productivity and people's living standards. Second, discriminations against the floating population widen the income inequality, and keep the already high urban and rural income gap intact. Third, as urban construction is slow, it is difficult for farmers to get the treatment as townspeople do. Often, they have to invest their limited funds in building houses back home, and these houses may well be abandoned with the development of urbanization in the near future, which leads to a substantial waste of resources. Fourth, limited financial resources make residents in small towns live in dirty and chaotic urban space. Meanwhile, overpopulation and poor management result in traffic congestion, soaring house prices and air pollution in large cities. Fifth, local governments make their own decisions and blindly build local infrastructures, which may cause resource waste with the entry of the floating population. Finally, poor employment mobility hinders knowledge spillover and reduces the possibility of productivity improvement in regions.

The solution to the abovementioned problems will depend on further institutional building and policy liberalization. These policies include: (1) promoting financial equalization and financial system building, so that cities of different tiers can access fiscal and financial resources equally; (2) relaxing the Hukou system in a coordinated way nationwide, so that people can gather in economically developed coastal regions and big cities in accordance with the law of economics. According to the international experience, cities with a population of more than 10 million are basically distributed in coastal regions along big rivers to ensure low levels of pollution. However, the capital cities of inland provinces are often big. With the increased consumption of automobiles and other energy-consuming products, the problem of pollution will inevitably hinder the development of cities. Therefore, the government should make efforts to develop large cities in coastal regions; and (3) promote labour mobility and employment system reform among enterprises and institutions, so as to improve the specialized division of labour, knowledge spillover and overall productivity of cities.

5.2 Developing Cities: The Government Should Avoid a "Caring Father Mentality"

Currently, China faces multiple challenges in its urbanization process: on the one hand, Beijing, Shanghai, Guangzhou, Shenzhen and other eastern coastal cities constantly attract the entry of labourers, leading to higher population densities. However, traffic congestion, air pollution and rising house prices in these cities are all indicative of a prominent problem of carrying capacity constraints; on the other hand, there is still a clear average income gap between central and western regions and eastern cities. It seems that more capital accumulation and a benign cycle of income improvement are needed to achieve the growth of the central and western regions.

It is against this background that the current policy tends to limit the population size of large cities and to build infrastructures in the central and western regions to attract capital and labour. This is like a father with an egalitarian tendency who takes away some food from his full boy to his other hungry child. To restrict the development of large cities in the eastern region, it is a common practice of the central government to take away funds from the eastern region to invest in infrastructures in the central and western regions, such as building industrial parks to attract capital and labour. However, the practice of limiting big cities and striving to develop the central and western regions calls for some reconsideration.

It is not without good reason why people are enthusiastic about large cities. According to the international experience, industrial restructuring is characterized by a general trend of rising labour productivity in the manufacturing industry and a falling proportion of the employed population, while the services sector will gain higher labour productivity and a higher share of employment. The United States went through this process at the end of the last century. As the services industry develops, manufacturing productivity rises and scientific and technological innovation progresses and generates positive externalities, an inevitable process is that the population will constantly concentrate in big cities. This is because only densely populated areas like big cities can boost demand-induced innovation and maximally drive the development of the services sector that needs to be close to users. By contrast, the manufacturing industry is not much restricted by geographic proximity. Therefore, the further expansion of large cities also means better use of their high productivity. This conforms to the laws of industrial transformation and upgrading, and it is not a bad thing. We do need to promote the further development of other places, but this should be done on the basis of a reasonable industrial structure and a correct understanding and rational utilization of local comparative advantages.

Usually, one of the most intuitive concerns about the further expansion of large cities is as follows: if we allow those already big cities to expand without restriction, it may lead to the concentration of the whole society's capital in the rich regions, thus causing the consequence of the richer regions getting richer and the poorer regions poorer. However, if we consider it more carefully, we will find that if capital and high-end human resources gather to rich regions without restriction, and the only means of production left in relatively poor regions are land, little capital and fewer labourers, the ultimate result will be lower marginal productivities of capital and labour in the rich big cities, while the marginal productivities of capital and labour in relatively resource-scarce regions will decline, which will lead to higher incomes for local people and narrow the per capita income gap between regions. Only the free flow of capital and labour can achieve the ultimate goal of a paternalistic government, while restricting the development of big cities can only be counterproductive.

In the process of urban development, the market will show and measure its cost and benefit. Apart from more efficient use of externalities and improvement of efficiency, the expansion of large cities will also generate more economic and social costs: the spillover effect of high productivity in big cities will lead to higher land rents in their suburbs. As a result, the marginal cost of developing large cities will be higher than that of developing small and medium-sized cities, and improper planning will also cause congestion and pollution. The market will automatically measure the cost and benefit of urban expansion, and determine the direction of capital and labour flows. In other words, under the premise that big cities accommodate means of production and labour to the maximum extent, the maximum city size will be ultimately limited, but it will be the optimal result of balanced regional development. Existing studies on urban development experiences in various countries in the world have shown that the relative population proportion of large cities follows the Zipf's Law: with the development of urbanization, the population of the largest city of a country tends to be a fixed proportion of the total population of the country, while the second, third and even the *n*th largest cities all have their size rules. Before reaching the optimal proportion, any blind effort to restrict the development of large cities will be equivalent to directly limiting the scope of diffusion for positive externalities, which will undoubtedly lead to efficiency loss. After a city reaches its optimal size, the market will automatically restrain its further expansion, with no need for government control. Responsible parents often have a pair of "restless hands" and always want to control the allocation of resources. Consequently, they do bad things despite their good intentions. Similarly, any forced transfer of capital to the central and western regions is also facing the danger of efficiency loss. In the past decade or so, many industrial parks have been built in China's central and western regions. Despite the preferential supporting policies from the government, few of them have been successful. Many industry parks become empty sites in the end. This is also a reflection of the failure of the government's "caring father-like" work style, which is resisted by the market. The government should change from always thinking of controlling the economy to passively serving the economy. As such, the "caring father" mentality is the last thing it needs.

In general, the flow of capital and labour should follow the decentralization decisions of the market. What the government needs to do most is to ensure the equitable and fair distribution of factors and returns, maximally leverage the market potential, and amplify the positive externalities of production. Instead of adopting a "caring father" mentality, it is better for the government to adopt a "good friend" mentality and adapt to the needs of productivity development. Instead of blindly pursuing the superficial equality of fixed assets investment and other indicators between different regions, the government should ensure that there is a good market order in all regions, and let factors play their maximum part. The convergence of per capita output can be ultimately achieved through the market-oriented flow of resources. This is the only way to achieve both efficiency and true balance among regions.

5.3 Urban Development Philosophy: Letting Supply Meet Demand

As the urbanization rate in China surpasses 50%, in recent years the government has issued many related plans to steer the direction of further development of cities. For example, the Central Committee of the Communist Party of China and the State Council issued *Several Opinions on Further Strengthening the Management of Urban Planning and Constr*uction in February 2016, emphasizing the decisive role of government planning in urban development. At the local level, various local governments have adopted different Hukou system provisions, measures to diffuse some industries in cities, and other policy measures to control the development scale and form of large cities, highlighting the strong desire of the government to control the development of cities from the supply side.

The government plays an irreplaceable role in the development of cities in China. The sole reason is that the government controls enormous resources for urban development. First, city land belongs to the public, and government approval, land acquisition, competitive bidding and auction are all essential steps to go through if any land is to be used for residential or commercial property development or other industrial or public utility purposes. This way, the government can decide the form, content, and scale of urban development. At the same time, the government also has other resources, such as supply of education, public security, healthcare, transportation and other public services. Even corporate recruitment and site selection processes are also directly affected by government decisions. All these directly determine how people evaluate and choose cities for work, thus affecting the inflow, outflow, development pattern and size of urban population.

In the meantime, urban development has its own patterns, and the size and characteristics of a city are largely determined by market demand. Cities worldwide entered a stage of rapid development after the Industrial Revolution, because technological advancement liberated the rural labour force, and fast industrial development in cities generated labour demand and attracted labourers. As industries often had the characteristic of economies of scale, their rapid development gradually led to the formation of large cities. The services industry followed on the heels of industries: most service enterprises rely more on the creation and consumption of products within close distances, which resulted in the further expansion of cities. Though the restriction of geographical space on urban development has decreased with the development of infrastructures and the advancement of the Internet and other communication technologies, it has nevertheless not fundamentally reversed the trend of urban growth. In larger cities, people can get higher incomes, more diversified consumption modes and higher degrees of satisfaction.

The history of urban development in China also reveals that government intervention has an important impact on the speed and rationality of urban development. However, two different conceptual ideas about the role of the government in urban development in China have not been well clarified in the past decade or so. One view holds that the government should dominate the development of cities and proactively control it, and the other view is that the government should obey the law of cities, serve the law and passively adapt to urban development. Currently, cities in China face enormous development opportunities. Without clarification on these two misleading development concepts, the government will inevitably make big or small mistakes in urban management.

Under the planned economic management model after the founding of New China, the government has a long history of controlling the development of cities. For almost 30 years before the reform and opening up, the government forcefully kept the rural population out of cities through the Hukou system, and developed the secondary industry out of proportion in cities, while restricting the development of the tertiary industry. This led to a rather low urbanization rate and an irrational industrial structure. After the reform and opening-up started, the relaxation of the Hukou system and the market-oriented development of industries have duly corrected the distortions caused by a planned economy. However, this does not mean that the government has clarified its thinking on urban development. Problems still surface from time to time in the government's regulation and control of urban development. One clear characteristic is that the government often wants to play a dominant role in urban development: in recent years, many cities have stressed the need to solve their "urban diseases" through dispersing the population and reducing city size. This can be seen in the government's actions to restrict urban expansion and artificially causing supply shortage through tightening Hukou control, limiting residential land supply and moving industries away. However, Tiers 2 and 3 cities still face the problem of oversupply. Many industry parks are built, and land supply is increased for many real estate projects. Many of these projects have now shown the adverse consequences of excessive investment.

History shows that when the government provides corresponding supply for urban development in order to meet market demand, considerable social benefits are often available. On the contrary, when the government intentionally controls market demand and artificially restricts urban development through reducing supply, it will make obvious mistakes, thus causing social welfare loss and long-term economic distortion. Many of the problems in cities are not caused by the existence of too many people, nor can they be solved through government control on population. The government should respect the laws of urban development and the ultimate demand created by the market and provide supply to meet such demand. Ideally, the government should mainly pursue passive adaptation rather than proactively change city size. The government only needs to provide guidance at an appropriate time, increase supply through improving planning and providing administrative and technical support, and adapt to the growing urban demand. This should be the basic philosophy for the government to manage urban development.

The optimal size of a city cannot be imposed from the above. Rather, it follows its endogenous development path. The pattern of urban development depends on the choice of the people or enterprises: people pursue better material conditions and service quality, and enterprises seek higher productivity and profit. In the short term, the resources and environment of a city are fixed. Under such constraints, there will be a price mechanism to regulate everyone's choices. On the one hand, rising prices will reduce the benefits which people can get from entering big cities, thus leading to a decline in the growth of the population entering cities. On the other hand, rising prices will expand the profit space for enterprises in the long term, and encourage enterprises to continuously increase their supply until such supply no longer contributes to marginal positive profit. At this point in time, supply and demand will reach a balance in the long run, and the optimal scale can be achieved without government regulation. The government should then provide an environment in which public goods can create a better combination of supply and demand, so that supply can maximally meet people's growing demand. For example, the South-to-North Water Transfer Project has alleviated the water shortage problem in Beijing. The West-to-East Electric Power Transmission Project mentioned above is also a classic example of the government's change of supply. The size of a city should be determined by the adjustment of the price mechanism, and the role of the government in urban development is to increase the sort of supply which goes beyond market control, and to through meet the growing urban demand by improving on management and technical deficiencies.

Currently, the supply of public service infrastructures in China's large cities is seriously behind the actual demand, which results in uneconomic city sizes and restricts the benign development of large cities. First, there is a shortage of public transport supply: in big cities like Beijing, public transport infrastructures are often built with no sufficient consideration of future demand. As a result, the capacity of the built public rail transits falls far short of actual demand. Once built, infrastructures are difficult to change. Outdated transport infrastructures may force people to abandon public transport, thus leading to traffic congestion and urban efficiency loss. Obviously, this is a big city disease caused by inadequate public services. Second, there is a serious undersupply of residential buildings in city centres. After the total land use quota is given, the government will increase the amount of industrial land as much as possible in order to maximize its own tax revenue. For the small amount of commercial and residential land available, the government will allocate commercial land as much as possible in order to attract investment, thus reducing the availability of residential land. Such a mechanism will lead to a serious shortage of housing supply at city centres. As a result, people must work in downtown areas but live in the suburbs and even farther away, thus spending much time on the road every day. On the one hand, the separation of working place from residential place lowers people's work efficiency in large cities. On the other hand, it also increases traffic congestion in big cities. These problems are essentially not caused by a big population but are a distortion caused by government planning. Third, there is insufficient diversification of service and commerce due to the housing construction mode in big cities. Residential quarters in Chinese cities are often too big and inaccessible, and urban streets and roads are wide but few. Existing traffic experience shows that more intersections and narrow roads are conducive to walking, and more pedestrians will brew service and commerce. According to experiences both at home and abroad, places with more intersections have higher restaurant density and consumption diversity. With the increased availability of services and commerce, people's consumption will no longer be concentrated at one point. Rather, people will choose to go to alternative venues close to them. This will reduce people's travel radius, as well as mobility demand and traffic congestion. By contrast, there are too few streets in China's large cities today, which leads to a serious lack of diversity in service and commerce, and people have to drive to commercial centres far away. This inevitably increases traffic congestion. In other words, by improving urban planning, it is possible to give full play to the role of street commerce and services to alleviate traffic pressure in large cities. All these issues are closely related to government decisions on supply.

In short, many of the problems that exist in China's large cities are not caused by the existence of too many people. Rather, these problems are a result of government-provided infrastructure falling short of the needs of the people, and the government's urban planning is often not the most efficient way of response. Active population control by the government cannot solve these problems. The solution to these problems will depend on the government providing necessary management services and technical support through better urban planning, so as to adapt to the demand of urban growth with increased supply. This is an important implication for urban supply side reform. Most fundamentally, the government should conceptually clarify its role as the service provider and the passive adaptor. The current practice of proactively regulating city size by limiting supply is not advisable.

Part II

Discussion of Issues Related to Family Planning Policy

As China's basic national policy, family planning has had a profound impact on the demographic, economic and social development of the country. Such impact has long been a hot research topic among academic circles. In particular, one widely accepted conclusion in the academic community is that a 'quantity-quality' tradeoff should be made to improve the educational level of the population. In recent years, as the problem of population ageing aggravates and natural population growth slows down in China, labour shortage has become a more serious issue. As a result, restrictions on second babies for couples who are the single child in their respective families (known as 'single-child couples' or 'onlies couples') have been gradually relaxed. After a brief period when couples were allowed to have a second baby if either of them is from a one-child family, a universal second-child policy has been put into implementation since 2016. While the effect of this second-child policy is still under debate, the academic circles have nevertheless started to argue about whether the government should subsidize couples to have a second baby.

In this part, I will briefly introduce the background of China's family planning policy first and discuss the issue of whether subsidies should be given to second babies. From Chapter 7 to Chapter 9, I will make an empirical examination of the family planning policy's impact on residents' marriage match decisions, childbirth, entrepreneurship, and old-age care. Because there are already too many studies on the family planning policy's impact on the improvement of people's educational level, all the chapters of this part will focus on the other impacts of the policy.

In Chapter 7, we adopt an empirical design of difference-in-differences to analyse Becker's economic theory of marriage, and find that the policy of allowing single-child couples to have a second baby actually increases the match between onlies, while reducing the 'mixed match' between onlies and non-onlies.

In Chapter 8, the author uses CGSS data for analysis and makes the following findings: (1) the possibility of entrepreneurship is significantly lower among onlies. This is not a problem of 'personality', but may be due to the lack of social security associated with onlies; (2) onlies do have a lot of

DOI: 10.4324/9781003288091-7

friends and are more acceptive to the idea of hard work. Compared with non-onlies, however, they are less intimate with relatives and friends and generally have a low sense of happiness. Consequently, the suppression of entrepreneurship by demographic changes resulting from the family planning policy should not be ignored.

In Chapter 9, the author finds that compared with multi-child families, one-child families are more inclined to choose a model of old-age care by living together. This phenomenon can be explained by the self-interest lifecycle theory, while social customs, especially the requirement for males to shoulder the old-age care responsibility for their parents, have also encouraged children to live with their parents. The author also demonstrates that while the living-together model has no significant impact on the welfare of the elderly, it nevertheless offers an at least not bad choice for old-age care.

6 History of Family Planning Policy and Current Debate

6.1 Historical Development of Family Planning

To control the drastic population surge at the time, the Chinese government started to implement family planning in the early 1970s. The policy was mainly about encouraging 'later, longer and fewer' births ('later' means that males get married at least after they reach the age of 25, and females at 23; 'longer' means a longer interval, usually at about four years, between two births; and 'fewer' means a couple could only have two children at most). It was not until the end of 1979 that the central government announced the mandatory family planning policy of 'one couple can only have one child', which is known as the one-child policy. This compulsory policy was introduced amidst a rising call for 'controlling the population and pursuing the modernisation drive' after the Cultural Revolution was ended (Bongaarts and Greenhalgh, 1985). In 1983, the State made family planning China's basic national policy. After the one-child policy was introduced, implementation efforts reached an unprecedented level of intensity. Those children born unplanned could not get Hukou, which would deny them free public education. Children without an ID card would find constraints in all aspects of their life in the future. Those couples who gave extra births were also at risk of high fines from the government and dismissal by their employers. Starting from 1983, the government also pushed forward with compulsory ligation and sterilization, causing more public to resent against the family planning policy.

In 1984, the government quickly became aware of some incidents of violence, abuse of power and other problems in the implementation of the family planning policy, and duly adjusted and relaxed childbirth restrictions on some sectors of society. Except that all urban residents and rural residents in six of the country's provinces and municipalities still implemented the original 'one child' policy, a new 'one-child-and-half' policy was adopted for rural residents in 19 provinces. In other words, if the first child of a family was a girl, the couple would be allowed to have a second child. But, if their first child was a boy, no more birth would be permitted for the couple.

DOI: 10.4324/9781003288091-8

In the remaining five ethnic minority provinces and autonomous regions, rural residents were generally allowed to have two children.

In the late 1980s, the government again relaxed the family planning policy for urban and rural residents, allowing two babies for those couples who were from one-child families themselves. The time of such relaxation varied significantly between provinces and municipalities. We will collect statistics based on the time when this policy was officially written into the provincial or municipal family planning regulations. Beijing, Tianjin and Jiangsu were the first municipalities or province to introduce the policy of 'two babies for couples from one-child families'. They did so in the late 1980s and the early 1990s respectively. Henan followed suit as late as 2011, the last province to adopt the policy. There were many reasons behind the time difference in the adoption of the policy between provinces and municipalities. Gu et al. (2007) mentioned two possible factors: one was the demographic factor, which meant that provinces like Henan with a high fertility rate or a large population base tended to adopt the policy late, and the other was the historical factor, whereby the expectation of whether the population control goal could be achieved was likely an important determinant of family planning policy relaxation. Beijing, Tianjin and Jiangsu were the first minimalities or province to strictly implement the one-child policy in an all-round way. Their fertility rates were substantially lowered and remained low for a long time. As a result, they were the first in the country to relax family planning control (Greenhalgh, 1986). In addition, as population ageing became a serious issue due to their vigorous implementation of the 'one child' policy, these municipalities and province were more motivated to relax the policy earlier.

In 2012, China's working-age population began to decline in absolute terms, with a fall of 3.45 million people from the previous year. This directly promoted the further liberalization of the birth control policy. In 2013, the Third Plenary Session of the 18th CPC Central Committee decided to introduce the policy of 'two babies for couples with either side from a one-child family'. On December 28, 2013, the *Resolution on Adjusting and Improving the Birth Control Policy* was adopted at the Sixth Meeting of the Standing Committee of the 12th National People's Congress, and the policy of 'two babies for couples with either side from a one-child family' officially came into implementation. Subsequently, all provinces successively formulated their separate measures to relax the birth limit on couples with either side from a one-child family.

Despite more births, the new policy fell short of expectations in increasing the number of new babies born. As a result, the government further relaxed birth control to allow all couples to have a second child. In October 2015, the Fifth Plenary Session of the 18th CPC Central Committee called for promoting balanced population development, adhering to the basic national policy of family planning, improving the population development strategy, comprehensively implementing the two-child policy for all couples, and proactively coping with the problem of population ageing. In early 2016, all provinces basically put the universal two-child policy into implementation. However, data show that while two years of implementation of the policy led to an increase in childbirths, it still fell far short of the expected effect. Consequently, a new issue has arisen whether to continue to relax the policy further or even encourage childbirths.

The once strict family planning policy has resulted in a growing proportion of onlies in Chinese society, which becomes an important demographic factor affecting both family decisions and the macro economy. Chinese census does not have a separate entry for the proportion of onlies. However, some sampling data show a significantly higher proportion of onlies born after 1980. Using the data of China General Social Survey ('CGSS') in 2006 and 2008 to calculate the proportion of onlies in different birth years, we have found that the proportion of onlies in China has followed a U-shaped curve of change, as shown in Figure 6.1. Before 1940, the proportion of onlies was only 10.67%, and the figure continued to fall from 1949 to the end of 1960s, implying that most families had more than one child thanks to the policy of encouraging births. After that, with the introduction of a mild population control policy in the early 1970s and a strict population control policy after the 1980s, the proportion of onlies rose higher and higher. In 1980 and the ensuing years, onlies accounted for 36.10% of the population born. Onlies have now become a hugely influential group among the Chinese population, and their collective characteristics will significantly affect the economic outcome of the whole country.

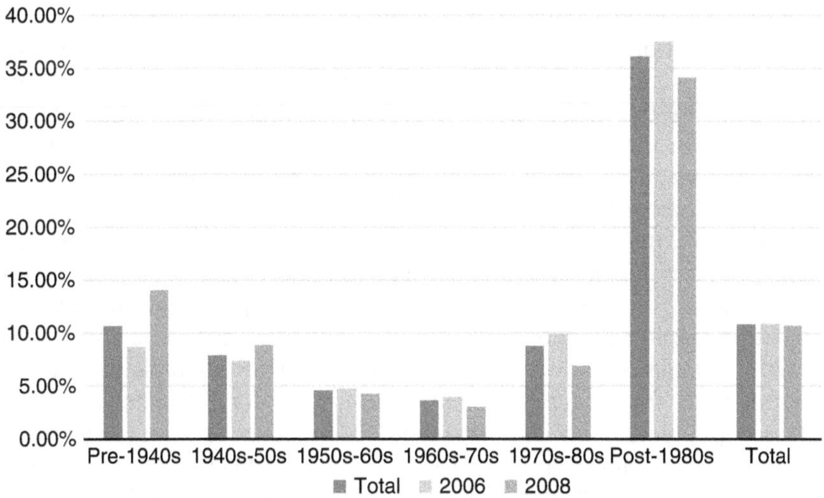

Figure 6.1 Proportion of Onlies by Year of Birth.

Source: CGSS survey data in 2006 and 2008, 'all' refers to the mixed data of the two years.

6.2 General Debate on Population Policy

On 29 October 2015, the Fifth Plenary Session of the 18th CPC National Congress announced that China would implement a 'policy of allowing two babies for all couples'. Such announcement practically put an end to the long debate on whether birth control should be relaxed, while giving those scholars who opposed opposing family planning the hope of further programs to support population growth. Scholars who support the liberalization of birth control have even made policy recommendations for boosting childbirths, such as introducing financial subsidies and making changes to marriage and childbearing cultures.[1] In this context, it is of great significance to examine the logic behind the demographic impact on economic growth, reflect on the current policy, and think about the future population policy.

The relationship between population and economy was a topic of discussion hundreds of years ago. Anyone who has studied textbooks on macroeconomic principles should know their conclusions. Classic textbooks generalize the impact of population growth on economic growth into two aspects: on the one hand, population growth may dilute capital stock, which causes per capita natural resources shortage—this logic is behind the conclusion which Malthus reached in his population theory at the end of the 18th century that the geometric increase of population leads to economic collapse. And, this conclusion is still true in many countries today. On the other hand, population growth may promote innovation, provide the labour force needed to match with capital, and boost economic development.

There are numerous cases of population growth as both a negative and a positive factor. For example, when the People's Republic of China was founded in 1949, the country already had a very large population base, while a large proportion of the population was illiterate and the economy was backward. But, more and more people were actually born, making it difficult to improve the quality of the population and the quality of life in per capita terms in the ensuing years. Under normal circumstances, when per capita income and population quality are low, a country may be more likely to decline if it gets a bigger population. During periods of big abnormal falls in population after a war or disaster (such as after major wars in ancient China), the new regime often encourages childbirths to increase the population in order to cultivate idle land. At such times, per capita income and population quality may be low, but the increased population can substantially stimulate production because there is a considerable amount of capital waiting for labourers to match with it. As for the conclusion that increased population boosts innovation, I have a personal experience to prove the point: a few years ago, I was on an academic visit to the United States. My host was Professor McFadden, who won the Nobel Prize in Economics in 2000 for advancing the theory and method of discrete data analysis. Professor MacFadden was the youngest son of his family. One can imagine that had the United States implemented a family planning policy, the world would not have had the service of Professor McFadden. As a result, the discovery of the discrete selection method would be delayed for several years. When McFadden was in his school days, the United States was already the world's largest economy, offering universal high school education and establishing a basically mature scholarship system in university education. It meant that even though Professor McFadden was born into a poor peasant family, he could still successfully complete his college education.

As for population growth, a natural question is where the boundary between the positive and negative effects of population growth lies. In other words, under what circumstances population growth is good for the economy, and under what circumstances it is not. A rational answer is that the boundary is determined by the quality of population—if it can be guaranteed that the newly born population has enough human capital after they grow up, they will be able to provide high-quality labourers for economic growth, and their output will be higher than their social cost. Usually, when per capita income reaches a certain level, both education and technological innovation will also attain a certain level. The accumulation of material wealth and the maturity of the government will be sufficient to make newborn babies grow up well, receive adequate education, get good health, and make enough contributions to society after adulthood. After mankind fully enters an industrial society, progress in productivity and technology has gradually freed population growth from resource constraints, turning it into a positive factor for further economic growth. Of course, with the advancement of knowledge, the per capita income threshold also increases accordingly.

6.3 Should Subsidies Be Given to Second Babies at Present?

From the brief analysis above, it is clear that after a certain living standard is reached, population growth can promote economic development. Of course, consideration should also be given to the distribution of income and the government's ability to subsidize education. If income distribution is far from even and the proportion of low-income groups is too high, it will be equally difficult for them to provide good family and school education for the more children they have. A poor social environment will not be adequate to ensure the healthy growth of teenagers. There are many such examples in some Latin American countries. In addition, the issue of absolute population size must also be considered. If China's already big population base increases further, no existing theory or experience may be able to predict its possible negative impacts, because no matter how innovative society is, the total amount of resources is always limited. The family planning policy involves all people. Over a considerable length of time, the birth of one social group will exert pressure on other people's enjoyment of resources such as employment, housing prices, and education. More consumption will lead to all sorts of problems such as traffic congestion, pollution, food shortage, and declining quality of living. A cautious approach is therefore warranted.

In China, people of marriageable age already have a relatively high level of education, basically at or above senior high school. Moreover, China has reached the middle-income stage, and the government provides nine-year compulsory education for all. All these give the country the basic leverage to relax the family planning policy to a proper extent. Moreover, the one-child policy in the past has mostly restricted the birth of high-quality people, which is not conducive to the improvement of population quality. These are all good reasons for revising the strict one-child policy. However, the time has yet to come to promote or even encourage childbirths through financial subsidies.

Most people who hold the view that subsidies should be provided for childbirths draw upon the experience of developed countries. For example, the Japanese government recently set an explicit goal of maintaining Japan's population at about 100 million from 2060 to 2070. This goal aims to address the grave population situation in Japan. To achieve this goal, the Japanese government plans to implement intensive response measures around 2020 to curb the trend of population decline. The main measure is to double the childbearing and parenting subsidies for parenting families. At the same time, the Japanese government has also clearly called for 'boldly shifting the focus of resource allocation from the elderly to children'. Similarly, because the United States implements a family-based system of collecting taxes and providing subsistence allowances, the more children a family gets, the less taxes it will pay and the more subsidies it will receive. Therefore, this is also a childbirth incentive policy in disguised form. In addition, Nordic countries all take a series of measures of their own to subsidize childbirths. Currently, China cannot follow the example of other countries to subsidize the birth of second babies, mainly for the following reasons:

First, China has not yet reached the national wealth level of those developed countries. China's per capita income is less than one-fifth of Japan's. Currently, the Chinese government needs to devote its limited resources to boost economic growth. At the same time, educational quality, social environment, and other factors in China can hardly ensure that the newborn population can get enough resources to grow up.

Second, subsidies distort childbearing decisions, and most of them are likely to flow into low-income families, because rich families' childbearing decisions will not be affected by the government's subsidies for childbirths. From a macro perspective, it is not a wise decision to encourage low-income families to have more children, because their family environment may not ensure that their newborn babies can get adequate human capital support. This is clearly evidenced in developed countries. Under the policy of disguised childbirth subsidies in the United States, the proportion of black and other coloured people among newborn babies is already more than that of white babies, and this may change the future outlook of the whole United States.

Third, there is another kind of fairness to be considered if subsidies are provided. In China, in fact, there are still many families that have no children for infertility or other reasons. These families do want to have babies. For health reasons, however, they can only have babies through surgery or IVF technology. This requires them to overcome psychological barriers, while incurring relatively high and financial costs. It is estimated that there are as many as 40 million people in this group. If childbirth subsidies are to be given, from the perspective of fairness, it is better to subsidise this segment of the population which has limited financial resources, so that they can have children through medical means. This will both enhance fairness and boost population growth.

Fourth, China has a large population. To maintain a relatively high standard of living, the country is already struggling with various adverse effects, such as shortage of natural resources, environmental pollution, rising house prices, and so on. At the same time, China enjoys abundant overall labour supply, and its working-age population alone is more than the total population of any developed country in the world. In the context of postponed retirement, there is no need for China to encourage childbirths to increase its population.

Fifth, there are better ways to promote population growth while concurrently boosting economic efficiency. In one of my studies, I have found that the floating population's willingness to have children has been declining due to their low income and low welfare benefits available to them in cities. However, people in the establishment previously restricted by the family planning policy do have a high willingness to have more children after the two-child policy was introduced. Given this, it is possible to both enhance equality and increase child births by amending the unfair Hukou system so that all people can be treated fairly.

To sum up, most experts who support subsidizing second babies only consider things from their own research perspective or take a demographic point of view, without taking into account more realistic situations. Currently, changing the distorted economic system and better looking after vulnerable groups in childbearing are better ways for China to boost childbirths than to subsidise second babies. Moreover, as China's population is already too big, the family planning policy still needs to be kept for a long time. If subsidizing second babies is to explicitly give up the original intention of total population control, it will be an absolutely unadvisable thing to do.

Note

1 For example, some of Liang Jianzhang's comments on population policy suggest that China should further expand childbirth by offering financial subsidies, allowing female students to skip grades to have children as soon as possible, changing marriage and childbearing cultures like allowing unmarried children, and expanding city size. For details, refer to http://business.sohu.com/20151207/n429981424.shtml.

7 Are People Willing to Have More Children?

7.1 Introduction

In many circumstances, the goals of public policy implementation are all related to family composition, as in the case of health insurance policy (Yelowitz, 1998) and welfare policy (Bitler et al., 2004) in the United States, social pension policy in Sweden and tax and subsidy policies in many countries (Baker et al., 2004). For economists, the goal of the research is to reveal how these policies affect individual motivations and behaviours. In this study, the author will examine how China's fertility policy affects the choice of partners in the formation of marriages.

Becker (1973, 1974a, 1981) laid the foundation of family economics. He pointed out that the formation of marriage and family is the outcome of people weighing and comparing the economic utilities with and without marriage. Especially, Becker argued that 'The most important purpose of marriage is for people to have and raise their own children'. From this argument, a direct inference can be made about marriage matching: because utility can be increased through the division of labour between participating in the labour market and raising children, it also gives individuals in the marriage market the incentive for reverse matching according to the potential wage rate. Though the economic connotations of Becker's theory are easy to understand, there has been little empirical evidence to support the theoretical inference of reverse matching according to wage rate in the marriage market. One possible explanation is that there may also exist motivations for positive matching in the marriage market. For example, Lam (1988) believes that the utilities which more similar family members can get from consuming similar public goods may give individuals the motivation to make positive matching according to the wage rate. If this is the case, Becker's prediction of the need for the division of labour for the sake of child-rearing and the resultant state of reverse matching with wage rate may be offset and cannot be identified.

In this chapter, we will use a 'shock' that directly acts on 'child-rearing' to study the match between individuals who have different birth quotas in the marriage process. To control its rapidly growing population, China began to

DOI: 10.4324/9781003288091-9

implement a 'one-child' policy in 1979. This policy started to be relaxed in the mid-1980s, and different provinces have gradually allowed couples who are both from one-child families to have a second child. This study will look at how the policy of granting different birth quotas to different types of families affects the match pattern in the marriage market.

We firstly construct a simple search and match pattern in the marriage market. In the model, individuals differ in whether they are the only child in their families, who are usually referred to as 'onlies'. After couples from one-child families are allowed to have a second child, onlies have the motivation to marry those who are also onlies. In this way, they will be permitted to have a second child in the family. In the matching process, onlies will be more tolerant to partners who are also onlies, but more critical about those who are not. In a state of equilibrium after the policy of 'allowing a second child for couples with both sides being onlies', partners with the same status (i.e. both are onlies or non-onlies) will account for a higher proportion of married couples, while those with mixed status (i.e. one side is an only, but the other side is a non-only) will make up a falling proportion of married couples.

The empirical analysis of this chapter is based on the 1% random sampling data of China's 2005 population census. By comparing the marriage compositions before and after the implementation of the policy of 'allowing a second child for couples with both sides being onlies', the simple differences method reveals an 8.8% increase in the proportion of female onlies who looked for male onlies as their spouses and a 14.3% increase in the proportion of male onlies who looked for female onlies as their spouses. In the meantime, the proportion of female non-onlies looking for make non-onlies as their spouses increased by 2.2%, and the proportion of male non-onlies looking for female non-onlies as their spouses rose by 1%. Traditional Chinese culture tends to consider children as the offspring of husbands' families. Therefore, the above differences also show that the policy of 'allowing a second child for couples with both sides being onlies' may asymmetrically influence people of different genders.

To remove the influence of time-varying factors (such as the proportion of onlies, etc.) on marriage matching between provinces, we further adopt the empirical analysis method of 'Difference-In-Differences'. In those provinces where the one-child policy is more strictly implemented, the policy of 'allowing a second child for couples with both sides being onlies' is likely to have a bigger influence, because couples who have an extra child would receive more severe punishment under the former policy. In these regions, relaxing birth quota control will bring greater potential benefits. Based on existing literature (Ebenstein, 2010; Scharping, 2003), we use the over-birth fine rate as a measure of the severity of the family planning policy. This empirical study finds that if the over-birth fine/average annual local household income ratio is increased 100%, the proportion of female onlies looking for male onlies as their spouses will rise by 12.7%, while the probability of male onlies looking for female onlies as their spouses will be up by 19.6%. By contrast, the probability of female non-onlies looking for male non-onlies as their spouses will increase by 2.5%, while that of male non-onlies looking for female non-onlies as their spouses will rise by 0.7%.

A series of econometric tests show the robustness of the above results, which is in line with what we have expected. We find that the fertility rate of couples who both come from one-child families has a small but significant increase after the implementation of the new policy.

In addition to the literature on marriage matching, this study is also linked with numerous research articles on the effects of the family planning policy. As an extreme case of natural experiments of family planning, China's one-child policy has attracted the research interest of economists and demographers. For example, Greenhalgh et al. (1994) studied the impact of the family planning policy on fertility rate, Ziegler et al. (2008) examined the influence of the family planning policy on maternal health and Edlund et al. (2013) expounded on the impact of the family planning policy on the crime rate. However, there is no research on the influence of the family planning policy on marriage matching in the existing literature. Because raising children is one important purpose of marriage, the family planning policy will inevitably affect the benefits of marriage, which will influence marriage matching from the other way around.

7.2 Theoretical Model

We construct a search-match pattern to describe the matching behaviours of different individuals with different statuses either being onlies or non-onlies in the marriage market, and portray the equilibrium state. We use the framework of Chiappori, Oreffice and Quintana-Domeque (2010) to deal with situations when personal characteristics are a discontinuous variable. Moreover, we extend their framework to allow two-way random search in the model.

7.2.1 Model Construction

Consider a marriage market like this: both males and females who can be either onlies or non-onlies are equal in numbers, and match freely in the marriage market. Use Variable x to represent whether a female is an only, and Variable y to represent whether a male is an only, and $x, y \in \{0, 1\}$, with '1' representing 'being an only', and '0' being a non-only. The proportion of female onlies in all females is expressed as α_w, while that of male onlies in all males is expressed as α_m. For the sake of simplicity, we assume that $\alpha_w = \alpha_m = \alpha$, wherein α is an exogenous variable which does not change over time.

Individuals meet randomly in the marriage market. Assume that time is discrete, and the intertemporal discount factor of utility is $\rho \in (0, 1)$. In each period, each person will encounter a potential mate of the opposite sex whose type (expressed as x or y) is a random variable. Individuals cannot anticipate the type of the other side before they meet. When they meet, they will find each other's type, and both sides decide whether they want to get married or not. If both sides are willing to get married, they form a family. Otherwise, individuals will continue to search in the next period. Assume that the utility of staying single in each period is kept at 0. If a man of Type y and a woman of Type x get married, the utility of each period is $u_{x,y}$, which can be simplified and assumed to follow the following form:

$$u_{x,y} = q + I_{x,y}\lambda,$$

Wherein: q represents the exogenous matching quality, which obeys the random distribution law in the interval $|\underline{q}, \bar{q}|$, and its probability density function (p.d.f) is $f(q)$ and distribution function (c.d.f.) is $f(q)$; λ expresses the utility increment brought by the quota for a second child; $I_{x,y}$ is a dummy variable, indicating whether a couple has a second child quota. Before the implementation of the 'policy of allowing a second child for couples with both sides being onlies', $I_{x,y} = 0$ holds true for all families. After the implementation of the policy, we have:

$$I_{x,y} = \begin{cases} 1, & \text{if } x = y = 1 \\ 0, & \text{otherwise} \end{cases}$$

To make the model simpler, we assume that the proportion of both males and females are onlies is exogenous, and that the proportion does not change over time. If a husband of Type y marries a wife of Type x, they will exit the marriage market, and in the next period, a single man and a single woman of the same type will enter the marriage market as supplements.

7.2.2 Equilibrium Analysis after Implementation of the Policy of 'Allowing a Second Child for Couples with Both Sides Being Onlies'

To simplify the analysis, we can regard the equilibrium state prior to the policy implementation as a special case of the equilibrium after the policy liberalization. In this special case, we may take $\lambda \to 0$ as true.

Let V_1 denote the expected utility of the life cycle of the only child brought by marriage, and V_0 denote the expected utility of the life cycle of the non-only child brought by marriage. A male of Type y would want to marry a female of Type x if $\frac{u_{x,y}}{1-\rho} \geq \rho V_y$. Similarly, a woman of Type x would want to marry a man of Type y if $\frac{u_{x,y}}{1-\rho} \geq \rho V_x$. When both conditions are met, namely $\frac{u_{x,y}}{1-\rho} \geq \max(\rho V_x, \rho V_y)$, the benefits of marriage for both sides will be greater than the benefits of continuing search for spouses in the next period. At this time, they get married and cease further search.

We can make equilibrium analysis according to the three situations below:

Situation 1. two onlies meet. In this situation, both sides choose to marry if and only if $\frac{u_{x,y}}{1-\rho} \geq \rho V_1 \Leftrightarrow q \geq \hat{q}_1$, wherein: $\hat{q}_1 = (1-\rho)\rho V_1 - \lambda$.

Situation 2. an only meets a non-only. In this situation, both sides choose to marry if and only if $\frac{q}{1-\rho} \geq \max(\rho V_1, \rho V_0)$. Naturally, we tend to think that after the policy of 'allowing a second child for couples with both sides being onlies' is implemented, onlies will have a higher expected utility than non-onlies, because the onlies will have a chance to have a second child, while non-onlies are not allowed to have a second child regardless of what type of partner they have. Then, we have $\max(\rho V_1, \rho V_0) = \rho V_1$. Therefore, both sides agree to marry if and only if $q \geq \hat{q}_2$, wherein: $\hat{q}_2 = (1-\rho)\rho V_1$.

Situation 3. two non-onlies meet. Both sides are willing to marry if and only if $\frac{q}{1-\rho} \geq \rho V_0 \Leftrightarrow q \geq \hat{q}_3$, wherein: $\hat{q}_3 = (1-\rho)\rho V_0$.

From the matching quality thresholds obtained from the above three situations, we can further get the expressions of V_1 and V_0:

$$V_1 = \frac{1}{1-\rho}\left\{\alpha\int_{\hat{q}_1}^{\bar{q}}(q+\lambda)f(q)dq + (1-\alpha)\int_{\hat{q}_2}^{\bar{q}} qf(q)dq\right\} + \rho[\alpha F(\hat{q}_1) + (1-\alpha)F(\hat{q}_2)V_1] \tag{7.1}$$

and

$$V_0 = \frac{1}{1-\rho}\left\{\alpha\int_{\hat{q}_2}^{\bar{q}} qf(q)dq + (1-\alpha)\int_{\hat{q}_3}^{\bar{q}} qf(q)dq\right\} + \rho[\alpha F(\hat{q}_2) + (1-\alpha)F(\hat{q}_3)V_0] \tag{7.2}$$

The economic meaning of Equation (7.1) is relatively straightforward. Consider a single male who randomly searches for a partner in the marriage market. He meets an only-child woman at a probability of α. If the matching quality q between the two sides is higher than the threshold $\hat{q}_1$, they will get married and obtain a utility of $q+\lambda$ in each period. Otherwise, he will remain single and go to the next period of search. Similarly, he meets a non-only child woman at a probability of $1-\alpha$. If their matching quality is higher than the threshold $\hat{q}_2$, the two sides will get married and obtain a utility of q in each period. Otherwise, he will remain single and go to the next period of search. If he chooses to remain single during the current period, his utility will be ρV_1. Similarly, we can make the above analysis on non-onlies and obtain Equation (7.2).

We can calculate the expected utilities of life V_0 and V_1 of individuals and find out the nature of the relevant thresholds by substituting the threshold values $\hat{q}_1$, $\hat{q}_2$, $\hat{q}_3$ which are obtained in the three situations above into Equations (7.1) and (7.2). In doing so, the following theorems and inferences can be obtained.

Theorem 1. $\frac{\partial \hat{q}_1}{\partial \lambda} < 0,\ \frac{\partial \hat{q}_2}{\partial \lambda} > 0,\ \frac{\partial \hat{q}_3}{\partial \lambda} < 0$

Proof: From the expressions of $\hat{q}_1$, $\hat{q}_2$, $\hat{q}_3$ and Equations (7.1) and (7.2), we can easily get:

$$\frac{\partial \hat{q}_1}{\partial \lambda} = (1-\rho)\rho\frac{\partial V_1}{\partial \lambda} - 1 = \rho\alpha(1 - F(\hat{q}_1)) - 1 < 0$$

$$\frac{\partial \hat{q}_2}{\partial \lambda} = (1-\rho)\rho\frac{\partial V_1}{\partial \lambda} = \alpha(1 - F(\hat{q}_1)) > 0$$

$$\frac{\partial \hat{q}_3}{\partial \lambda} = (1-\rho)\rho\frac{\partial V_0}{\partial \lambda} = (1-\rho)\rho\frac{\partial V_0}{\partial \hat{q}_2}\frac{\partial \hat{q}_2}{\partial \lambda} = -\rho\alpha\hat{q}_2 f(\hat{q}_2)\frac{\partial \hat{q}_2}{\partial \lambda} < 0$$

The economic meanings of $\frac{\partial \hat{q}_1}{\partial \lambda} < 0$ and $\frac{\partial \hat{q}_2}{\partial \lambda} > 0$ are relatively easy to understand. When λ increases, onlies will be more tolerant $\left(\frac{\partial \hat{q}_1}{\partial \lambda} < 0\right)$ towards the only-child partners they meet, but pickier about the non-only child partners they come across. This is because an only-child spouse means a quota to have a second child, which increases the possible utility level of marriage.

The impact of the policy of 'allowing a second child for couples with both sides being onlies' on non-onlies is an 'indirect' or 'spillover' effect, because the policy does not directly affect non-onlies. For families with one or both sides being a non-only, the birth quota is the same as before the policy was implemented. The negative impact of non-only child status after the policy implementation comes from the fact that onlies will raise their matching quality threshold for spouses who are non-onlies. In other words, onlies become pickier when choosing non-onlies as their spouses. As a result, non-onlies will have a lower match success rate than before the new policy is implemented, or they will have to spend more time searching for the right spouse. Therefore, the policy of 'allowing a second child for couples with both sides being onlies' reduces non-onlies' expected utility of life

$\left(\frac{\partial V_0}{\partial \lambda} = \frac{\partial V_0}{\partial \hat{q}_2}\frac{\partial \hat{q}_2}{\partial \lambda} = -\frac{1}{1-\rho}\alpha \hat{q}_2 f(\hat{q}_2)\frac{\partial \hat{q}_2}{\partial \lambda} < 0\right)$. For non-onlies, their response to behaviour optimization will be to lower the threshold of matching quality $\left(\frac{\partial \hat{q}_3}{\partial \lambda} < 0\right)$.[1]

At equilibrium, onlies have a probability of $\alpha(1 - F(\hat{q}_1))$ to marry onlies of the opposite sex and a probability of $(1 - \alpha)(1 - F(\hat{q}_2))$ to marrying non-onlies of the opposite sex, while non-onlies have a probability of $(1 - \alpha)(1 - F(\hat{q}_3))$ to marry onlies and a probability of $\alpha(1 - F(\hat{q}_2))$ to marry non-onlies. The implementation of the policy of 'allowing a second child for couples with both sides being onlies' can be regarded as being equivalent to an increase in the value of Parameter λ. Thus, Theorem 1 enables us to predict changes in these proportions after the policy implementation and obtain Inference 1.

Inference 1. Onlies are more inclined to marry onlies, while non-onlies are more inclined to marry non-onlies.

Furthermore, we can conclude that provinces and cities with big increases in λ will see significant changes in the match proportion mentioned in Inference 1 after the policy of 'allowing a second child for couples with both sides being onlies' is implemented. In provinces and cities where family planning is relatively relaxed, families are more likely to have two children through various channels, and the policy change will not bring significant increases in λ. By contrast, in provinces and cities where strict family planning is implemented, birth control policy relaxation will significantly increase λ.

Inference 2. The policy of 'allowing a second child for couples with both sides being onlies' will have a bigger effect in those provinces and cities with strict family planning in the past.

7.2.3 Model Expansion: Possible Impacts of the Policy 'Allowing a Second Child for Couples with Both Sides Being Onlies' and the 'Universal Two-Child' Policy

In early 2014, Zhejiang, Anhui and Jiangxi became the first provinces in China to amend their family planning regulations, allowing couples to have a second child if either of them comes from a one-child family. Subsequently, Beijing, Jiangsu and Hubei followed suit.

After the second-child policy is extended to couples with either side coming from a one-child family, onlies will no longer require higher matching quality for non-onlies as before. This has led to an increase in the proportion of marries between onlies and non-onlies. The new policy allows onlies to have a second child whether they marry an only or a non-only. As a result, they do not have to raise the requirements when they consider non-onlies for marriage. It also means that they need not to lower the requirements when they meet onlies for marriage. Consequently, the number of marriages between onlies has fallen than under the policy of 'allowing a second child for couples with both sides being onlies'. Contrary to the situation under the old policy, non-onlies become stricter under the new policy when they consider fellow non-onlies for marriage. This has resulted in a decline in the proportion of marriages between non-onlies. Under the joint action of the above channels, the second-child policy for couples with either side coming from a one-child family will increase the proportion of marriages between onlies and non-onlies, something which is opposite to the situation under the former policy of 'allowing a second child for couples with both sides being onlies'.

After January 1, 2016, the Chinese government further relaxed the second-child policy at the national level, which made the only-child status totally irrelevant to birth quotas. Corresponding to the above model, λ will be permanently 0, and random matching will prevail as if the relevant restrictive policies were non-existent.

7.3 Data and Empirical Method

7.3.1 Data Description and Preliminary Analysis

This empirical study mainly uses the 1% random sampling data from China's 2005 census, which include basic demographic information such as gender, marital status, year of first marriage, birth date, level of education, Hukou types, relationship with household head and other variables. In particular, for the entire population aged 32 and under (who were born in 1974 and after), the census contained data on the number of siblings in households. From this information, we can infer the one-child status of an individual. Since the statutory minimum age for marriage is 20 for women and 22 for men, we limit the samples to the married population aged 20–32 in 2005.

We assume that the marriage market in China mainly involves searching and matching within a province, which has been statistically proved by multiple studies (Wei and Zhang, 2011). After data screening, we finally selected 15 provinces as the sample provinces for study. In these 15 provinces, the proportion of onlies among men and women aged 20–32 does not significantly change over time.

Table 7.1 presents the descriptive statistics of the various characteristics by gender and one-child status of the sampled families before and after the policy of 'allowing a second child for couples with both sides being onlies' were implemented in the 15 provinces. It shows a higher proportion of Han Chinese and urban residents among the onlies. This is consistent with the fact that Han Chinese and urban residents have long faced a stricter one-

Table 7.1 Descriptive Statistics of Families in 15 Provinces by Gender and Only-Child Status

	Female Samples		*Male Samples*	
	Onlies	*Non-onlies*	*Onlies*	*Non-onlies*
Number of years of education	9.371	8.350	10.115	9.049
	(3.394)***	(3.129)	(3.171)***	(2.781)
Age at first marriage	22.029	21.564	23.744	23.280
	(2.495)***	(2.494)	(2.551)***	(2.586)
Proportion of Han Chinese	0.864	0.771	0.871	0.778
	(0.342)***	(0.420)	(0.335)***	0.415
Proportion of urban residents	0.347	0.175	0.431	0.198
	(0.476)***	(0.380)	(0.495)***	(0.399)
Self-declared level of health	1.008	1.007	1.008	1.008
	(0.112)	(0.106)	(0.124)	(0.113)
Proportion of marriage with onlies	0.403	0.064	0.444	0.075
	(0.491)***	(0.244)	(0.496)***	(0.262)

Notes: 1. Table 7.1 presents the means, as well as standard deviations (in brackets) of the samples.
2. *, ** and ***, respectively indicate that the means of the samples of onlies and the samples of non-onlies are different at 10%, 5% and 1% levels.

child policy, while rural residents and ethnic groups enjoy a more relaxed family planning policy. Table 7.1 also shows that onlies have a relatively higher level of education on average and an older age at first marriage. Finally, both male and female onlies tend to marry onlies. Another possible reason for this, apart from the influence of selective matching channels mentioned earlier, is that most people look for spouses in their own provinces. Therefore, provinces where the one-child policy is more strictly implemented have a higher proportion of onlies, which means more one-child families.

In Figure 7.1, we plot the proportions of different types of marriage matching in different years. 'Year' is defined as the year relative to the time point when the policy of 'allowing a second child for couples with both sides being onlies' was implemented. Figure 7.1 shows several important characteristics of the changes in the proportions of different matching types at different time points: there was a clear fall in the proportion of matching between onlies and non-onlies at the time of the policy implementation, but jumps occurred in the proportions of matching between onlies and onlies and between non-onlies and non-onlies at Year 0 (the first year of the policy implementation). The evidence in Figure 7.1 supports Inference 1 from the model, which states that when couples with both sides being onlies get a quota to have a second child, the proportions of marriage between onlies and between non-onlies will both rise, while the proportion of 'mixed' marriages (i.e. marriages between onlies and non-onlies) falls.

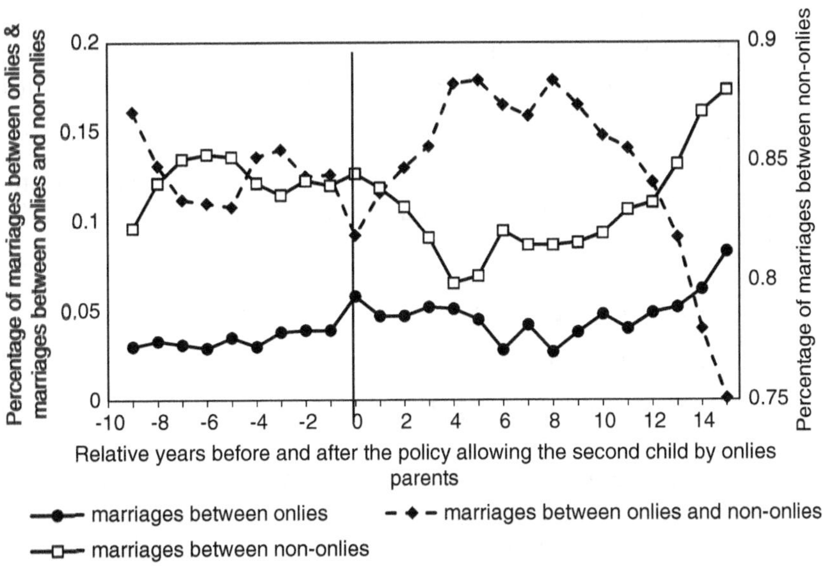

Figure 7.1 Time Trends of Different Types of Marriage Match.

However, changes in the proportion of different types of marriage matching in Figure 7.1 should not be directly construed as being indicative of the impact of the policy of 'allowing a second child for couples with both sides being onlies' on the marriage market, especially when there are systematic differences in social and economic variables between onlies and non-onlies as shown in the descriptive statistics in Table 7.1. Therefore, we adopt the more accurate empirical estimation method of Differences-In-Differences to make further estimates.

7.3.2 Empirical Method

In our empirical estimation, we concurrently use the difference in the implementation time of the policy of 'allowing a second child for couples with both sides being onlies' and the difference in the implementation intensity of the previous one-child policy in different provinces to estimate the difference-in-differences. According to the method provided by Scharping (2003) and Ebenstein (2010), we take the over-birth fine rate as a measure of the implementation intensity of the one-child policy. In Attached Table 7.1, we provide a province-by-province description of the family planning policies, over-birth fine rates and the years in which the policy of 'allowing a second child for couples with both sides being onlies' was officially written into the family planning regulations of the provinces under study. Our empirical analysis focuses attention on the differences in policy effects in different provinces. If the only-child status means that one can get a quota for having a second child by marrying a one-child spouse, then our model can infer that the policy of 'allowing a second child for couples with both sides being onlies' will produce a greater impact in places where the former one-child policy is more strictly implemented.

From the model, we can easily get the difference in the proportion of marriages between onlies before ($\lambda = 0$) and after ($\lambda > 0$) the implementation of the policy of 'allowing a second child for couples with both sides being onlies':

$$\begin{aligned} D(\lambda) &= \alpha[1 - F(\hat{q}_1(\lambda > 0, t)) - (1 - F(\hat{q}_1(\lambda = 0)))] \\ &= \alpha[F(\hat{q}_1(\lambda = 0)) - F(\hat{q}_1(\lambda > 0, t))] \\ &= \alpha[F(\hat{q}_1(\lambda = 0)) - F(\hat{q}_1(\lambda > 0))] + \eta(t) \end{aligned} \tag{7.3}$$

Because $\frac{\partial \hat{q}_1}{\partial \lambda} < 0$, we have $\alpha[F(\hat{q}_1(\lambda = 0)) - F(\hat{q}_1(\lambda > 0)) > 0]$. However, $D(\lambda)$ may include the trend of change in time of the proportion, which is denoted by $\eta(t)$, of matching among individuals with both sides being onlies. If provinces with different $D(\lambda)$ values have the same $\eta(t)$, we can remove $\eta(t)$ by subtracting $D(\lambda)$ between different regions.

As Inference 2 states, the benefits (λ) of marriage between onlies are greater in provinces where the one-child policy is more strictly implemented. By subtracting the values of $D(\lambda)$ of provinces with different λ values, we can get:

$$\begin{aligned} DD(\lambda) \equiv D(\lambda^S) - D(\lambda^L) &= \alpha[F(\hat{q}_1(\lambda^L,\ t)) - F(\hat{q}_1(\lambda^S,\ t))] \\ &= \alpha[F(\hat{q}_1(\lambda^L)) - F(\hat{q}_1(\lambda^S))] > 0 \end{aligned} \tag{7.4}$$

Wherein: λ^S and λ^L respectively represent the utility increment brought by only-child families obtaining a quota to have a second child in provinces where the one-child policy is strictly implemented and in provinces where the one-child policy is implemented relatively loosely. We have $\lambda^S > \lambda^L > 0$. If provinces with different values of λ have the same $\eta(t)$, our difference-in-differences estimates will no longer include the time trend $\eta(t)$ of marriages between onlies.

Similarly, we can make estimates for non-onlies. We get following the inter-provincial difference in the proportion of marriages between non-onlies before and after the implementation of the policy of 'allowing a second child for couples with both sides being onlies':

$$\begin{aligned} DD(\lambda) \equiv D(\lambda^S) - D(\lambda^L) &= \alpha[F(\hat{q}_2(\lambda^L,\ t)) - F(\hat{q}_2(\lambda^S,\ t))] \\ &= \alpha[F(\hat{q}_2(\lambda^L)) - F(\hat{q}_2(\lambda^S))] > 0 \end{aligned}$$

7.3.3 Discussion of the Rationality of Difference-in-Differences Empirical Design

7.3.3.1 The Proportion of Onlies May Change over Time

Our empirical identification method requires that the proportion of onlies among males and females remains unchanged over time.[2] Otherwise, our difference-in-differences estimates will include both the impact of the policy and the impact of changes in the proportion of onlies. This can be illustrated from the model, where the proportion of onlies α affects $D(\lambda)$ in two different ways. First, α directly influences the matching results by changing the probability of encounter between onlies in the search process. As shown in Equation (7.3), if α increases at the same time, the effect on the increase of λ will be overestimated. Second, α will also affect the threshold value of matching. If α increases, onlies will raise their threshold, because an increase in α will reduce the search cost of finding an only-child spouse in the marriage market. So, if α and λ increase together, the effect of falling $\hat{q}_1$ will be underestimated. In summary, α will have an impact on the proportion of matching, but the direction of such impact is uncertain.

To address this problem, we have pre-screened the samples. Assuming that most people choose spouses within their own provinces (Wei and Zhang 2011),[3] we remove those provinces where the proportion of onlies among males and females in the population aged 20–32 has significantly changed, so as to prevent estimation errors. Specifically, we take out provinces with a trend of significant changes (rising or falling proportions) in male onlies or female onlies, as well as provinces with significant differences in the average proportion of onlies before and after the implementation of the policy of 'allowing a second child for couples with both sides being onlies'. In Attached Table 7.2, we detail how we obtained the desirable samples. Among the 15 provinces included in the samples of the current study, the level of onlies among the males and females born in the 1974–1985 period remained stable among the population of different age groups in the provinces.

7.3.3.2 Whether the Time to Implement the Policy of 'Allowing a Second Child for Couples with Both Sides Being Onlies' Is Related to the Proportion of Onlies

The second issue of identification to be discussed is whether the time of implementation of the policy of 'allowing a second child for couples with both sides being onlies' is related to the 'proportion of onlies' (meaning an increase in λ) is related to the proportion α of onlies. If the two are related, our difference-in-differences estimates may be biased.

Any doubt about the possible existence of correlation between α and λ should not be ignored. As we mentioned in the background introduction in

Table 7.2 Effect on Marriage Matching of the Policy of 'Allowing a Second Child for Couples with Both Sides Being Onlies'—Evidence from OLS Regression

Dependent Variable	*Whether Married to Onlies*		*Whether Married to Non-onlies*	
Samples	*Female Onlies*	*Male Onlies*	*Female Non-onlies*	*Male Non-onlies*
	(1)	*(2)*	*(3)*	*(4)*
Relaxation	= 0.088**	= 0.143***	= 0.022***	= 0.010
	(0.043)	(0.048)	(0.008)	(0.008)
Chow Test	Null: = 0.44 Prob > = 0.5070 Prob> =0.5070		Null: = 0.63 Prob > = 0.4278 Prob> =0.4278	
Age at first marriage	0.012	−0.083	0.003	0.011
	(0.050)	(0.059)	(0.007)	(0.010)
Square of age at first marriage	0.000	0.002*	−0.000	−0.000
	(0.001)	(0.001)	(0.000)	(0.000)
Number of years of education	0.005	0.002	−0.002***	−0.001
	(0.003)	(0.004)	(0.001)	(0.001)
Whether being Han Chinese	0.036	0.025	−0.008	−0.010**
	(0.032)	(0.032)	(0.005)	(0.005)
Urban Hukou	0.123***	0.042*	−0.055***	−0.022***
	(0.024)	(0.024)	(0.006)	(0.006)
Observed value	2,971	2,704	23,444	23,743
R-squared	0.064	0.049	0.038	0.029

Notes: 1. The standard deviations are clustered at the province—year-of-marriage level.
2. ***, ** and * respectively represent being significant at the level of 1%, 5%, or 10%.
3. The regression equation also contains constant terms and the fixed effects of year-of-marriage and province.

Section 2, the timetable for the implementation of the policy of 'allowing a second child for couples with both sides being onlies' may be related to the demographic factor of each region and the time when the one-child policy was initially implemented. Specifically, provinces with historically low fertility rates or regions that have strictly implemented the one-child policy are more inclined to adopt the policy of 'allowing a second child for couples with both sides being onlies' earlier. In the meantime, these provinces also have a higher proportion of onlies.

In our data analysis, we find that in the 15 provinces included in our samples, the proportion of onlies is roughly 12%–13% among the 20–30 age group. When the mean proportion of onlies in the experimental group ($\lambda > 0$, where the policy of 'allowing a second child for couples with both sides being onlies' is implemented) is compared with that of the control group ($\lambda = 0$, where the policy of 'allowing a second child for couples with both sides being onlies' is not yet implemented), *T* test could not reject the hypothesis that the two sub-samples have an equal mean.[4]

7.3.3.3 Systematic Differences between Onlies and Non-onlies

When we assume that the only-child status only indicates 'a possibility of obtaining a quota for a second child by marrying onlies', the difference-in-differences estimates can reflect the effect of the policy of 'allowing a second child for couples with both sides being onlies'. However, there may be differences between onlies and non-onlies in other aspects, and such differences may also affect the marriage matching results. One difference that people can most easily think of is that there may be significant differences in the human capital level between onlies and non-onlies. In his famous article on the relationship between child quantity and quality, Becker and Tomes (1976) reveals that there is a negative correlation between the two. The descriptive statistics shown in Table 7.1 also reveal that onlies receive longer school education than non-onlies. In a recent empirical study comparing the personal characteristics of people who were born before and after the one-child policy was introduced, Cameron et al. (2013) point out that onlies are less trustful, difficult to win trust, more risk-averse, less competitive and more pessimistic and have a lesser sense of justice. In their research, Sun Wenkai et al. (2016) believe that onlies in China lack entrepreneurship because they have no natural networks of contact of their own. Moreover, onlies may come from families which lack social contacts and have a low level of wealth, thus unable to get around the one-child policy or pay over-birth fines.

If these social and economic factors related to the one-child status have no effect on the marriage market over time, by comparing the simple differences between and after the policy implementation, it will be possible to remove the impact of such differences on marriage matching. However, the influence of these social and economic variables on the marriage market may change over time. For example, the rate of return on education may change over time (due to economic growth), making people with a high level of education more popular in the marriage market. If onlies have a higher level of education, then the simple difference will include the impact of the higher returns on education. In this situation, if we assume that the impact of social and economic variables on the marriage market have the same trend of change in provinces with different λ values, then our difference-in-differences estimates can remove the impact of these time trends.

In the robustness test to be discussed in Section 5, we will further allow these social and economic variables to have different effects on the marriage market among different provinces. We control the cross terms of dummies for social and economic variables and individuals' professed time of marriage after the implementation of the policy of 'allowing a second child for couples with both sides being onlies'. If the difference-in-differences estimates thus obtained do not change significantly, this robustness test can to a great extent alleviate the above concerns.

7.3.4 Discussion of the Rationality of Using Cross-Sectional Samples

Our regression analysis uses the samples of China's 2005 census. In this study, we focus on individuals aged 20–32. Only after one is married can we observe his or her marriage composition. In this way, individuals who choose to make more searches in the marriage market are automatically removed from the samples. This situation could be more common among the younger population.

Specifically, our model shows that λ will make the thresholds $\hat{q}_1$ and $\hat{q}_3$ fall but $\hat{q}_3$ rise. This shows that after the policy of 'allowing a second child for couples with both sides being onlies' is implemented, marriages between onlies, as well as between non-onlies can come about faster, while marriages between onlies and non-onlies will become slower than before the implementation of the policy. Because of this, our samples are likely to include more matching between people with the same, but less matching between people with different one-child status. As a result, we may overestimate the changes in the matching pattern.

In the robustness test in Section 6, we will restrict our samples to the older age groups, which will reduce the possible errors due to the use of cross-sectional data. By comparing estimation differences between the older samples (over 25 years old) and all the samples of the 20–32 age group, we can roughly find out whether the use of cross-sectional samples may cause greater estimation errors.

7.4 Evidence from Regression Analysis

7.4.1 Evidence from OLS Regression

We report the results of OLS regression first. These are the results of the 'simple differences' before and after the implementation of the policy of 'allowing a second child for couples with both sides being onlies'. If the marriage matching pattern has no trend of change over time, namely $\eta(t) = 0$ in Equation (7.3), it will be reliable to use the OLS method to estimate the policy effect. As whether any trend of change over time exists in the marriage matching pattern, we can roughly see the situation with the help of Figure 7.1. In Figure 7.1, marriages between people with the same status (i.e. being an only child in their families) and marriages between people with different personal status did not show a significant trend of change over time before the policy was implemented (Year 0). In fact, our data screening process ensures that this trend does not change much over time. Therefore, we carry out OLS regression and use the results as preliminary reference.

We respectively use the samples of male onlies and female onlies to fit Equation (7.5a).

$$SPOC_i = \alpha + Relaxation_i \cdot \beta_g + X_i\rho + \tau + \theta + \varepsilon_i \tag{7.5a}$$

Wherein: Result Variable $SPOC_i$ is a dummy variable, which indicates whether the only-child person i marries an only-child partner. On the right side of the equation, the independent variable of greatest concern to us is the dummy variable $Relaxation_i$, which indicates whether i's time of marriage is after the policy of 'allowing a second child for couples with both sides being onlies' was implemented in his or her province. If i was married after the province implementation, $Relaxation_i = 1$. Otherwise, $Relaxation_i = 0$. β_g is the regression coefficient obtained by using the male and the female samples respectively. Control Variable X_i includes i's age, level of education, ethnic affiliation, possession of urban or rural Hukou; τ is the fixed effect of the year of marriage; and θ is the fixed effect of the province where i resides. The estimated standard deviations are clustered at the province-marriage year level.

To test whether the proportion of marriages between non-onlies has increased after the policy implementation, we respectively use the samples of non-only males and female non-onlies to fit Regression Equation (7.5b):

$$SPSIB_i = \alpha + Relaxation_i \cdot \gamma_g + X_i\rho + \tau + \theta + \varepsilon_i \tag{7.5b}$$

Wherein: Result Variable $SPSIB_i$ is a binary dummy variable, which indicates whether the non-only person i marries a non-only; and γ_g is the regression coefficient obtained by using the male and female samples respectively. The clustering methods for the other regression factors and standard deviations of statistics are the same as those in Equation (7.5a).

The estimated results are reported in Table 7.2. Columns (1) and (2) respectively show the policy effects on marriage between female onlies and onlies, and between male onlies and onlies. $\beta_{women} = 0.088$, which implies an increase of 8.8% in the probability of female onlies to marry male onlies after the implementation of the policy of 'allowing a second child for couples with both sides being onlies'. This increase is significant at the 5% level. $\beta_{men} = 0.143$, which indicates a rise of 14.3% in the probability of male onlies to marry female onlies after the policy implementation. This increase is significant at the 1% level.

The probability increase and its significance may vary with the respective use of male and female samples. Chiappori, Oreffice and Quintana-Domeque (2010) explain that such 'asymmetry' in the matching process may be a result of stable equilibrium of matching. In the matching process, even if λ increases by the same amplitude for both males and females, the gender group with a fewer population may react more strongly, because it is easier for them to find partners of the same personal status of whether they are onlies or non-onlies. Our sample population includes a total of 26,405 couples. Among them, 2,971 are female onlies, and 2,704 are male onlies, which are less than the number of female onlies. On the other hand, the utility increment (λ) of the policy implementation may vary between males and females. In traditional Chinese culture, children are generally considered as the offspring of the husband's family, so λ is likely to increase the utility for males. In other words, male onlies have more motivations to find female onlies for marriage. The results in Table 7.2 tend to support the latter interpretation more. We employ Chow test to test the null hypothesis, and the X^2 value in Table 7.2 shows that the null hypothesis cannot be rejected. The reason might be that there is no significant gap in λ between males and females.

In Table 7.2, Columns (3) and (4) respectively show an increase of 2.2% in the proportion of female non-onlies seeking male non-onlies for marriage and a rise of 1% in the proportion of male non-onlies seeking female non-onlies for marriage. The difference in policy effect as indicated by the simple differences is not statistically significant, and Chow test cannot reject the = hypothesis.

7.4.2 Evidence from Difference-in-Differences Regression

To get more consistent estimates, we next adopt the more robust statistical difference-in-differences estimation method. If there is the same trend of change over time in the marriage matching pattern between provinces with different λ values, the difference-in-differences estimation method will enable us to remove the impact of this time trend.

For the samples of male onlies and female onlies, we respectively fit Equation (7.6a):

$$SPOC_i = \alpha + Fine_{pt} \times Relaxation_{it} \cdot \omega_g + fine_{pt} \cdot \varnothing + Relaxation_i \cdot \delta + X_i \rho + \tau + \theta + \varepsilon_i \quad (7.6a)$$

For the samples of male non-onlies and female non-onlies, we respectively fit Equation (7.6b):

$$SPSIB_i = \alpha + Fine_{pt} \times Relaxation_{it} \cdot \varsigma_g + fine_{pt} \cdot \varnothing + Relaxation_i \cdot \delta + X_i \rho + \tau + \theta + \varepsilon_i \quad (7.6b)$$

In Equations (7.6a) and (7.6b), the explanatory variable we are concerned about is the cross term of the dummy variables that indicate whether individuals marry after the policy implementation and over-birth fines. For the fine rate here, we take the mean of the rates of fine on Individual *i* before marriage. The control variables and the fixed effects are the same as those in Equations (7.5a) and (7.5b).

Columns (1) and (2) in Table 7.3 show that if the increase in over-birth fines before the policy implementation is twice the average annual family income in the province, the policy of 'allowing a second child for couples with both sides being onlies' will lead to an increase of 12.7% in the proportion of female onlies to marry male onlies and a rise of 19.6% in the proportion of male onlies to marry female onlies. The difference in policy effect is not statistically significant, and Chow test cannot reject the hypothesis of $\beta_{men} = \beta_{women}$. Columns (3) and (4) in Table 7.3 reveal that if the increase in over-birth fines before the policy implementation is by the same amount as the average annual family income in the province, the policy of 'allowing a second child for couples with both sides being onlies' will lead to an increase of 2.5% in the proportion of female non-onlies to marry male non-onlies and a rise of 0.7% in the proportion of male non-onlies to marry female non-onlies. The difference in policy effect is not statistically significant. In other words, Chow test cannot reject the hypothesis of $\varsigma_{men} = \varsigma_{women}$.

As in Table 7.2, the cross-term coefficient has some 'asymmetry' between different gender samples, which may be equally due to the asymmetrical increases in λ between the male and the female samples. If males care more about getting a birth quota, male onlies will benefit more from the implementation of the policy of 'allowing a second child for couples with both sides being onlies'. In the marriage market, this response will be manifested as bigger changes in the marriage matching pattern of male onlies. If females care relatively less about birth quotas, male non-onlies will suffer less harm than female non-onlies after the policy implementation. Consequently, male non-onlies will also make fewer changes in their marriage matching pattern.

7.5 Supplementary Evidence: Fertility Rate

The key hypothesis in the current study is that individuals are willing to have more children, so the policy of 'allowing a second child for couples with both sides being onlies' can bring about utility increment, namely an increase in λ. In this section, we will test this hypothesis. Specifically, if onlies are indeed driven to marriage by a willingness to have children, it should be possible for us to observe that those families which have obtained the second child quota do have given birth to one more child. We will test this hypothesis by fitting Equation (7.7).

$$\text{Fertility}_j = \alpha + \mathit{Eligibility}_j \times R_j \cdot \gamma + \mathit{Eligibility}_j \cdot \delta + R_j \cdot \mu + X_j \rho + t + \theta + \varepsilon_j \tag{7.7}$$

Table 7.3 Effect on Marriage Matching of the Policy of 'Allowing a Second Child for Couples with Both Sides Being Onlies'—Evidence from Difference-in-Differences Regression

Dependent Variable	*Whether Married to Onlies*		*Whether Married to Non-onlies*	
Samples	*Female Onlies (1)*	*Male Onlies (2)*	*Female Non-onlies (3)*	*Male Non-onlies (4)*
Fine × Relaxation	= 0.127*	= 0.196**	= 0.025***	= 0.007
	(0.075)	(0.097)	(0.009)	(0.014)
Chow Test	Null: 0.11 Prob > = 0.7433		Null: 0.86 Prob > = 0.3542	
Relaxation	−0.663	−1.019*	−0.123**	−0.031
	(0.441)	(0.575)	(0.050)	(0.084)
Fine	0.036**	0.046	0.018	0.012
	(0.012)	(0.032)	(0.015)	(0.015)
Age at first marriage	0.011	−0.085	0.003	0.011
	(0.050)	(0.059)	(0.007)	(0.010)
Square of age at first marriage	0.000	0.002*	−0.000	−0.000
	(0.001)	(0.001)	(0.000)	(0.000)
Number of years of education	0.005	0.002	−0.002***	−0.001
	(0.003)	(0.004)	(0.001)	(0.001)
Whether being Han Chinese	0.036	0.026	−0.008	−0.010**
	(0.032)	(0.032)	(0.005)	(0.005)
Urban Hukou	0.123***	0.041*	−0.055***	−0.022***
	(0.024)	(0.024)	(0.006)	(0.006)
Observed value	2,971	2,704	23,444	23,743
R-squared	0.064	0.050	0.038	0.029

Notes: 1. The standard deviations are clustered at the province—marriage year level.
2. ***, ** and * respectively represent being significant at the level of 1%, 5% or 10%.
3. Fine represents the fine rate, defined as the mean of the rates of fine on the individual in the years before his or her marriage.
4. the regression equation also contains constant terms and fixed effects of marriage year and province.

$Fertility_j$ is the number of children born in Marriage *j*.$Eligibility_j$ is a binary dummy variable, which indicates whether Marriage *j* consists of two onlies. R_j is a binary mute variable, which indicates whether the province where the family is located implemented the policy of 'allowing a second child for couples with both sides being onlies' nine months before the population census was conducted. Since it usually takes nine months for females to get pregnant, the effect of the policy change on fertility rate can only be observed at least nine months later. This shows that the dummy variable R_j for policy implementation is defined according to the likely pregnancy time, which is slightly different from Relaxation$_j$ defined as the time of marriage above. M_j, respectively, represents the age, level of education, ethnic affiliation and Hukou type of husband and wife in Marriage j. t is the fixed effect of the year of marriage, and θ is the fixed effect of province. Since China's family planning policy generally does not allow couples to have more than two children, those families with three or more children are not representative. In our samples, we only focus on families with not more than two children.

The estimated results of Equation (7.7) are presented in Table 7.4. Column (1) shows that in those provinces where the policy of 'allowing a second child for couples with both sides being onlies' is implemented, on average, only-child families give birth to 66 more children per 1,000 households than non-only-child families. This effect is significant at 10%. It should be noted that because our samples only include families of couples aged 20–32, the fertility rate reflected in the data is likely to be lower than the total fertility rate. Besides, females generally get pregnant after the policy liberalization. Due to the existence of these measurement errors, we can see that the results in Table 7.4 may be less than the actual effect. We may consider the results as the lower limit of the effect on fertility rate of the policy of 'allowing a second child for couples with both sides being onlies'.

Columns (2) and (3) respectively show the number of boys and the number of girls born. The cross-term coefficient in Column (2) indicates that only-child families give birth to 52 more children per 1,000 households than non-only-child families after the policy implementation. This coefficient is very close to being significant at the 10% level. Column (3) shows that the policy of 'allowing a second child for couples with both sides being onlies' leads to an increase in the birth of 13 girls per 1,000 households. The cross-term coefficients in Columns (2) and (3) are not statistically significant, which may be due to expect to have btoo small values of the explained variables. The finding that the policy implementation affects the fertility rate differently for different genders is consistent with existing literature on gender-biased abortions in China. Previous literature (Ebenstein, 2010) has found that the gender structure of first births is very close to the natural level, while the gender structure of second births is severely unbalanced. And, these families with two children are more likely to be those who expect to have boys. There is a greater possibility for these families to make gender-biased abortions.

7.6 Robustness Test

7.6.1 Allowing Observable Influencing Factors to Change over Time

In this section, we will examine how our estimates are affected by the possibility that the coefficient of factors influencing marriage matching changes

Table 7.4 Effect on Fertility Rate of the Policy of 'Allowing a Second Child for Couples with Both Sides Being Onlies': Evidence from Difference-in-Differences Regression

Result Variable	*Number of Children Born (1)*	*Number of Boys Born (2)*	*Number of Girls Born (3)*
Eligibility × R	0.066*	0.052	0.013
	(0.038)	(0.037)	(0.039)
Eligibility	−0.088**	−0.080**	−0.008
	(0.035)	(0.033)	(0.035)
R	0.072***	0.033	0.039*
	(0.021)	(0.022)	(0.020)
Wife's number of years of education	−0.053***	−0.028***	−0.025***
	(0.005)	(0.005)	(0.005)
Husband's number of years of education	−0.010**	−0.003	−0.007
	(0.005)	(0.005)	(0.005)
Wife's age	0.007***	0.001	0.006***
	(0.002)	(0.002)	(0.002)
Husband's age	−0.000	0.001	−0.001
	(0.002)	(0.002)	(0.002)
Wife is Han Chinese	−0.001	−0.014	0.013
	(0.014)	(0.017)	(0.016)
Husband is Han Chinese	0.008	0.026	−0.018
	(0.014)	(0.017)	(0.016)
Wife has urban Hukou	−0.023**	0.000	−0.023*
	(0.012)	(0.013)	(0.013)
Husband has urban Hukou	−0.046***	−0.030**	−0.017
	(0.011)	(0.012)	(0.012)
Observed value	25,774	25,774	25,774
R-squared	0.384	0.146	0.090

Notes: 1. The standard deviations are clustered at the province—marriage year level.
2. ***, ** and * respectively represent being significant at the level of 1%, 5% or 10%.
3. The regression equation also includes constant terms and the fixed effects of year of marriage and province.

over time and the trend of change varies between provinces. In Equations (7.6a) and (7.6b), we respectively add the cross terms of individuals' number of years of education and the dummy variables for Hukou type, ethnic affiliation and implementation of the policy of 'allowing a second child for couples with both sides being onlies'. The regression results are shown in Table 7.5. The cross-term coefficients obtained from regression of different sub-samples are very close to those in Table 7.3. The consistency between Table 7.5 and Table 7.3 shows that there is little possibility that different

Table 7.5 Effect on Marriage Matching by the Policy of 'Allowing a Second Child for Couples with Both Sides Being Onlies': Evidence from Difference-in-Differences Regression (Allowing Observable Factors to Have Different Time Trends of the Rate of Return in the Marriage Market in Different Provinces)

Dependent Variable	*Whether Married to Onlies*		*Whether Married to Non-onlies*	
Samples	*Female Onlies*	*Male Onlies*	*Female Non-onlies*	*Male Non-onlies*
	(1)	*(2)*	*(1)*	*(2)*
Finexpolicy liberalization	0.127*	0.198*	0.024***	0.008
	(0.074)	(0.106)	(0.009)	(0.014)
Policy liberalization	−0.649	−1.130*	−0.126**	−0.023
	(0.432)	(0.620)	(0.051)	(0.085)
Fine	0.030*	0.042	0.011	0.012
	(0.016)	(0.032)	(0.015)	(0.016)
Age at first marriage	0.011	−0.085	0.003	0.011
	(0.050)	(0.059)	(0.007)	(0.010)
Square of age at first marriage	0.000	0.002*	−0.000	−0.000
	(0.001)	(0.001)	(0.000)	(0.000)
Number of years of education	0.006	0.002	−0.003**	−0.003***
	(0.007)	(0.007)	(0.002)	(0.001)
Whether being Han Chinese	0.056	−0.026	−0.007	−0.010
	(0.080)	(0.085)	(0.010)	(0.012)
Urban Hukou	0.116**	0.011	−0.052***	0.001
	(0.052)	(0.040)	(0.008)	(0.008)
Number years of education × policy liberalization	−0.001	0.000	0.002	0.003**
	(0.008)	(0.008)	(0.002)	(0.001)
Han Chinese × policy liberalization	−0.022	0.059	−0.001	−0.001
	(0.080)	(0.091)	(0.011)	(0.013)
Urban Hukou × policy liberalization	0.009	0.041	−0.004	−0.034***
	(0.058)	(0.049)	(0.011)	(0.012)
Observed value	2,971	2,704	23,444	23,743
R-squared	0.064	0.050	0.038	0.030

Notes: 1. The standard deviations are clustered at the province—year-of-marriage level.
2. ***, ** and * respectively represent being significant at the level of 1%, 5% or 10%.
3. Fine is defined as the mean of the rates of fine on the individual in the years before his or her marriage.
4. The regression equation also contains constant terms and the fixed effects of year of marriage and province.

marriage matching trends between different provinces have caused errors in the difference-in-differences regression results.

7.6.2 *Double Difference-in-Differences Estimates of the Sample Population over 25*

To deal with the problem of selective samples that may arise from the use of cross-sectional data estimates, we limit the sub-samples in the regressions represented by Equations (7.6a) and (7.6b) to those born in the 1974–1979 period, i.e. those aged 26 to 32 at the time of population census. Since the marriage rate of the population over 25 is significantly higher than that of the population under 25, studying the matching pattern of the population over 25 can alleviate the possible estimation errors caused by the limitation associated with the use of the cross-sectional data mentioned above. This limitation is that because it takes a longer time for onlies to find matching non-onlies, their marriages are less observable from the cross-sectional data. In other words, the proportion of marriages between onlies and non-onlies observed in the cross-sectional data is lower than the real proportion. Such under-sampling will lead to an overestimation of the effect on changes in the marriage matching pattern.

Table 7.6 reports the regression results of the older age samples. In Table 7.6, the regression coefficient shows a greater policy effect than in Table 7.3. At the same time, the regression coefficient also has a higher level of significance. Since there is a lower probability of selectivity bias in the sampled population over 25, we can easily conclude that the policy effect estimated using all the samples as reported in Table 7.3 is not much affected by the selectivity bias.

7.7 Conclusion

Family economics attributes the formation of a family to individuals' desire to improve their utility by way of family. The 'functions' that can be realized by forming a family include division of labour (Becker and Tomes, 1976), public goods for joint consumption (Lam, 1988), joint insurance (Rosenzweig and Stark, 1989), extended credit (Borenstein and Courant, 1989), among others. The various hypotheses about the 'functions' of a family can be tested by observing the matching pattern in the marriage market. However, there has been no empirical study to test the most important 'function' of family, namely raising children (Becker and Tomes, 1976).

A series of changes in China's family planning policy has made this study possible. In 1979, China started to implement a strict one-child policy. Subsequently, this policy has been gradually relaxed, as reflected in allowing families with both husband and wife being onlies to have a second child. We

Table 7.6 Effect on Marriage Matching of the Policy of 'Allowing a Second Child for Couples with Both Sides Being Onlies': Evidence of Difference-in-Differences Regression for the Samples over 25 Years Old

Dependent Variable	*Whether Married to an Only*		*Whether Married to a Non-only*	
Samples	*Female Onlies* *(1)*	*Male Onlies* *(2)*	*Female Non-onlies* *(3)*	*Male Non-onlies* *(4)*
Fine × policy liberalization	0.193**	0.228**	0.039***	0.004
	(0.088)	(0.092)	(0.010)	(0.015)
Policy liberalization	−0.935*	−1.176**	−0.180***	−0.018
	(0.494)	(0.540)	(0.054)	(0.086)
Fine	0.030*	0.042	0.011	0.012
	(0.016)	(0.032)	(0.015)	(0.016)
Age at first marriage	−0.024	−0.155**	0.001	0.033**
	(0.081)	(0.076)	(0.017)	(0.013)
Square of age at first marriage	0.001	0.003**	0.000	−0.001**
	(0.002)	(0.002)	(0.000)	(0.000)
Number of years of education	0.012**	0.000	−0.002**	−0.001
	(0.006)	(0.005)	(0.001)	(0.001)
Whether being Han Chinese	−0.045	0.022	−0.006	−0.008
	(0.049)	(0.041)	(0.006)	(0.006)
Urban Hukou	0.088***	0.028	−0.057***	−0.019***
	(0.032)	(0.027)	(0.007)	(0.007)
Observed value	1,554	2,059	11,791	17,519
R-squared	0.064	0.055	0.032	0.028

Notes: 1. The standard deviations are clustered at the province—year-of-marriage level.
2. ***, ** and * respectively represent being significant at the level of 1%, 5% or 10%.
3. Fine is defined as the mean of the rates of fine on the individual in the years before his or her marriage.
4. The regression equation also contains constant terms and the fixed effects of year of marriage and province.

estimate the difference in differences using the policy changes over time and the difference in the strictness of implementation of the one-child policy in different provinces before the policy liberalization. We find a greater increase in the proportion of marriages between onlies, as well as between non-onlies in the provinces where a stricter one-child policy is implemented. In the meantime, the proportion of 'mixed' marriages, namely marriages between onlies and non-onlies, has fallen more in these provinces after the implementation of the policy of 'allowing a second child for couples who both come from one-child families'

The empirical results of this study provide direct evidence for Becker's proposition that 'The most important function of family is for people to raise their own children'. At the same time, this study also shows that if the family is taken as the unit for implementing a policy and the applicability of the policy is decided by family composition, then such a policy is bound to change the matching pattern in the marriage market. Besides, this study may also be seen as a test of Becker's family economics theory, namely 'family matching is the result of comparing the economic benefits inside and outside marriage'.

This study also provides a meaningful reference for policy-making in China. Firstly, under the policy of 'allowing a second child for couples with both sides being onlies', the dependency rate of one-child families will be much higher than that of non-only families. For families with two children, the high dependency rate comes from not only the pressure to raise the second child, but also from the pressure for one couple to support four elderly dependents. As a result, allowing a second child for couples who already have the highest dependency rate will increase their dependency rate further. The extra birth quota they get may be at the cost of 'squeezing out' the resources of other family members, which is likely to harm the wellbeing of the elderly people in the only-child families. Implementing the policy of 'allowing a second child for couples with either side being an only child' and the universal second-child policy will lead to fewer family structures like families with both husband and wife being onlies, because they have a high dependency rate in the marriage market. This will be of great significance for reducing the burden of old-age care on families. Secondly, relaxing birth control will help to increase the fertility rate in China. In recent years, China's fertility rate has been constantly declining, while population ageing is deepening. Some people argue that even birth control is relaxed, it will still not lead to an increase in the number of births because young people face high pressure to care for the elderly and cope with the demand of the workplace. Our research and identification results suggest that relaxing birth control will have a significant effect on raising the fertility rate and may even affect family formation, thus further expanding the overall impact of fertility policy reform on births. Though we use the policy of 'allowing a second child for couples with both sides being onlies' as the means of identification, the conclusion is of the same significance for understanding the effects of the policy of 'allowing a second child for couples with either side being an only-child' and the policy of 'universal second child'.

Appendices to this Chapter

Table 7.7 Regional Differences in Family Planning Policies

Province	*Inclusion of the Policy of 'Allowing a Second Baby for Couples Who Both Come from One-Child Families' in Provincial Family Planning Regulations*	*Fertility Quota Set Forth in Provincial Family Planning Policy*		*Range of Change in Fine Rate since 1980 (Multiplier of Average Annual Family Income)*
		Cities	Countryside	
Jilin	July 1988	One child	One child	
Anhui	December 1988	One child	One and half children	5
Fujian	July 1988	One child	One and half children	2–3
Hunan	January 1990	One child	One and half children	2–6
Sichuan	July 1987	One child	One child	6–8
Chongqing	July 1987	One child	One child	2–6
Guizhou	January 1988	One child	One and half children	2–3
Yunnan	April 1991	One child	Two children	5–10 (urban); 5–8 (rural)
Qinghai	April 1992	One child	Two children	3–4
Ningxia	January 1991	One child	Two children	2–6
Jiangxi	September 1995	One child	One and half children	3.5
Hubei	January 2003	One child	One and half children	2–6
Hainan	November 1995	One child	One and half children	3–4
Xinjiang	January 2003	One child	Two children	3
Guangdong	January 2009	One child	One and half children	3–6

Table 7.8 Sampled Provinces

Status of Implementation of the Policy of 'Allowing a Second Child for Couples with Both Sides Being Onlies' in the 1994–2005 Period	*Province*
Implemented before 1994	Beijing, Tianjin, Hebei, Shanxi, **Jilin**, Liaoning, Heilongjiang, **Anhui**, **Fujian**, Shandong, **Hunan, Sichuan, Chongqing, Guizhou, Yunnan**, Shaanxi, **Qinghai,** and **Ningxia**;
Implemented between 1994 and 2005	Inner Mongolia, Shanghai, Jiangsu, Zhejiang, **Jiangxi, Hubei**, Guangxi, **Hainan**, Gansu and **Xinjiang**;
Implemented at the end of 2005	Henan and **Guangdong**

Notes

1 The reason for especially mentioning the lowering of threshold for non-only spouses here is that we are only concerned with the side with a high threshold (only when matching quality is higher than the thresholds of both sides can the match be successful). As discussed above, onlies hold higher requirements for non-onlies. Therefore, if one-child status is the only difference between individuals, the success of matching will be determined by the threshold of the one-child side. Only when both sides are non-onlies will the non-only threshold play its role.

2 In the model, we also assume the same proportion of onlies among males and females. If this assumption is not made, changes in marriage match will only be observed among the gender group with a lower proportion of onlies (Chiappori, Oreffice and Quintana-Domeque, 2010).

3 Wei and Zhang (2011a) used different data to summarize the locality (i.e. within-province matching) of China's marriage market.

4 In particular, Beijing, Tianjin and Jiangsu, which were the first municipalities and province to implement the policy of 'allowing a second baby for couples with both sides being onlies', also have a significantly higher proportion of onlies than the other provinces. For this reason, we do not include Beijing, Tianjin and Jiangsu in our samples.

8 Family Planning and Entrepreneurship

8.1 Introduction

This chapter aims to study the differences between onlies and non-onlies in entrepreneurial behaviour, social communication and subjective attitude. These research topics are roughly related to entrepreneurship and its influencing factors. As an important human capital, entrepreneurship influences the development potential of a country. One perspective to directly test this linkage is to study at the individual level whether onlies show different entrepreneurship after they reach adulthood. We will also test the factors that may theoretically affect such differences and provide a wider basis for improving the family planning policy.

Compared with existing research, this chapter is expected to make the following four main contributions. First, it directly links onlies with entrepreneurship, which is different from existing micro research on personality differences between onlies and non-onlies, and studies that indirectly examine the influence of gender on entrepreneurship. Second, this chapter uses micro data to test the differences between onlies and non-onlies in entrepreneurial behaviour, and attempts to explain the underlying reasons. The micro data set used in this chapter can help to unravel the differences between onlies and non-onlies in their actual job choices after adulthood. This is different from past micro analyses using the data of minors and college students or experimental data, as well as from the studies of entrepreneurship from a demographic structural perspective with the use of macro data. In other words, our data are more targeted and realistic compared with the micro data used in the existing research, while being capable of avoiding the measurement errors of variables and other problems associated with macro data. Third, this chapter utilizes a series of instrumental variable sets provided by Ebenstein (2010) to effectively address the problem of possible endogeneity of the only-child status and better identify its influence on entrepreneurship. Fourth, we analyse and discuss the micro mechanisms behind the formation of entrepreneurship among onlies, which is also a contribution in its own right.

DOI: 10.4324/9781003288091-10

8.2 Literature Review

Certain quantitative studies have been conducted on the two topics of onlies and entrepreneurship, which are summarized below.

8.2.1 Research on the Individual Characteristics of Onlies and Their Economic Effects

As a special demographic phenomenon, onlies have long attracted attention from the psychological and sociological circles abroad. Bohannon (1896) was the first to study the characteristics of onlies. Early studies by Fenton (1928) and Hooker (1931) pointed out some bad personal characteristics of onlies, such as excessive self-indulgence and insufficient affinity to society. However, mixed and even pro-onlies conclusions have been subsequently emerged. For example, Dyer (1945) sampled female students from college freshmen, compared 100 onlies and 100 non-onlies and found no significant difference between them in all aspects. Polit and Falbo (1987) discovered that onlies are no different from non-onlies except that they have greater motivations for pursuing success. Falbo and Polit (1986) summarized more than 100 studies on onlies, which focus on their school work, personality, intelligence, parent-child relationship and social abilities, with family size of non-onlies taken into account for comparison. Onlies were found to outperform non-onlies in almost all aspects, except being close, in terms of school work and intelligence, to the first children of those families with two children.

Following the implementation of the family planning policy in the late 1970s, a large number of onlies have been born in China, leading to the formation of a unique demographic characteristic in society and growing research on the personality of onlies. Feng Xiaotian (2002) reviewed 305 research articles on onlies in Chinese academic journals from 1980 to 2001. These papers were published in various domestic journals, involving psychology, education, sociology, demography, sports science and other different disciplines, but economic research on onlies was lacking. With the passage of time and the growth up of the onlies generation, research on onlies has gradually expanded. Summarizing the conclusions of the papers above, Feng Xiaotian (2002) found that most research in the early 1980s agreed on one thing: onlies have serious personality problems. In the early 1980s, scholars in various fields believed that onlies suffered some common personality weaknesses such as poor independence, excessive self-centrism and psychological vulnerability. In 1986, *Guangming Daily* initiated a nationwide discussion about the issue of education of onlies, and reached the general conclusion that onlies have much more shortcomings. However, a subsequent large sample survey revealed a different picture and drew mixed conclusions. There have even been studies pointing out that onlies have their own strengths (Gao Wenli, 1992). Based on an analysis of the data obtained from five large-scale surveys, Feng Xiaotian (2000) showed that on the whole urban young onlies have normal social development patterns and share more things in common with non-onlies of the same age in all aspects of socialization. Onlies and non-onlies were found to have their respective advantages, with onlies being a bit poorer at living skills but stronger in social communication. The differences between the two in many aspects gradually disappear with the passage of time.

Negative views on onlies are more often merely a kind of social prejudice. Based on a large amount of data collected from the media, Feng Xiaotian (2010) provided a systematic interpretation of the image of onlies in mass media reports. According to the account of Feng Xiaotian (2010), even in the West, onlies and their parents are often considered as a negative label. Ordinary people and public opinion often assume that onlies have some kind of adverse consequences. This is the direct reason why many parents choose to have a second child simply to avoid making their children from becoming onlies (Falbo, 1984). In China, this phenomenon also exists, as any search of news websites would show. Negative coverage of onlies is prevalent, but this does not conform to the actual situation of onlies.

There are two key deficiencies in the current studies on the personality of onlies. The first deficiency is that the research subjects are mainly preschool- and school-age onlies, including infants aged 3–6, children aged 7–12, middle school students aged 12–10 and college students who are much older. There is seldom analysis on the differences between onlies and non-onlies of the working age. This is a deficiency arising from the practical situation, because most onlies were still relatively young when these studies were conducted and it was relatively easier to sample students. The second deficiency is that existing research lacks in-depth analysis of causal relationships. Most studies adopt some metrics to make comparative analysis of onlies and non-onlies, while regression analysis is rare. These methods fail to effectively address possible endogenetic problems associated with onlies. In a recent study, Cameron et al. (2013) came up with a better approach to solve the issue. They employed street surveys to collect samples before and after the implementation of family planning, conducted different experiments (including dictator experiment, trust experiment, risk experiment and competition experiment) to identify different personality characteristics and looked for causal relationships by taking whether family planning was implemented as an instrumental variable for onlies. Their research found that onlies trust others less and are also less trusted by others, and are more risk-averse, less competitive, pessimistic and self-centred. The problem of this study is that it gave no consideration to the actual economic behaviours of onlies and the characteristics of onlies in a more realistic environment, thus resulting in the possibility of deviating from reality. Moreover, the study mainly analysed the personalities of onlies rather than their economic characteristics.

In addition, a few economists have examined the possible macroeconomic effects of the one-child policy. Choukhmane et al. (2013) studied the effect of the family planning policy on household savings rate and found that demographic structural changes induced by the family planning policy could explain 60% of household savings growth. Ebenstein (2010) found that the family planning policy has led to 'missing girls', resulting in an unbalanced sex ratio. Wei and Zhang (2011a) further pointed out that a high sex ratio leads to higher savings rate. In their study, Edlund et al. (2013) believed that China's high sex ratio has caused a high crime rate.

8.2.2 Research on Entrepreneurship

Schumpeter (1934) was the first to recognize the importance of entrepreneurship in economic growth. To him, entrepreneurship refers to some personal traits that promote entrepreneurs to start a business. Since then, numerous research articles have been published examining the effects of entrepreneurship on enterprises and macroeconomy. Entrepreneurship is seen as a source of knowledge spillover, technological progress and innovation, all of which are the most important factors which promote long-term economic growth and ultimately spur macroeconomic growth (Audretsch and Keilbach, 2004). Entrepreneurship can also promote knowledge progress and growth by encouraging competition and differentiation (Jacobs, 1969). In the China case, Li et al. (2012) used regional data to show that entrepreneurship boosts macroeconomic growth. As for the factors influencing entrepreneurship, Wei and Zhang (2011b) used data from the China region for analysis and found that imbalanced sex ratio stimulates competition and entrepreneurship. Li and Wu (2014) examined the effect of rising housing price on individuals' entrepreneurial behaviours, and concluded that entrepreneurship is negatively affected by rising housing price.

By Schumpeter's definition, entrepreneurship mostly refers to some personal characteristics, such as innovation, adventurousness, cooperation, honesty, pursuit of achievement and entrepreneurial vision. These characteristics have been subsequently studied and redefined (Djankov et al., 2006; Lee et al., 2004). Li et al. (2012) used the proportion of self-employed persons in the labour force and the proportion of employments offered by private enterprises as macro measures of entrepreneurship. Though the concept of entrepreneurship is generally accepted, the specific measures and analyses of entrepreneurship are variable with data and environment.

8.2.3 Research on the Linkage between Onlies and Entrepreneurship

Among the existing research, only a few studies have linked onlies with entrepreneurship for analysis. These analyses are closely related to the current study.

Based on a job intent questionnaire survey of 1,210 college students, Zhou Delu (2009) found that onlies are more confident in job seeking: college students who are onlies are 68% more in numbers than those who are non-onlies in thinking that personal abilities are more important for getting jobs. Meanwhile, onlies are relatively more rational about expected incomes than non-onlies, with 10.5% fewer of them expecting higher incomes than non-onlies. Besides, onlies are more motivated for entrepreneurship. This is more apparent among rural onlies. Finally, college students who are onlies are more willing to accept employment in less developed areas. The results of the survey show the advantages which onlies have in seeking employment, but the study did not do enough to identify the causal relationships behind.

In their research, Wei and Zhang (2011b) found that a higher sex ratio leads to more proactive entrepreneurial behaviours, which indirectly points out the effect of the family planning policy on entrepreneurship. There are other studies showing that the one-child policy has made parents in a society where boys are preferred to girls more inclined to have boys, thus resulting in an imbalanced sex ratio (Ebenstein, 2010), which in turn may stimulate competition and entrepreneurship. They use the number of private enterprises per 10,000 people at the county level as the variable representing entrepreneurship. However, such macro metrics may face potential problems such as measurement errors.[1]

One study which is related to this study and well solves the identification problem is carried out by Cameron et al. (2013). They used micro experimental data to comprehensively compare the personalities of onlies and non-onlies, and adopted the instrumental variable method to solve the problem of possible endogeneity of onlies. They found that the one-child policy has produced a generation who are more risk averse, more pessimistic, less trustworthy, less competitive and less conscientious, calling onlies 'little emperors'. If these conclusions are established, the family planning policy will greatly harm entrepreneurship and be detrimental to China's long-term economic growth. However, because the research was conducted under the research framework of street interviews in combination with experiments, the characteristics of onlies with regard to employment and entrepreneurship still need to be analysed through the use of survey data.

To sum up, there are many studies on the characteristics of onlies, and their conclusions vary from one another. Generally speaking, with the passage of time, onlies' early disadvantages in personality are gradually transformed into advantages, which is termed as 'wear-down and convergence' by Feng Xiaotian (2000). The topic of entrepreneurship is attracting more and more attention in China, but studies are still rare which analyse entrepreneurship by linking it with the one-child policy, and use micro survey data to effectively solve the problem of identification.

We surmise that onlies are less entrepreneurial mainly due to three main possible reasons: (1) excessive doting by parents makes onlies lack self-initiative and over self-centred, while absence of siblings may make them less keen to communicate with others and go for the team spirit. These factors influence the personality of onlies since childhood and will ultimately leave an imprint on their employment choice, social communication ability and subjective attitude after adulthood; (2) compared with individuals with siblings, onlies naturally lack 'social assurance', namely the support of siblings and relevant social networks, making it impossible for them to start a business; and (3) onlies shoulder greater family responsibilities and have to support their elderly family members and raise children all on their own, making them dare not venture to start a business. The first surmise is about the personality characteristics of onlies. Existing research has reached different conclusions on the personality issue. Moreover, studies on the topic basically take children and college students as the object for observation, but there is a lack of analysis of their differences in the actual workplace. There are few studies on the second and third surmises, because micro research on the entrepreneurial behaviour of onlies is quite rare. As for the personality issue, there may be a phenomenon that social learning leads to the disappearance of onlies' personality defects. For example, Feng Xiaotian (2000) pointed out that as onlies' personality characteristics gradually change from childhood to adulthood, their personality differences from non-onlies gradually disappear. However, lack of risk-taking actions arising from absent social network support and social assurance always constitutes a constraint on onlies in making rational choices, which may lead to a persistent reduction of risk-taking actions and the loss of entrepreneurship among onlies. As the proportion of onlies continues to rise today, lack of entrepreneurship as a trait of onlies may result in less entrepreneurial activity in China.

8.3 Data and Method

8.3.1 Data Source

The data used in this study come from the Chinese General Social Survey ("CGSS") conducted jointly by the National Survey Research Center of Renmin University of China and the Survey Research Center of Hong Kong University of Science and Technology. As of 2015, CGSS had published the data of seven surveys (which were respectively conducted in 2003, 2005, 2006, 2008, 2010, 2011 and 2012). CGSS surveys non-tracking mixed cross-sectional data and covers all the provinces and municipalities in China except Hong Kong, Macao and Taiwan. It has the characteristics of stratified random sampling, large sample size and comprehensive content.

The current study uses data from the two random sampling surveys of CGSS in 2006 and 2008, because the questionnaires in the other years cannot effectively identify onlies. The data are confined to the labour force population aged from 18 to 60. The sample size was 9,061 for 2006 and 5,224 for 2008. Onlies make up more than 10% of the total sample size (Figure 2.1), which means that there are roughly more than 130 million onlies in China.

8.3.2 Selection and Description of Variables

The main independent variable we analyse is the dummy variable for only-child status, while many alternative surrogate metrics exist for the dependent variable entrepreneurship. In some macro analyses, the number of private enterprises is used to represent entrepreneurship, as in the case of Wei and Zhang (2011b). A similar method is also adopted by Li et al. (2012). With micro data, we can use more personal characteristics and economic behaviours to reflect entrepreneurship. Intuitively, whether people start a business is a direct measure of their entrepreneurship. It is the most important explanatory variable in this study. In addition, according to Schumpeter and some subsequent scholars, entrepreneurship mainly refers to the following personal characteristics: innovation, adventurousness, cooperation, dedication, learning, persistence, integrity and service attitude. The CGSS questionnaire includes subjective questions about attitude towards risks. Moreover, answers to such subjective questions as 'friendly relationship with people around', 'importance of hard work' and 'degree of plan execution' can all to some extent reflect the personality characteristics of the respondents. Finally, the number of friends visited during holidays can reflect the social networking situation of the respondents. Analyzing such subjective characteristics and social networking is helpful in examining the causes of onlies' different entrepreneurial outcomes.

Table 8.1 shows the descriptive characteristics of the explained variables of concern to us in the current study based on the only-child status.

In our data, "post-1980" onlies, referring to onlies who were born after 1980s, make up 36%, while "pre-1980" onlies, namely onlies who were born before 1980, account for less than 6% (Figure 2.1). This is largely the result of the implementation of the one-child policy in the late 1970s and the early 1980s. However, because 'post-1980' individuals only account for less than 14% of the total sample size, we put all the samples together in our subsequent regression analysis, rather than only use the samples after the implementation of family planning. From Table 8.1, it can be seen that for all age groups and both genders, a significantly smaller proportion of onlies start their own business than that of non-onlies, while male onlies have a slightly higher propensity for entrepreneurship than their female counterparts.

As far as the subjective metrics are concerned, onlies generally consider themselves as being willing to take risks. Compared with non-onlies, fewer onlies regard them as happy and think hard work is important. There is no not much difference between the two in terms of relationship with people around and plan execution. As for the objective metrics, onlies visit fewer friends than non-onlies.

On the time dimension, there is not much difference in overall entrepreneurial behaviour between pre-1980 and post-1980 individuals. However, a slightly higher proportion of non-onlies choose to start their

Table 8.1 Descriptive Statistics of Explained Variables

	All			*Post-1980*			*Pre-1980*		
	All	*Onlies*	*Non-onlies*	*All*	*Onlies*	*Non-onlies*	*All*	*Onlies*	*Non-onlies*
Entrepreneurship	0.17	0.12	0.18	0.20	0.12	0.25	0.17	0.13	0.17
	(0.38)	(0.33)	(0.38)	(0.40)	(0.32)	(0.43)	(0.37)	(0.34)	(0.38)
Males	0.20	0.14	0.21	0.21	0.13	0.26	0.20	0.15	0.21
	(0.40)	(0.35)	(0.41)	(0.41)	(0.34)	(0.44)	(0.40)	(0.35)	(0.40)
Females	0.15	0.11	0.15	0.19	0.11	0.23	0.14	0.11	0.14
	(0.36)	(0.31)	(0.36)	(0.40)	(0.31)	(0.42)	(0.35)	(0.31)	(0.35)
Number of friends visited	24.25	22.47	24.46	27.42	24.06	29.03	23.57	20.50	23.76
	(23.96)	(23.18)	(24.05)	(26.78)	(24.99)	(27.47)	(23.26)	(20.60)	(23.40)
Willingness to take risks	3.59	3.24	3.63	3.23	2.99	3.35	3.67	3.55	3.68
	(1.64)	(1.57)	(1.65)	(1.53)	(1.46)	(1.55)	(1.66)	(1.64)	(1.66)
Fondness of venture investment	3.63	3.31	3.67	3.32	3.18	3.39	3.70	3.48	3.71
	(1.66)	(1.52)	(1.67)	(1.53)	(1.46)	(1.57)	(1.68)	(1.59)	(1.68)
Happiness	3.53	3.72	3.51	3.72	3.82	3.67	3.50	3.62	3.49
	(0.85)	(0.82)	(0.85)	(0.81)	(0.78)	(0.83)	(0.85)	(0.85)	(0.85)
Importance of hard work	1.81	1.86	1.80	1.74	1.81	1.70	1.82	1.93	1.82
	(0.77)	(0.80)	(0.76)	(0.74)	(0.80)	(0.71)	(0.77)	(0.81)	(0.77)
Good relationship with people around	1.84	1.82	1.84	1.82	1.81	1.82	1.84	1.84	1.84
	(0.59)	(0.61)	(0.59)	(0.59)	(0.59)	(0.59)	(0.59)	(0.64)	(0.59)
Strong plan execution	1.98	1.95	1.99	1.95	1.92	1.97	1.99	1.98	1.99
	(0.54)	(0.54)	(0.54)	(0.54)	(0.53)	(0.55)	(0.54)	(0.55)	(0.54)

Note: Figures in brackets are standard errors. From "Willingness to take risks" to "Plan execution", the larger the value is, the higher the degree of 'disagreement' with the statement. 'Post-1980' refers to individuals born in 1980 and after it. This statistical distinction is made because strict family planning was implemented starting from 1980.

own business than onlies. Moreover, post-1980 individuals show some advantages in respect of the number of friends they have, willingness to take risks, considering hard work as important and plan execution, though they have a lower sense of happiness.

Table 8.2 shows some differences between onlies and non-onlies, and such differences vary with different subjective and objective metrics, which may be a result of the one-child attribute or their different personal characteristics. We have summarized some of the personal and family characteristics available in the database in Table 8.2.

Table 8.2 shows a high proportion of males among the onlies, which is in line with the conclusion reached in some studies that family planning leads to an imbalanced sex ratio. Onlies are relatively young, which is a result of the intensified implementation of family planning over time. They have relatively longer years of education and better state of health, and are more likely to be Han Chinese and unmarried, hold an urban Hukou and have urban parents who work in the establishment and a high-income father. It can be seen that there are systematic differences between onlies and non-onlies. This may be the reason why onlies differ from non-onlies in respect of subjective and objective metrics that are a concern to us, such as type of employment and entrepreneurship. To identify the effect of the only-child attribute on entrepreneurship, we, therefore, need to control these variables. Moreover, even if these variables are controlled, there may still be errors caused by missing variables, especially those variables unobservable at the family level.

8.3.3 Method Description

This study mainly adopts the OLS method, which is expressed as:

$$Y_i = \alpha_1 + \alpha_1 only_i + \alpha_2 X_i + F_I + Prov_i + \varepsilon_i \tag{8.1}$$

Wherein: *only* represents the one-child variable of concern to us; X the set of an individual's demographic characteristics; F the family economic and demographic variable, and Prov is the dummy variable for the province where the concerned individual is located. When the explained variable is a 0–1 variable (such as entrepreneurship), the Probit model is adopted.

As mentioned above, analyzing the effect of the only-child attribute—which is the variable of interest, on entrepreneurship may face the problem of missing variables. Especially when some family characteristic variables are omitted, and these family characteristics may affect the formation of onlies or the current employment status of their children. In such situations, the OLS estimation coefficient of the only-child variable will face the problem of errors. Ebenstein's (2010) research provides a set of possible instrumental variables, namely the birth quota, amount of fines and amount of

Tables 8.2 Differences in Characteristics between Onlies and Non-onlies

		All			*Post-1980*			*Pre-1980*	
	All	*Onlies*	*Non-onlies*	*All*	*Onlies*	*Non-onlies*	*All*	*Onlies*	*Non-onlies*
Male	0.47	0.55	0.46	0.47	0.51	0.45	0.47	0.60	0.46
Age	42.7	33.8	43.7	22.7	22.2	23.0	46.4	46.3	46.4
Number of years of education	8.33	11.36	7.98	11.37	13.13	10.46	7.76	9.46	7.65
Han Chinese	0.93	0.97	0.93	0.92	0.97	0.90	0.93	0.96	0.93
Party member	0.10	0.08	0.10	0.04	0.04	0.03	0.11	0.13	0.11
State of health	3.20	3.44	3.18	3.60	3.64	3.57	3.13	3.22	3.13
Urban Hukou	0.53	0.79	0.50	0.57	0.87	0.41	0.53	0.71	0.52
Unmarried	0.12	0.46	0.09	0.64	0.80	0.56	0.03	0.08	0.02
Father_Party member	0.14	0.15	0.14	0.12	0.13	0.12	0.14	0.16	0.14
Father_Hukou	0.40	0.72	0.37	0.50	0.84	0.32	0.39	0.59	0.37
Father's income	8,351	16,692	6,964	14,104	19,858	10,847	6,411	11,079	6,066
Father's type of employment	0.27	0.43	0.25	0.26	0.49	0.15	0.27	0.38	0.26
Mother_Partymember	0.03	0.04	0.03	0.03	0.04	0.03	0.03	0.04	0.03
Mother_Hukou	0.37	0.70	0.33	0.48	0.83	0.30	0.35	0.56	0.33
Mother's type of employment	0.13	0.33	0.10	0.18	0.41	0.06	0.12	0.24	0.11

Note: Parents' type of employment refers to whether they work in the establishment i.e. whether they work in state-owned enterprises, government organs or public institutions. Father (mother)_Hukou refers to whether the father (mother) holds an urban Hukou. State of health is a self-evaluation metric whose value ranges from 1 to 5. The higher the value, the better the state of health.

subsidies and rewards in various provinces in China. These instrumental variables were first collected by Scharping (2003). In this study, we mainly use the set of instrumental variables proposed by Ebenstein (2010). These macro policies may be considered as strictly exogenous in the analysis of micro data, and the two-stage least square method (or IV + Probit) can be applied in such situations. In addition to directly using various policies as instrumental variables, we also construct a complex instrumental variable Z_1 as follows:

$$Z_1 = 0 * I[2] + fine * male * I[1.5] + fine * I[1] \quad (8.2)$$

Wherein: I [2], I [1.5] and I [1] respectively represent the situations where the policy allows couples to have two or more children, 1.5 children (which means that couples can have a second child if their first child is a girl) and one child one year after the birth of the first child; *fine* represents the ratio between the over-birth fines one year after the birth of an individual and the average income level of the local region. The policy and the fine rate of one year after are used because the family planning policy affects whether the next child is born; and *male* represents whether the child is male. Because only 'over births' are fined, the exact influencing process of whether the first child is an only child can be expressed by Equation (8.2). This instrumental variable is mainly used to compare the onlies and the first children of non-onlies.

In addition to the instrumental variable described in Equation (8.2), we also take the subsidy policy for onlies as an additional instrumental variable. Because these instrumental variables fall within the category of macroeconomic policies, they have nothing to do with the family- or individual-level variables that may be missed, but are rather related to whether they become onlies.

8.4 Estimated Results of Onlies' Entrepreneurial Behaviour

8.4.1 Overall Comparative Analysis of Onlies and Non-onlies

To analyse whether onlies choose to start their own business, we focus on the non-student samples and the sample of labourers aged over 18 but under 60. On-campus students are removed from the samples. First, Probot estimates are made for all the samples of the working age, and the results are shown in Column (1) of Table 8.3. Then, the samples listed in Column (2) of Table 8.3 are confined to the Han Chinese population, while Column (3) further limits the samples to the registered urban population. The samples are so divided because the Han Chinese population and urban residents are more likely to be strictly affected by the family planning policy.

It can be seen from Table 8.3 that after controlling the individual and family characteristics and the fixed effect of province, the effect of the one-child attribute on entrepreneurship is significantly negative. In the

Table 8.3 Simple Probit Estimates of Whether Onlies Are Inclined to Start Their Own Business—Dependent Variable: Whether to Start a Business

	(1)	*(2)*	*(3)*
Bring an only	−0.2517***	−0.2534***	−0.1746***
	0.0503	0.0515	0.0640
Male	0.3283***	0.3195***	0.2698***
	0.0264	0.0274	0.0393
Age	−0.0264***	−0.0276***	−0.0301***
	0.0015	0.0016	0.0024
Number of years of education	0.0106***	0.0080*	−0.0354***
	0.0041	0.0043	0.0067
Han Chinese	0.0816		
	0.0554		
Party member	−0.4759***	−0.4547***	−0.5391***
	0.0560	0.0577	0.0789
State of health	−0.0821***	−0.0834***	−0.0924***
	0.0152	0.0157	0.0225
Unmarried	−0.3344***	−0.3558***	−0.3813***
	0.0463	0.0483	0.0700
Father's Hukou type	−0.0231	−0.0255	−0.0887
	0.0618	0.0636	0.0880
Father works in the establishment	−0.1215***	−0.1113***	−0.1170**
	0.0417	0.0431	0.0501
Mother's Hukou type	0.0071	−0.0062	0.1035
	0.0607	0.0624	0.0823
Mother works in the establishment	−0.1252***	−0.1393***	−0.1088**
	0.0504	0.0520	0.0551
Fixed effect of province and year of sampling survey	Controlled	Controlled	Controlled
Sample size	13,753	12,785	6,691
Pseudo R2	0.0778	0.0807	0.1034

Note: Columns (1), (2) and (3) are general Probit estimates, which respectively correspond to the sample population excluding students and people over 60, the sample population excluding students, people over 60 and ethnic groups and the sample population excluding students, people over 60 and ethnic groups and rural residents. Figures under the coefficients are robust standard errors. ***, ** and * represent the 1%, 5% and 10% significance levels respectively. The definitions apply to the tables below.

regression results reported in Columns (1), (2) and (3), the marginal effects dF/dX of the one-child attribute on entrepreneurship are −5.9%, −5.9% and −3.7% respectively. It means that onlies lack entrepreneurship. Among the other influencing factors, individuals who are male, young, highly educated, married and healthy are more likely to start their own business, while Party members and individuals whose parents work in the establishment are much less likely to do so.

As mentioned above, OLS regression may face the problem that onlies themselves are endogenous. Some family characteristic variables may also be omitted in the regression equation, and these variables affect not only the

Table 8.4 Analysis of Whether Onlies Are Inclined to Start a Business (Instrumental Variable Method)

	(1)	*(2)*	*(3)*
Onlies	−0.9498***	−0.9705***	−0.8618***
	0.2451	0.2480	0.2582
Fixed effect of province and year of sampling survey, and other control variables	Controlled	Controlled	Controlled
Stage I Results			
Allowing only one child	0.3421***	0.3624***	0.5232***
	0.0397	0.0422	0.0688
Allowing 1.5 children	0.1564***	0.1761***	0.3501***
	0.0392	0.0418	0.0688
Allowing two children	−0.0045	0.0296	0.1313
	0.0464	0.0508	0.0840
Extra fines	−0.0760***	−0.0818***	−0.1199***
	0.0123	0.0129	0.0204
Fine/income ratio	−0.0316*	−0.0290	−0.0467
	0.0185	0.0200	0.0312
Rewards for onlies	2.72E−06	−1.69E−05	−1.00E−04
	4.15E−05	4.41E−05	7.22E−05
Other control variables	Controlled	Controlled	Controlled
Sample size	13,753	12,785	6,691
Wald statistic	1,019.91	988.71	602.60

Note: There is no birth restriction on the reference group.

formation of onlies, but also the employment decision-making of individuals when they reach adulthood. The estimates in Table 8.3 may contain errors. We respectively select instrumental variables to re-estimate the three regression results in Table 8.3, and the new results are given in Table 8.4. Among them, Table 8.4 mainly selects and use instrumental variables from the set provided by Ebenstein (2010), which include: (1) the number of births allowed by the policy, i.e. one, 1.5 or two children, or no birth restriction (mainly before family planning was implemented); (2) whether there are incremental fines on over births; (3) the ratio between the amount of fines and the average pay level of the concerned province; and (4) whether there are rewards for onlies. These variables directly enter the estimation process in their original form, and are not reconstructed as in the case of Equation (8.2). Because these variables are changing with time and province, we can continue to use them by controlling the dummy variable for province in the main regression equation.

Columns (1), (2) and (3) of Table 8.4 correspond to the three regression results of Table 8.4, and report on the Stage I regression results. It can be seen that onlies are still less inclined to start a business, and the only-child status has a higher negative effect than in Table 8.3. The lower probability estimated by the instrumental variables indicates the existence of endogeneity caused by missing variables. For example, the more a family understands the law, the more likely it is to start its own business and comply with the law to have only one child. In such a situation, omitting the variable of family's legal knowledge may lead to higher estimates with the OLS method. Any similar omission of unobservable factors such as family ability is likely to cause a problem of endogeneity. There is not much change in the results of the other variables. In the Stage I results, the policy of limiting the number of births and the incremental fines on over births significantly explain whether children are onlies.

8.4.2 Segmentation of Non-onlies

To apply our instrumental variables more rationally and observe differences within non-onlies, we divide non-onlies into two types: first children and others. As mentioned in the literature review, many studies have suggested that there are differences between the first children and the non-first children among non-onlies. We can use CGSS data to observe the differences among onlies, the first children of non-lines and the non-first children among non-onlies. Table 8.5 shows their sample size distributions in the database used in this study. On the whole, the other children of non-onlies make up the majority of the sample population.

Table 8.6 gives the estimated coefficients of entrepreneurial behaviour differences between onlies and non-onlies (Column (1)), and between onlies and the first children among non-onlies and the other children among non-onlies (Column (2)). Compared with the other children among non-onlies, onlies and the first children among non-onlies show the characteristics of being less inclined to start a business. Among them, onlies get a lower coefficient, meaning that they are even more reluctant to start their own business. In addition, the first children among non-onlies are also more reluctant to start a business than the other children among the non-onlies. Therefore, it can be inferred that if below we only compare the first children

Table 8.5 Distribution of Onlies, the First Children among Non-onlies and the Other Children of Non-onlies

	2006	*2008*
Onlies	1,069 10.53%	621 10.35%
First children among non-onlies	2,428 23.92%	2,510 41.83%
Other children of onlies	6,654 65.55%	2,869 47.82%
Total	10,151	6,000

Table 8.6 Analysis of Whether Onlies Are Inclined to Start a Business (The Entire Sample Population)

	(1) Probit	*(2) Probit*
Onlies	−0.2534***	−0.3171***
	0.058	0.0542
First children among non-onlies	–	−0.1674***
	–	0.0302
Other control items	Controlled	Controlled
Sample size	12,785	12,785
Pseudo R2	0.081	0.083

Note: The objects for analysis in the above table are all non-student adult Han Chinese residents under 60. 'Other control items" refers to the same control variables as 'Other variables' in Table 8.3. Due to limited space, their coefficients are not reported here. Overall, the results are not much different from those in Table 8.3. 'Other control items" has the same meaning in the tables below.

Table 8.7 Analysis of Whether Onlies and the First Children among Non-onlies Are Inclined to Start a Business (Instrumental Variable Method)

	(1) IV	*(2) IV*	*(3) IV*
Onlies	−1.8443***	−1.8316***	−1.3918**
	(0.3646)	(0.3669)	(0.5493)
Other control items	Controlled	Controlled	Controlled
	Stage I Results		
Population control policy	0.0431**	0.0338*	0.0125
	(0.0178)	(0.0184)	(0.0277)
Reward for onlies	0.0001***	0.0001***	0.0002***
	(0.0000)	(0.0000)	(0.0000)
Other control items	Controlled	Controlled	Controlled
Sample size	5,427	5,090	2,939
Wald statistic	743.15	711.14	350.29

Note: Columns (1), (2) and (3) respectively correspond to the sample population excluding students and people over 60, the sample population excluding students, people over 60 and ethnic groups, and the sample population excluding students, people over 60, and ethnic groups and rural residents. Figures under the coefficients are robust standard errors.

among non-onlies and non-onlies, the overall hindrance effect of the only-child status on entrepreneurship will be even underestimated.[2] In Table 8.6, we only use the Han Chinese population data, but adding the ethnic group samples will not change the conclusion.

In Table 8.7, the instrumental variable method listed in Equation (8.2) is used to estimate and compare the entrepreneurial behaviours of onlies and the first children among non-onlies. For all the samples, it is found that onlies are significantly less likely than non-onlies to start a business.

The above results confirm a significantly low probability of entrepreneurship among onlies. As mentioned above, there are three possible reasons for the lower probability of entrepreneurship among onlies compared with non-onlies: (1) differences in some personality characteristics and entrepreneurship formed by living habits; (2) inability to start a business due to lack of social networks; and (3) lack of courage to start a business due to huge family responsibilities. The first two possible reasons are examined below, and the third reason is not tested due to lack of data.

8.5 Test of Possible Paths of Influence

8.5.1 Possible Path of Influence 1: Difference in Subjective Attitude

In this section, we make an attempt to analyse whether there is any difference in personality between onlies and non-onlies. To use the instrumental variables in Equation (8.2), we only compare onlies and the first children among non-onlies.

Adopting the same method as in the previous section, Row 1 of Table 8.8 shows the estimated differences between onlies and the first children among non-onlies in two risk metrics, namely 'Yearning for a life full of risks' and 'Yearning for venture investment'. A higher value means a higher degree of disagreement with the statement. Because the explained variables are

Table 8.8 Comparison between Onlies and the First Children among Non-onlies in Terms of Subjective Attitude towards Risks

		(1)	*(2)*	*(3)*
Dislike risk-taking life	**Oprobit**			
	Onlies	−0.0730	−0.0988	0.0015
		(0.0819)	(0.0843)	(0.1024)
	Sample size	1,291	1,207	725
	Pseudo R2	0.043	0.037	0.040
	IV			
	Onlies	0.3908	0.5588	0.6164
		(0.7145)	(0.7095)	(0.6070)
	Sample size	1,291	1,207	725
	Pseudo R2	0.0434	0.0368	0.0401
Dislike venture investment	**Oprobit**			
	Onlies	0.0072	−0.0102	0.0586
		(0.0803)	(0.0824)	(0.1004)
	Sample size	1,291	1,207	725
	Pseudo R2	0.040	0.035	0.033
	IV			
	Onlies	0.4737	0.5365	0.6199
		(0.7679)	(0.7658)	(0.6489)
	Sample size	1,291	1,207	725
	Pseudo R2	0.0402	0.0347	0.0337

Note: A higher value means a higher degree of negation.

Table 8.9 Comparison between Onlies and Non-onlies in Terms of Other Subjective Characteristics

		(1) Oprobit	*(2) IV*
Importance of hard work	Onlies	0.0435	−0.4527
		(0.0907)	(0.8301)
	Sample size	1,202	1,202
	Pseudo R2	0.037	0.0372
Degree of plan execution	Onlies	0.0505	−0.2096
		(0.0726)	(0.0330)
	Sample size	2,345	2,345
	Pseudo R2	0.033	0.033
Relationship with people around	Onlies	−0.0662	0.9118
		(0.0724)	(0.5902)
	Sample size	2,380	2,380
	Pseudo R2	0.0410	0.0415
Degree of happiness	Onlies	0.0869**	1.7009***
		(0.0405)	(0.3929)
	Sample size	5,090	5,090
	Pseudo R2	0.0540	0.0556

Note: A higher value means a higher degree of negation.

discrete evaluation values in the range from 1 to 5, we adopt an Ordered Probit (Oprobit) model for all the rows in Table 8.8. The results show that there is no significant difference in the subjective attitude towards risks between onlies and non-onlies, whether it is the common method or the instrumental variable method (taking Equation (8.2) as IV).

Table 8.9 analyses the differences in work attitude, relationship with people around and degree of happiness between onlies and the first children among non-onlies. Work attitude is reflected by two subjective metrics: ‘Recognizing the importance of hard work’ and ‘Status of execution after plan formulation’. Again, a higher value means a higher degree of disagreement with the statement. The results show that there is no significant difference in work attitude and plan execution between onlies and non-onlies. Row 3 of Table 8.9 shows the relationship between onlies and the people around them, but no conclusion can be reached that they are significantly different from non-onlies in terms of such relationship. Only Row 4 of Table 8.9, which examines onlies’ degree of happiness, shows that onlies are less happy. This is consistent with the estimated results obtained by ordinary Oprobit and instrumental variables. Among them, the IV results show that onlies are less happy, which is related to the possible missing variables mentioned above.

8.5.2 Possible Path of Influence 2: Social Network Effect

The natural characteristics of onlies may make them lack social network support, including the lack of siblings and the possible lack of relatives and friends. We may adopt the number of relatives or friends to represent the social network of an individual. In the database, there are several questions that reflect social networking: (1) How many relatives/friends did you visit during the Spring Festival? (2) On a normal day, apart from those family members who live with you, how many other family members or relatives do you roughly make contact with, in whatever way? (3) On a normal day, apart from family members and relatives, how many non-relatives do you make contact with, in whatever way? 'Contact' here refers to one-to-one contact, including by phone, e-mail, Internet, etc. For Question (1), the survey questionnaire directly gives different numbers of relatives and friends visited during the Spring Festival. For Questions (2) and (3), the options given in the survey questionnaire include 0 person, 1–4 persons, 5–9 persons and 10 or more persons.

Table 8.10 examines whether there is any significant difference in the number of friends between onlies and the first children among non-onlies, respectively adopting the OLS method and the instrumental variable method. For the first two questions, the general OLS method is adopted. For the last two questions, the Probit method is employed. It can be seen that when the OLS method is adopted, the number of relatives and friends visited by onlies during the Spring Festival is significantly less than that visited by the first children among non-onlies. However, the result is reversed after instrumental variables are used. This implies that the relatively fewer number of relatives and friends visited by onlies in the OLS results is not due to their only-child status, but may be caused by other missing variables, especially the family-level factors mentioned above. After these variables are controlled, it can be

Table 8.10 Differences between Onlies and the First Children among Non-onlies in Terms of Number of Relatives and Friends

		(1) OLS	*(2) IV*
Visiting relatives during the Spring Festivals	Onlies	−2.1434***	16.7861**
		0.7305	6.6752
	Sample size	2,397	2,397
	R2/Wald	0.113	224.69
Number of friends visited during the Spring Festival	Onlies	−1.7165**	5.2835
		0.8065	5.6447
	Sample size	2,397	2,397
	R2/Wald	0.107	346.88
		(1) Oprobit	(2) IV
Number of non-co-resident relatives in contact	Onlies	0.0326	−0.1551
		0.0668	0.5875
	Sample size	2,397	2,397
	Pseudo R2	0.012	0.012
Number of friends who are not relatives	Onlies	0.0346	0.1362
		0.0651	0.5999
	Sample size	2,397	2,397
	Pseudo R2	0.010	0.010

Table 8.11 Differences between Onlies and Non-onlies in Terms of Attitude towards Relatives and Friends

		(1) Oprobit	*(2) IV*
Give preferential consideration to relatives or friends when employing personnel	Onlies	−0.0722	−1.2380*
		0.0833	0.7439
	Sample size	1,207	1,207
	Pseudo R2	0.033	0.0337
Take pride when fellow countrymen play an important role in society	Onlies	−0.1524*	−2.0872***
		0.0880	0.7509
	Sample size	1,207	1,207
	Pseudo R2	0.049	0.0501

Note: The bigger the value is, the more onlies agree with the statement.

found that onlies visit more relatives and friends and are more proactive in establishing social networks. However, this conclusion is only limited to such one-off behaviour during the Spring Festival. There is no obvious difference between onlies and non-onlies in everyday behaviour.

The potential problem with the use of the above metric is that the number of relatives and friends visited may not represent the real establishment of effective social networks, because one-off or daily communication may not necessarily allow one to establish a real relationship of mutual support when in need of help. In the CGSS questionnaire, there are also two questions about the subjective attitude towards these relatives and friends, which can be seen from the psychological intimacy of individuals to their relatives and friends. The two questions are respectively '(If you are a boss), do you give more preferential consideration to your relatives or friends when you hire employees', and 'Do you take pride if your fellow countrymen play an important role in society?' Oprobit estimates are used to answer these two questions, and the results are shown in Table 8.11. It can be seen that in the results estimated by both general regression or instrumental variables, compared with the first children among non-onlies, onlies do have negative emotions about the two questions, which means that onlies are psychologically alienated from their relatives and friends. Though Table 8.10 shows an enthusiasm for onlies to establish social networks, they have less close relationships with relatives and friends than non-onlies, possibly because of the psychological problems caused by their living habits. Consequently, social networking may indeed be a factor that restrains onlies' entrepreneurship.

8.6 Summary

Using the mixed cross-sectional data of two CGSS surveys, this chapter has examined the differences in entrepreneurial behaviour between onlies and non-onlies. Mainly adopting the methods of OLS and instrumental variable regression, an attempt is made to explain the causes of the differences by personality formation and social networking. The research results show that onlies demonstrate obvious prudence in their entrepreneurial behaviours, and are less inclined to start a business than non-onlies. This conclusion is very robust, and becomes more obvious after endogeneity is controlled.

As for the possible influencing factors, we have found no significant difference between onlies and non-onlies in respect of subjective attitude towards risks, plan execution ability and interpersonal relationship. The only difference is that onlies are less happy than non-onlies, which indicates that onlies are less optimistic. However, it is difficult to further explain the source of such unhappiness. It may be due to the personality factor which has formed over a long time, or a psychological burden arising from a lack of social networks. In short, as far as most subjective attitudes are concerned, onlies are not the 'little emperors' as described in some literature. As for the social networks that can be described by other subjective and objective metrics, though descriptive statistics and simple regression analyses seem to suggest that onlies have a relatively small number of relatives and friends, once possible endogenous problems are controlled, we can see that the only-child attribute does not reduce the number of relatives and friends. On the contrary, it even has a positive effect. However, in terms of inner affinity, onlies do have relatively poor relationships with relatives, friends and fellow countrymen, which means that they may lack truly effective social networks.

These results show that as far as personality is concerned onlies do not significantly fair worse than non-onlies. In other words, onlies are not in a disadvantageous position when it comes to most personality characteristics. However, because they are the only child in their families, onlies are nevertheless significantly less entrepreneurial than non-onlies. This is more likely due to the lack of social networks and 'social assurance' brought by their only-child attribute than the lack of personality.[3] Due to limited data, we are unable to further test the 'social assurance' mechanism. We can only make rough inferences from the above results. The mechanism behind the less entrepreneurial activities of onlies will be the topic for analysis at the next step.

Notes

1 For example, some entrepreneurs may set up multiple companies, which implies that the increase in the number of private enterprises does not necessarily mean an increase in the number of entrepreneurs.

2 When the comparative samples of onlies and the first children among non-onlies and the comparative samples of the first children among non-onlies and the other children among non-onlies are analyzed separately, it is also found that onlies and the first children among non-onlies are significantly less likely to start a business than other children among non-onlies. This further verifies the conclusion of Table 8.6. Due to limited space, the results are not listed here.

3 As mentioned above, onlies are more likely to avoid risks in family decision-making, because there is no one to share the risks with them. To give a specific example: if there is only one child in a family, the child is more likely to stay with and look after his or her parents. But, if the family has more than one child, then one child may stay with their parents, while the other children can engage in some risk activities and take care of each other.

9 Family Planning and Old-Age Care

9.1 Introduction

China has now entered a period of population ageing. In 2010, over 8% of the country's population were over 65. The ratio rose to 9.7% in 2013, while the dependency ratio of the elderly population reached 13.1% in the same year. The total dependency ratio began to reverse the previous downward trend in 2011. At the same time, average family size has also been declining (see Table 9.1), with two-person and three-person families gradually making for the largest proportion of all family types. The one-child family planning policy implemented in the 1980s has played a significant role in the decline of family size.

Currently, growing public concern in China about the issue of old-age care has led to increasingly heated debate, with insufficient pension funds attracting the most attention. This is the most important perspective to examine the old-age care issue from the angle of social provision for the aged. From the perspective of household economics, we need to examine how the model of family provision for the aged can make up for the lack of social support. In particular, more than 30 years have passed since the early 1980s, and the onlies have gradually entered the age of providing old-age care for their parents. Onlies will face more pressure in providing for the aged, because they have no siblings to share the burden. China's demographic structural changes may also cause more prominent problems in the family provision for the aged. In light of these two phenomena, this study examines the differences in old-age care between one-child and multi-child families, reveals changes in the model of old-age care in the context of increased onlies and analyses the motives behind family provision for the aged and its impact on the well-being of elderly people.

Analysing this issue has several implications. First, distinguishing dependency structures, especially co-residence structures, is helpful for predicting changes in family structure, thus making it possible to forecast changes in the number of families, housing demand and other economic metrics. This will have an effect on the prediction of such important economic dimensions as urbanization and the real estate market. Second, if

DOI: 10.4324/9781003288091-11

Table 9.1 Changes in Family Size and Percentage of Elderly People in China as Revealed in Successive Population Censuses

	1953	*1964*	*1982*	*1990*	*2000*	*2010*
Household size (persons/household)	4.33	4.43	4.41	3.96	3.44	3.1
Percentage of people over 65	4.41	3.56	4.91	5.57	6.96	8.87

family support can effectively bear the burden of old-age care, it will reduce the adverse effects of the possible pension funds gap in the future. Third, by comparing one-child with multi-child families, it is possible to effectively identify motives behind the provision of old-age care, and offer theoretical supplements to the existing literature.

9.2 Summary of Relevant Literature

9.2.1 Literature Review

Internationally, there are few specific studies on the issue of old-age care in one-child families, because few countries implement a family planning policy, and one-child families do not form enough groups of concern. In China, the issue of population ageing has received growing attention in recent years, but there is still a lack of analysis of the issue of providing for the aged by onlies. There are only some simple analyses which find that onlies face a bigger economic burden to provide old-age care for their parents. There is little in-depth research to compare one-child with multi-child families and examine the impact on well-being.

There are many international studies on the driving factors behind the co-residence model of old-age care. Numerous studies have been conducted in East Asia, especially Japan, and there are also some related studies in the United States. Basically, the widely recognized theories of the driving factors for co-residence include 'the theory of family lineage succession', 'the theory of self-interested life cycle', 'the theory of altruistic behavior' and 'the theory of social norms'. These theories explain the motives of both parents and children.

Among them, the theory of self-interested life cycle is the absolutely dominant explanatory theory of old-age care. Modigliani and Brumberg (1954) assume that both parents and children are self-interested. If children do not take care of their parents, then parents will not leave their bequests to their children. Many other studies hold similar views. For example, Lucas and Stark (1985) find that if immigrants have wealthy parents, they have to give their parents more money than those whose parents are poor. This phenomenon shows these immigrants' motive to fight for bequests, and the logic behind is that there are more children who compete for bequests.

Therefore, the game theory is adopted in a considerable number of studies to study multi-child families (Bernheim et al., 1985). If parents have more wealth and their children want to fight for it, they may act strategically in front of their parents, such as making more transfers to their parents to cover their expenses. Wakabayashi and Horioka (2006) find such a strategic bequest motive among Japanese children. Many studies on Japan have found that parents live with their children out of a self-interested motive, using bequests to attract their children to live with them (Horioka, et al., 2000).

Parents' welfare benefits are also often regarded as a kind of public goods between children (Bergstrom et al., 1986). Children may expect their siblings to take care of their parents and get a free ride to enjoy their parents' welfare benefits. However, if children take care of their parents without considering the contribution of other siblings, which is called warm-glow giving, then their care for the elderly will go independently and does not affect one another (Andreoni, 1990). Barro (1974), Becker (1974) and Wakabayashi and Horioka (2006) call this characteristic the altruism of children. In fact, the 'theory of family lineage continuation' mentioned above can also be regarded as the altruism of parents. In the altruistic model, Barro (1974) and Becker (1974a, 1981) assume that parents are altruistic, defined as parents leaving bequests to their children, live with and take care of their children, regardless of whether their children will provide old-age care for them or not. If the children are also altruistic, they will also live with and take care of their parents when they grow old, regardless of whether their parents will leave bequests to them or not. The altruistic model holds that possible bequests bear no relation to co-residence between parents and children.

The theory of social norms or social tradition emphasizes other factors such as social customs and other social traditions to explain co-residence (Sakudo, 2007). Tsuya and Martin (1992) find that parent-child co-residence in Japan is partly determined by social customs, in that co-residence is more likely to happen to sons living in small towns or rural areas, sons with arranged marriage, the eldest sons and daughters who are not married to the eldest sons of others. This is a typical Japanese custom. But, Martin and Tsuya (1991) also discover that the custom weakens over time.

There are some studies that test the well-being effects of parent-child co-residence in China. For example, Chen and Short (2008) use a micro data set to study the impact of different living arrangements with children on the subjective well-being of old people over 80. It is found that living arrangements do affect subjective well-being, but the impact pattern is very complex. Chyi and Mao (2012) examine whether the co-residence model affects the happiness of elderly people, but find that living with children has no positive effect on the happiness of the elderly people. Currently, no one has studied the issue of motives and wellbeing corresponding to old-age care provided by onlies.

9.2.2 Roadmap of This Study

The first issue to be addressed in the current study is to provide a statistical description of the differences in old-age care model between one-child and multi-child families, so as to understand changes in the overall model of social provision for the aged in the context of a rising proportion of onlies.

The second issue is to identify the motives behind the provision of old-age care in China. The theories of self-interested life cycle, altruism and social norms are the most important theories to explain the behaviour of co-residence. However, past studies can hardly solve the problem of identification of these determining factors. In other words, it is difficult to eliminate the problem of unreliable coefficient estimates caused by missing variables. In China, a natural experiment like the one-child family planning policy provides an opportunity for such identification. If we think that children have similar motives to provide old-age care for their patents, in both situations of onlies and non-onlies, the difference in co-residence arrangements for old-age care between one-child and multi-child families can be used to identify the motives behind the provision of old-age care. Because onlies have no motive to fight for bequests through co-residence—they have no rival to compete for bequests with them, such motive only exists in multi-child families. So if the motive for co-residence is to compete for bequests, then one-child and multi-child families will have very different co-residence behaviours. In other words, by observing the difference between these two kinds of families, it is possible to identify whether the theory of self-interested life cycle holds true in China.

The third issue is whether co-residence significantly increases or reduces the wellbeing of elderly people. Analysing this issue based on a sound identification of the motives for co-residence will help to reach more intuitive explanations.

9.3 Data Description

This study uses the data of the China Health and Retirement Longitudinal Study (CHARLS) conducted by Peking University in 2011. Focusing on elderly people, the data come from a large sample size and are representative of the whole country. The CHALRS data of 2011 cover 150 county-level units, 450 village-level units and 17,000 people of approximately 10,000 households. The CHALRS data survey the personal characteristics, family assets, family member information (including spouse, children) and personal subjective attitude towards old-age care of the respondents (basically parents), as well as information on their personal subjective satisfaction and other aspects of well-being. This enables us to control as many factors as possible in regression analysis. After the families with no children still alive and families with missing key variables are removed, a total of 9,787 families are left, of which 1,694 are one-child families and 8,093 multi-child families and 5,696 are co-resident families and 4,091 non-co-resident families.

Table 9.2 shows the descriptive statistics of parents in both types of families. Compared with multi-child families, one-child families have a slightly higher proportion (65% vs. 57%) of parent-child co-residence. Compared with multi-child families, parents in one-child families are younger, have higher incomes and are more likely to own houses, have better education and hold an urban Hukou. Among the one-child families, parents living with their children are generally younger and have bigger houses, more rooms and a relatively high level of education, though with a relatively low level of income. Besides, they are happier, less lonely and much healthier. Among the multi-child families, parents living with their children are also younger, have bigger houses, more rooms and a relatively high level of education, but there is not much difference in their income level and psychological state.

Table 9.3 shows the descriptive statistics of children in both types of families. Compared with non-onlies, onlies are younger and better educated and have a higher proportion of males among them. It can be seen that more onlies choose to live with their parents. Among non-onlies, more male females live with their parents, and they are younger and mostly unmarried. Among the non-onlies, those living with their parents are younger, mostly male, and well educated, but fewer are married.

It can be found that some of the groups living with their parents are children who are young, and have yet to take up formal employment and cannot live independently of their parents. This is more obvious among onlies, mainly because they are generally younger than non-onlies and many of them do not yet live independently of their parents. Because this study focuses on the issue of old-age care for parents, these samples should be removed. In the subsequent analysis, we will limit the samples to those with the age of at least one parent being 60 or older.

9.4 Differences in Old-Age Care Model between One-Child and Multi-Child Families

9.4.1 Brief Description

There are two main ways of providing old-age care for parents: (1) co-residence: children live with their parents and provide comprehensive support for their everyday life; and (2) economic support: children live separately from their parents but provide them with funds and necessary material support.

The CHALRS data contain a specific survey question on the economic relationship between parents and their non-co-resident children: 'In the past year, have you or your spouse received any economic support from your child/children who is/are not living with you?' This study mainly uses this

Table 9.2 Descriptive Statistics of Parents' Personal Characteristics

	One-Child Families			*Multi-Child Families*		
	All	*Co-resident*	*Non-co-Resident*	*All*	*Co-resident*	*Non-co-Resident*
Co-residence (1 = Yes)	0.65			0.57		
	0.48			0.50		
House floorspace	107.70	113.90	96.25	113.80	124.40	99.85
	72.08	71.58	71.64	71.21	72.15	67.46
Number of rooms	2.66	2.82	2.37	3.04	3.25	2.76
	1.68	1.61	1.75	1.94	1.90	1.96
Owning house (1 = Yes)	0.92	0.93	0.91	0.89	0.96	0.80
	0.27	0.25	0.29	0.31	0.20	0.40
Parents' average age	55.45	54.28	57.60	60.92	58.18	64.52
	9.42	9.52	8.85	10.42	10.24	9.52
Parents' average level of	7.06	7.15	6.91	4.14	4.46	3.71
education	4.73	4.76	4.68	3.77	3.79	3.71
Parents have an urban	0.61	0.61	0.60	0.41	0.39	0.43
Hukou (1 = Yes)	0.49	0.49	0.49	0.49	0.49	0.50
Both parents are alive (1	0.73	0.73	0.72	0.74	0.74	0.74
= Yes)	0.45	0.44	0.45	0.44	0.44	0.44
Parents' total income	18,584	17,853	19,931	7,842	7,884	7,788
	26,862	24,689	30,438	16,442	17,039	15,623
Parents' average sense of	1.52	1.470.80	1.61	1.62	1.58	1.67
loneliness	0.85		0.92	0.92	0.89	0.95
Parents' average sense of	3.08	3.15	2.95	2.89	2.89	2.89
happiness	0.96	0.93	1.01	1.00	1.01	1.00
Parents' average level of	3.12	3.14	3.10	2.93	2.96	2.90
health	0.78	0.76	0.83	0.78	0.77	0.78
Number of children	1.00	1.00	1.00	3.16	3.03	3.33
	0.00	0.00	0.00	1.33	1.27	1.39
Sample Size	1,694	1,098	596	8,093	4,598	3,495

Note: 'Sense of loneliness' has a value from 1 to 4, indicating a growing degree of lineless; "Sense of happiness" has a value from 1 to 4, indicating a growing degree of happiness; and "Level of health" has a value from 1 to 5, indicating a growing degree of health.

Table 9.3 Descriptive Statistics of Children

	Onlies			Non-onlies		
	All	*Co-resident*	*Non-co-Resident*	*All*	*Co-resident*	*Non-co-Resident*
Co-residence	0.65			0.26		
	0.48			0.44		
Education	11.34	11.15	11.64	7.75	8.89	7.40
	4.58	4.57	4.57	4.65	4.35	4.68
Gender	0.64	0.68	0.57	0.53	0.72	0.46
	0.48	0.47	0.50	0.50	0.45	0.50
Marital status	0.55	0.43	0.75	0.80	0.49	0.90
	0.50	0.50	0.44	0.40	0.50	0.30
Age	28.32	27.00	30.78	35.36	27.89	38.15
	9.09	9.28	8.17	10.82	9.97	9.76
No income (1 = Yes)	0.21	0.27	0.09	0.08	0.20	0.04
	0.41	0.45	0.28	0.27	0.40	0.19
Sample Size	1,694	1,103	591	25,256	6,641	18,615

Note: Income refers to the annual income of the child and his or her spouse.

Table 9.4 Analysis of Models of Old-Age Care in Different Families

Being onlies?	*Overall*	*One-Child Families*	*Multi-Child Families*	
Co-residence	58.33%	65.01%	56.93%	
Non-co-resident: children provide economic support	21.10%	9.35%	23.55%	
Non-co-resident: children do not provide economic support	20.57%	25.64%	19.51%	
Sample distribution	100%	17.31%	82.69%	
Parents' age	*Overall*	*Under 65*	*Aged 65–70*	*Over 70*
Co-residence	58.33%	65.06%	42.03%	40.66%
Non-co-resident: children provide economic support	21.10%	14.95%	35.74%	37.40%
Non-co-resident: children do not provide economic support	20.57%	19.99%	22.23%	21.93%
Sample distribution	100%	69.41%	10.54%	20.05%

question to investigate whether parents who do not live with their children get any form of economic support for their old-age care. As shown in Table 9.4, co-residence is the main model of old-age care for both only-child and multi-child families, and only 20% of the surveyed parents received economic support for old-age care. Because the survey question asks respondents to include 'any economic support' and all those small-amount and non-regular economic exchanges with children that do not play the role of old-age care are also considered as forms of old-age care, the proportion of families choosing economic support for old-age care is actually overestimated. In addition, it can be found that compared with multi-child families, a significantly less proportion of one-child families choose the model of economic support for old-age care. However, as parents become older, the proportion of families choosing co-residence for old-age care falls, while the proportion of families resorting to economic support for old-age care increases. When children are young, co-residence more reflects parents' care for their children than children providing old-age care for their parents. Therefore, we will focus on the group of parents over 60 in the analysis below.

The co-residence model of old-age care is relatively common. Moreover, it is a relatively low-cost way of old-age care when parents still have the ability to work. It does not require many funds, and children can make proper use of their parents' surplus labour resources. This study will mainly examine the differences between one-child and multi-child families in the co-residence model of old-age care, and verify the motives behind it and the effect of co-residence on the well-being of parents.

Table 9.5 Distribution of Age and Co-residence of Parents and Children

Parents' Age	*Under 65*	*65–70*	*Over 70*	
Proportion of onlies	21.12%	6.56%	8.26%	
Proportion of parent-child co-residence	64.93%	41.99%	40.50%	
Proportion of co-residence of one-child families	65.50%	62.86%	58.57%	
Proportion of co-residence of multi-child families	64.78%	40.52%	38.87%	
Sample distribution	69.41%	10.54%	20.05%	
Children's age	*The 1960s Generation*	*The 1970s Generation*	*The 1980s Generation*	*The 1990s Generation*
Proportion of onlies	1.30%	3.73%	11.37%	12.72%
Proportion of parent-child co-residence	8.01%	19.23%	43.57%	79.43%
Proportion of co-residence of one-child families	53.85%	52.78%	62.03%	90.33%
Proportion of co-residence of multi-child families	7.41%	17.93%	41.20%	77.84%
Sample distribution	18.58%	32.24%	30.27%	7.85%

Note: The 1990s, 1980s, 1970s and 1960s generations respectively refer to children born in 1990–1999, 1980–1989, 1970–1979 and 1960–1969. Children born before 1960 and after 2000 account for 11.06% of the total samples but are not reported here.

Table 9.5 shows the sample distribution and co-residence patterns of parents and children of different ages as calculated from the data used in this study. It can be seen that the number of parents under 65 with only one child has begun to increase significantly. At the same time, with the increase of parents' age, the proportion of children living with parents has declined for both onlies and non-onlies. As children become younger, the proportion of onlies has also increased continuously. The proportion of onlies among the 1990s generation is nearly 13 times that among the 1960s generation. In addition, with the decrease of age, the proportion of both onlies and non-onlies living with their parents increases, and more onlies live with their parents than non-onlies.

9.4.2 Regression Description

Generally speaking, there are three options which families may choose for old-age care (namely parents live with their children; parents do not live with their children, but their children provide economic support; and parents live with their children, but their children do not provide economic support). There is no obvious superiority between the three models, because there is no way to ascertain that the co-residence model of old-age care is better than the old-age care model in which parents live with their children, but their children do not provide economic support. Therefore, this study will use the multivariate unordered choice model to estimate the differences between one-child and multi-child families in the selection of old-age care models. We adopt a regression model to re-describe the differences in the co-residence model between one-child and multi-child families, and observe possible variations among different age groups. Compared with the descriptive analysis in Table 9.5, regression analysis can test the significance of the differences.

Family is taken as the unit for analysis. The control group consists of those families which choose the old-age care model of parents not living with their children but children providing economic support for their parents. The overall regression results are shown in Columns (1)~(3) of Table 9.6. It can be seen that relative to the old-age care model of parents not living with their children but children providing economic support for their parents, onlies tend to choose the co-residence model and the old-age care model of parents not living with their children and children not providing economic support for their parents. This may be because onlies do not have siblings to share the burden of old-age care for parents, which makes them go to extremes when choosing an old-age care model. From Column (2), it can be seen that onlies still keep this tendency after the parents' age variable is controlled. From the cross items in Column (3), it is clear that onlies are more likely to live with their parents and take no old-age care measures when their parents grow old.

Because of the big differences in the level of development, social customs and other aspects between cities and rural areas in China, we will respectively conduct regression analysis on the rural and urban samples and examine their differences. Here, rural and urban families are distinguished based on parents' Hukou status. If one of the parents in a family has an urban Hukou, the family will be considered as an urban family. Otherwise, it is a rural family. From the results of Column (4)~(7), the main conclusion is that there is no difference between urban and rural families in the selection of old-age care models. Relative to the old-age care model of parents not living with their children but children providing economic support for their parents, onlies tend to choose the co-residence model and the old-age care model of parents not living with their children and children not providing economic support for their parents. The difference is that compared with non-onlies, urban onlies are more likely to live with their parents when their parents grow older. Compared with non-onlies, rural onlies are more likely to live with them when their parents are older, or not to take old-age care measures.

Table 9.6 Regression Test of Relationship between Old-Age Care Model Selection and One-Child Status

	All			*Urban*	*Rural*	*Urban*	*Rural*
	(1)	*(2)*	*(3)*	*(4)*	*(5)*	*(6)*	*(7)*
Non-co-resident and no economic support							
Whether living together	1.096***	1.054***	0.425	1.026***	0.881***	0.588	−0.140
	(7.35)	(7.04)	(1.22)	(5.52)	(3.37)	(0.88)	(−0.31)
Parents' age = 65_70		−0.325**	−0.376**	−0.980***	−0.188	−1.041***	−0.284
		(−2.22)	(−2.35)	(−3.05)	(−1.09)	(−2.71)	(−1.56)
Parents' age > 70		−0.695***	−0.762***	−1.337***	−0.717***	−1.429***	−0.807***
		(−4.64)	(−4.65)	(−4.17)	(−3.73)	(−3.73)	(−3.99)
Onlies*65_70			0.575			0.193	1.488**
			(1.42)			(0.27)	(2.45)
Onlies*70			0.996**			0.800	1.394*
			(2.22)			(1.08)	(1.74)
Co-residence							
Whether living together	1.032***	0.983***	−0.155	0.797***	1.150***	0.0225	−0.463
	(7.53)	(7.13)	(−0.47)	(4.60)	(4.98)	(0.03)	(−1.16)
Parents' age = 65_70		−0.415***	−0.564***	−0.766**	−0.401***	−0.932***	−0.578***
		(−3.25)	(−4.10)	(−2.50)	(−2.76)	(−2.60)	(−3.78)
Parents' age > 70		−0.805***	−0.981***	−1.051***	−1.199***	−1.281***	−1.381***
		(−6.16)	(−7.00)	(−3.45)	(−7.29)	(−3.59)	(−7.99)
Onlies*65_70			1.133***			0.453	2.210***
			(3.00)			(0.65)	(4.12)
Onlies*70			1.668***			1.318*	2.297***
			(4.00)			(1.84)	(3.30)
Sample Size	4,992	4,992	4,992	2,634	2,358	2,634	2,358
Pseudo R2	0.007	0.013	0.015	0.013	0.021	0.015	0.025

Note: Parents' age is the average age of parents. Onlies*65_70 represents the cross term between parents' average age being 65–70 and the one-child family, and onlies*70 the cross item between parents' age being over 70 and one-child family. Values in brackets are the t values, the same below. ***, ** and * respectively represent the significance levels at 1%, 5% and 10%, the same in the tables below.

9.5 Results of Recognition of Motives behind Co-residence for Old-Age Care

This section will mainly discuss two of the three types of motives for old-age care mentioned above: (1) self-interest motives; and (2) social norms. Motives for altruism (including parents' altruism and children's altruism) are difficult to test directly. We mainly discuss them in an indirect way. If the co-residence model of old-age care does not come from a self-interest motive, it is very likely that the altruistic motive promotes children to undertake the heavy task of looking after their parents. However, social norms and parents' care for children when they live together may both have an influence.

9.5.1 Social Norms

The social norms theory emphasizes that social norms such as cultural tradition affect the co-residence arrangement. In Chinese social norms, there are strong ideas such as 'sons should care for their elders' and 'eldest children should provide for their elders'. In this study, children's gender, eldest son status, eldest daughter status, eldest child status and youngest child status are added to the regression analysis to test whether there exists an influence of 'sons should care for their elders' and 'eldest children should provide for elders'. In addition, other personal characteristics variables of parents and children which may have an influence are also controlled.

From Table 9.7, we can see that the idea of 'sons should care for their elders' is prevalent in Chinese society, and the probability of parent-child co-residence is significantly increased when children are males. In addition, in the case of eldest sons, the probability of co-residence with parents is also significantly higher. But, when the eldest children are females, it will reduce the probability of co-residence. This also reflects the common idea that sons not daughters are responsible for providing old-age care for their parents. Moreover, after eldest child status and youngest child status are taken into account, it is found that eldest child status does not increase the probability of co-residence, while youngest child status does increase the probability of co-residence. This may be due to the fact that in traditional Chinese practice children successively live independently of their families after marriage, leaving younger children to live with their parents. It may also be because parents tend to provide care for their younger children. One-child families only have one child. In Table 9.7, onlies are considered as both the eldest and the youngest children. If one-child families are taken out and only multi-child families are analysed, the conclusion remains unchanged.

We can find less co-residence when there are more children in a family and children become older or are married. However, children are more likely to live with parents who have their own houses, bigger houses or houses with more rooms, all of which provide the objective conditions for co-residence. In addition, parents' attitude towards co-residence is also important, and

Table 9.7 Effect of Social Norms on Co-residence for Old-Age Care

	(1)	*(2)*	*(3)*
Male children	0.835*** (36.57)	0.684*** (18.11)	0.641*** (15.87)
Eldest son	– –	0.152*** (5.21)	0.174*** (5.56)
Eldest daughter	– –	−0.0895** (−2.30)	−0.124*** (−3.08)
Eldest child	– –	– –	0.0334 (1.00)
Youngest child	– –	– –	0.136*** (4.28)
Number of children	−0.127*** (−12.63)	−0.129*** (−12.33)	−0.115*** (−10.27)
Onlies	0.367*** (8.04)	0.353*** (7.67)	0.277*** (5.31)
Children's age	−0.0352*** (−16.39)	−0.0381*** (−16.91)	−0.0345*** (−14.04)
Parents' age	−0.00381* (−1.75)	−0.000206 (−0.09)	−0.00326 (−1.34)
Children's marital status	−0.865*** (−33.11)	−0.869*** (−33.04)	−0.865*** (−32.84)
Both parents are alive	−0.0490 (−1.02)	−0.0477 (−0.99)	−0.0483 (−1.00)
Parents' health	−0.00688 (−0.47)	−0.00402 (−0.27)	−0.00436 (−0.29)
Children's education	0.000245 (0.09)	−0.000707 (−0.25)	−0.000931 (−0.33)
Parents' level of education	0.00142 (0.39)	0.00170 (0.46)	0.00198 (0.53)
House floorspace	0.00133*** (8.19)	0.00130*** (7.94)	0.00130*** (7.90)
Number of rooms	0.0128** (2.15)	0.0133** (2.22)	0.0136** (2.26)
Ownership of house	0.642*** (14.36)	0.632*** (14.03)	0.631*** (14.01)
Parents' income	0.000000515 (0.65)	0.000000437 (0.55)	0.000000463 (0.58)
Attitude Towards Co-residence 1	0.285*** (10.69)	0.282*** (10.51)	0.283*** (10.51)
Attitude Towards Co-residence 2	0.443*** (9.68)	0.437*** (9.46)	0.434*** (9.41)
Attitude Towards Co-residence 3	0.0904*** (2.82)	0.0938*** (2.90)	0.0969*** (3.00)
Parents holding urban Hukou	0.0987*** (2.65)	0.0951** (2.54)	0.0955** (2.55)

(*Continued*)

Table 9.7 (Continued)

	(1)	*(2)*	*(3)*
Fixed effect of province	Y	Y	Y
Size of observed samples	22,333	22,206	22,206
Pseudo R2	0.299	0.299	0.300

Notes: 1. Attitude Towards Co-residence 1: Have both spouse and children and should live with their children; Attitude Towards Co-residence 2: Have children but no spouse and should live with their children; Attitude Towards Co-residence 3: Rely on children for old-age care. Here, Attitude 1, Attitude 2 and Attitude 3 are respectively parents' attitude multiplied by corresponding conditions. For example, Attitude 1 asks if elderly people "have both spouse and children‘, then this study uses the product of the dummy variable of Have Both Spouse and Children and the original Attitude 1 as Attitude 1 in the regression.
2. All variables involving parents are the average values of parents, the same in the tables below.
3. Members of the control group for children's income have an income of RMB5,000 or less, including cases of no income.

such attitude is found to be consistent with actual co-residence action. Finally, if parents have an urban Hukou, it will also increase the probability of co-residence.

In addition, due to the huge urban/rural gap in China, it is very likely that social norms influence old-age care differently between urban and rural areas. Table 9.8 shows that if children are males, it will significantly increase the probability of parent-child co-residence in both urban and rural areas. However, the tendency of eldest sons providing old-age care for parents and elderly daughters not providing old-age care for parents is not as obvious in cities as in rural areas. In all situations, youngest child status does increase the probability of co-residence.

9.5.2 Self-Interest Motive

Onlies and non-onlies form natural control groups, which can be used to verify the self-interested life cycle theory. If parents are wealthy (such as having good incomes, businesses and realty), non-onlies are more likely to live with their parents for the sake of getting bequests, while onlies do not need to take initiative to live with their parents because they have no others to compete with them for bequests. Therefore, by adding the cross term of the parents' realty variable and the only-child status variable into the regression equation, it will be possible to identify whether onlies and non-onlies take different co-residence actions because of their parents' different wealth status.

In principle, we need to know the relative wealth of parents and children in order to identify the influence of parents' wealth. Even if parents are wealthy, such wealth will not become a motive for their children to live with them when their children have more assets. However, we do not have data or

Table 9.8 **Effect of Social Norms on Co-residence for Old-Age Care (Divided Into Urban and Rural Areas)**

	Rural	*Rural*	*Rural*	*Urban*	*Urban*	*Urban*
Male children	0.862*** (28.99)	0.670*** (13.70)	0.597*** (11.35)	0.814*** (22.44)	0.721*** (11.85)	0.710*** (11.02)
Eldest son		0.206*** (5.39)	0.248*** (6.07)		0.0831* (1.80)	0.0799 (1.61)
Eldest daughter		−0.104** (−2.09)	−0.156*** (−3.04)		−0.0638 (−1.00)	−0.0784 (−1.20)
Eldest child			−0.000895 (−0.02)			0.0817 (1.53)
Youngest child			0.165*** (3.99)			0.108** (2.14)
Number of children	−0.113*** (−8.05)	−0.114*** (−7.88)	−0.100*** (−6.39)	−0.140*** (−9.55)	−0.145*** (−9.41)	−0.132*** (−7.97)
Onlies	0.398*** (6.00)	0.371*** (5.55)	0.294*** (3.99)	0.364*** (5.66)	0.359*** (5.53)	0.275*** (3.61)
Other control variables	Y	Y	Y	Y	Y	Y
Fixed effect of province	Y	Y	Y	Y	Y	Y
Size of observed samples	12,971	12,895	12,895	9,360	9,309	9,309
Pseudo R2	0.300	0.300	0.301	0.308	0.309	0.310

information on children's assets. We can only control as many as possible such factors as age, gender and level of education which may reflect children's ownership of wealth. We assume that children's assets are given once these factors are fixed, so that parents' wealth can be used to directly identify the applicability of the self-interested life cycle theory.

We first measure parents' wealth using the variable of parents' financial assets, which include deposits, government bonds, stocks and funds. The cross item between parents' financial assets and onlies can reflect the identification of competition for bequests. Because onlies have no siblings competing for bequests with them, there is no incentive for them to live with their parents to compete for the inheritance of wealth. However, non-onlies will compete for bequests by living with their parents. If the cross item is significantly negative, it indicates that onlies are less affected by parents' wealth in their decision to live with parents. In other words, the motive to compete for bequests may be confirmed, and the theory of self-interested life cycle may stand true. Table 9.9 shows the Probit-estimated willingness to co-residence of all the samples and the urban and rural samples. The cross terms of biggest concern to us for identifying the self-interested life cycle are not significant among all the samples and the urban samples, but significant among the rural samples.

However, there are some problems in the above estimates, because compared with multi-child families, one-child families may have some non-observable characteristics of heterogeneity, which may affect their co-residence behaviour. Therefore, the one-child status variable we focus on has an endogenous problem, and the above estimates of its coefficient may be biased. To solve this problem, we draw on some of the instrumental variables provided by Ebenstein (2010), which mainly include the fines/income ratio, number of childbirths allowed by the family planning policy, rewards for onlies and other provincial regulation variables. These variables are adopted as instrumental variables for onlies, and estimates are made again. The results are shown in Table 9.10. Among all the samples and the

Table 9.9 Effect of Self-Interested Motives on Co-residence for Old-Age Care (Financial Assets)

	All	*Urban*	*Rural*
Parents' financial assets	−0.00000000787	−0.000000855	0.000000392
	(−0.20)	(−1.25)	(0.78)
Onlies	0.406***	0.377***	0.473***
	(8.67)	(5.79)	(6.77)
Financial assets*onlies	−0.000000909	0.000000220	−0.00000417*
	(−1.27)	(0.25)	(−2.29)
Fixed effect of province	Y	Y	Y
Size of observed samples	22,230	9,434	12,794
Pseudo R2	0.286	0.292	0.289

Table 9.10 Effect of Self-Interested Motives on Co-residence for Old-Age Care (Financial Assets; IV)

	All	*Urban*	*Rural*
Parents' financial assets	0.000000482***	0.000000481**	0.000000123
	(3.11)	(2.46)	(0.69)
Onlies	0.880***	0.715***	0.406
	(5.67)	(6.01)	(1.19)
Financial assets*onlies	−0.00000146***	−0.00000109***	−0.00000303
	(−4.65)	(−3.86)	(−1.06)
Other control variables	Y	Y	Y
Fixed effect of province	Y	Y	Y
Size of observed samples	22,301	9,427	12,874
R2	0.189	0.214	0.300

Table 9.11 Effect of Self-Interested Motives on Co-residence for Old-Age Care (Realty Ownership)

Probit	*All*	*Urban*	*Rural*
Parents owning realty	0.438***	0.504***	0.416***
	(12.64)	(9.52)	(8.85)
Onlies	0.629***	0.801***	0.335
	(4.86)	(5.16)	(1.35)
Parents owning realty *onlies	−0.286*	−0.518**	0.0819
	(−2.13)	(−3.19)	(0.32)
Other control variables	Y	Y	Y
Fixed effect of province	Y	Y	Y
Size of observed samples	22,365	9,386	12,977
Pseudo R2	0.296	0.305	0.297
IV	*All*	*Urban*	*Rural*
Parents owning realty	0.290***	0.248***	0.236***
	(5.58)	(5.35)	(5.68)
Onlies	6.280***	3.258***	9.545***
	(4.22)	(3.86)	(4.04)
Parents owning realty*onlies	−5.985***	−2.999***	−9.287***
	(−4.11)	(−3.70)	(−3.97)
Other control variables	Y	Y	Y
Fixed effect of province	Y	Y	Y
Size of observed samples	22,210	9,337	12,873

urban samples, onlies are found to see financial assets as less incentive for co-residence, which indicates the existence of self-interested motives.

Parents' income above is only one way to measure wealth. In China, realty is an important part of bequests from parents. However, due to limited data, it is

Table 9.12 Effect of Self-Interested Motives on Co-residence for Old-Age Care (Self-Employment)

Probit	*All*	*Urban*	*Rural*
Parents being self-employed	0.112**	0.00733	0.132**
	(2.87)	(0.10)	(2.84)
Onlies	0.376***	0.342***	0.428***
	(7.96)	(5.20)	(6.16)
Parents being self-employed*onlies	0.0747	0.281	−0.0600
	(0.56)	(1.48)	(−0.31)
Other control variables	Y	Y	Y
Fixed effect of province	Y	Y	Y
Size of observed samples	22,456	9,476	12,978
Pseudo R2	0.290	0.296	0.292
IV	*All*	*Urban*	*Rural*
Parents being self-employed	1.174***	0.692***	2.728***
	(6.18)	(5.49)	(4.69)
Onlies	0.0994***	0.0642**	0.150***
	(5.79)	(2.74)	(4.67)
Parents being self-employed*onlies	−0.833***	−0.376**	−2.250***
	(−4.99)	(−3.23)	(−4.33)
Other control variables	Y	Y	Y
Fixed effect of province	Y	Y	Y
Size of observed samples	22,301	9,427	12,874

impossible to identify whether all realties owned by a family are 100% owned by parents. In this study, such realties are simply assumed to be entirely owned by parents, because patents definitely have certain power to dispose of such realties even if they belong to all family members. The results in Table 9.11 show that when parents' wealth is measured by realty ownership, onlies have a significantly lower the probability of co-residence for the sake of parents' realties, which therefore indicates the existence of self-interested motives.

In addition, this study also uses whether parents are self-employed as another way to measure their wealth. If parents run their own businesses, their work can be inherited by their children. The results in Table 9.12 show that when parents' wealth is measured by self-employment, onlies have a significantly lower probability of living with self-employed patents, which therefore indicates the existence of self-interested motives.

9.6 Well-Being Effect of the Co-residence Model of Old-Age Care

This section analyses changes which co-residence brings to the well-being of elderly people. For the purpose of analysis, two subjective well-being metrics are used: degree of happiness, and degree of loneliness. These two variables are derived from the questionnaire survey of respondents' state of mental health, which mainly askes the respondents about their feelings in the previous week. Taking loneliness as an example, the questionnaire asks respondents how often they felt lonely in the previous week, and the answers were divided into four levels (1) Never or seldom feel lonely (less than one day); (2) Do not feel lonely too often (1–2 days); (3) Feel lonely sometimes or half of the time (3–4 days); and (4) Feel lonely most of the time (5–7 days)). Then, the average degree of parents' loneliness in a family is obtained as the metrics for loneliness. The bigger the value, the lonelier the parents feel. Similarly, the higher the happiness value, the happier the parents are. With reference to the method of Chyi and Mao (2012), we use the patents' attitude variable as the instrumental variable for co-residence. This study mainly chooses Attitude Towards Co-residence 1 (Have both spouse and children and should live with their children) and Attitude Towards Co-residence 2 (Have no spouse but children and should live with their

Table 9.13 Co-residence and the Happiness/Loneliness of Elderly People (IV)

	Happy One-Child Families	*Happy Multi-Child Families*	*Lonely One-Child Families*	*Only Multi-Child Families*
Co-residence	0.0888 (0.13)	0.0866 (0.31)	0.717 (1.41)	0.151 (0.59)
Other control variables	Y	Y	Y	Y
Fixed effect of province	Y	Y	Y	Y
Sample Size	1,569	7,456	1,570	7,453
R2	0.185	0.132	0.183	0.131
Stage I Regression				
Community average Attitude Towards Co-residence 1	0.133** (0.06)	0.104** (0.05)	0.135** (0.06)	0.102** (0.05)
Community average Attitude Towards Co-residence 2	0.174* (0.10)	0.620*** (0.10)	0.172* (0.10)	0.612*** (0.10)
Other control variables	Y	Y	Y	Y
Fixed effect of province	Y	Y	Y	Y
Size of observed samples	1,569	7,456	1,570	7,453
R2	0.146	0.199	0.145	0.199
Overidentification test				
Sargan statistics	0.044	0.024	0.002	0.008
P value	0.833	0.876	0.964	0.930
Basmann statistics	0.043	0.024	0.002	0.008
P value	0.835	0.876	0.964	0.930

children). However, the problem of endogeneity arises, if parents' attitude is adopted as the instrumental variable for co-residence. Many parent characteristics and family characteristics jointly determine parents' attitude towards and final choice of co-residence. Therefore, this section also uses the general attitude which the other families of the local community hold towards co-residence. To some extent, parents' choice of co-residence is affected by the attitude of other elderly people in the community, but such attitude has no direct effect on the happiness or loneliness of elderly people.

Stage I regression shows that parents' attitude is statistically significantly correlated with co-residence, and there is no such question called weak instrumental variables. Overidentification test also verifies the exogeneity of the instrumental variables. Table 9.13 shows the results re-estimated by the instrumental variable method. It can be seen that co-residence does not affect happiness in either one-child or multi-child families. When parents' loneliness is taken as a subjective well-being metric for analysis in Stage I regression, the results also show that it has no effect on co-residence. Because instrumental variables can better deal with the endogenous problem of co-residence, the conclusion reached here is more credible.

9.7 Brief Summary and Discussion of Macro Significance

This study has found that one-child families are more inclined to adopt the co-residence model of old-age care than multi-child families. We have compared the two to identify the motives behind co-residence, and discover that the theories of self-interested life cycle and social customs can explain the phenomenon of co-residence in China. Because it does not increase or reduce the well-being of elderly people, co-residence at least provides a good choice for old-age care. As the number of onlies increases, when they become old and require care from others, family miniaturization may slow down, thus affecting all dimensions of the economy.

Part III

Discussion of Issues Related to the Labour Market

This part focuses on issues related to employment and income in the labour market, with special attention to relevant management systems. Covering a wide range of aspects, this part is a collection of the author's discussions on various topics about the labour market, including market segmentation in the public sector, gender wage differentials, minimum wage and other hot issues.

Institutional factors have long played a certain role in the segmentation of China's labour market. In Chapter 10, the author uses data from China Family Panel Studies to examine the effect of working in the establishment on pay level, and finds that the overall income advantages of working in the establishment have been weakened, with a reduced number of labourers enjoying the premiums. Nevertheless, working in the establishment is still attractive to low-income labourers. This shows that there has been improvement in China's labour market segmentation, with market-oriented driving forces gaining steam.

In Chapter 11, the author looks at the issue of gender wage differentials between men and women. Based on existing academic research on traditional ideas and gender discrimination, the author further discusses the physiological characteristics, risk preferences, professional choices, as well as comparative advantages-induced output differentials of men and women, which provides new evidence for explaining gender wage differentials.

After analysing the gaps in return to labour arising from institutional and gender differences, the author goes on to discuss two policy effects on income gap from a more macro perspective in Chapter 12, so as to understand the causes of various income gaps in the labour market and the possible solutions to them.

DOI: 10.4324/9781003288091-12

10 Institutional Premiums in the Labour Market

10.1 Introduction

One basic conclusion of economics is that the market provides the most efficient way of labour resources allocation. However, during the period from 1949 to the reform and opening up, labour in China was mainly allocated through administrative means. Since the market-oriented reform began, a labour market has gradually taken shape in China. Labourers have much more freedom to choose and change jobs. Through wage adjustment, the market has started to regulate the allocation of labour resources. With the emergence of labour shortage, labourers have become more and more dependent on the market for job changes, which has promoted balanced pay in different sectors for labourers with the same background. Zhang Yibo (2012) divides the development of China's labour market into the following two stages: Stage 1, which was the period from the 1970s to the late 1990s. During this period, market capacity was gradually released, and returns on human capital from the market were gradually rationalized, and returns on labour capital from the market in non-public sectors rose substantially, offering income advantages; and Stage 2, which was the period from the mid- and later-1990s to the present. During this period, market competition has intensified, the government has been playing an increasingly important role in the market, and the public sector has gradually started to show its advantages. China's development history shows that labour market improvement inevitably faces multiple institutional obstacles. Under the framework of a socialist market economy, the state still retains a certain power to dominate the market, and China's labour market is still subject to the control of non-market forces. As the state has been stepping up economic regulation after the 2008 financial crisis, some have expressed the view that the public sector has advanced at the expense of the retreat of the private sector. Therefore, there is extra value in empirically testing the progress of China's labour market.

As far as the basic theory goes, in a fully developed labour market, individuals with the same human capital should have similar pay levels in different sectors. This means that inter-sectoral premiums can reflect the

DOI: 10.4324/9781003288091-13

degree of labour marketization. Because transitional economies have their special stages of development, the premiums between the state-owned and non-state-owned sectors often receive extra attention.

In China's transition from a planned into a market economy, the Chinese economy has been developing very fast. However, incomplete reform has inevitably led to the co-existence of two economic systems. Since the reform began, the within-establishment labour market and the outside-establishment labour market have long existed side by side. This dual labour market structure is not conducive to the efficient allocation of resources, while causing income distribution problems. This is because jobs inside the establishment often bring higher incomes than jobs in the competitive market. In recent years, state-owned enterprises have become college graduates' preferred employers, and there is a fever for college graduates to taking the national civil servant examination. To some extent, it shows that there are differences in returns from labour between the market inside the establishment and the market outside the establishment, and such differences actually guide the flow of labourers. In the Work Report to the 18th National Congress of the Communist Party of China, a call was made for

> unswervingly encouraging, supporting and guiding the development of the non-public sectors of the economy, ensuring that economies of all ownership types can access and use production elements equally according to law, participate in market competition fairly and receive equal protection of the law.

The current government policy encourages the full leveraging of the market in deepening economic reform and reducing income premiums in the establishment. Since 2003, China has continuously deepened its market economic reform. Changes in labour marketization and the achievements of economic system reform need to be tested by empirical analysis. Today, it is clear that public sector reform in China has achieved certain results, with more transparent management in place and rent-seeking behaviour under control from the source. According to a survey conducted by the Social Survey Center of China Youth Daily, 80% of the respondents believe that the advantages of working in the establishment have been weakened.[1] Though a large number of labourers still work in the establishment and taking the national civil servant examination remains popular with many people despite an extremely low recruitment rate, these phenomena may not necessarily prove that working in the establishment still has a greater advantage in terms of income. They may only reflect people's job choice, attitude towards risks and other considerations. By analysing the level of premiums of working in the establishment, it can be concluded that the degree of labour market segmentation is the key to objectively evaluating China's labour marketization process. At the same time, the income advantage may not necessarily be the main reason for the continuous popularity of working in the establishment or the chief source of premiums offered by the establishment. By analysing the level of premiums of working in the establishment and judging whether there are still advantages of working in the establishment, we can reveal the degree of labour market segmentation, which is the key to objectively evaluating China's *Labour* marketization process. By examining the issue of invisible welfare associated with working in the establishment, we will be able to find a supplementary explanation of the above phenomena.

This study is mainly concerned about the issue of wage differentials arising from the different ownership types of organizations where people work. This can be linked to the theory of labour market segmentation. In 1971, Doeringe and Piore put forward the theory of labour market segmentation, dividing the labour market into a primary labour market and a secondary labour market.[2] In the primary labour market, because of the high entry threshold and the low substitutability of each labourer, competition is not fierce. The wages of labourers are generally high and often affected by non-market factors, and employment is relatively stable. In the secondary labour market, because of the relatively low entry threshold and high labourer homogeneity, competition is fierce. As a result, the pay level is relatively low and often determined by marginal labour productivity, and employment is unstable.

Fields (2007) defines labour market segmentation in two dimensions: labourers with the same productivity earn different wages in different sectors, and jobs in high-paying sectors are scarce. In reality, the division between the public and private sectors meets these two criteria. Internationally, there are many studies comparing the wages of social servants with those of ordinary workers. Krueger (1988), for example, finds that federal employees in the United States are paid over 10% more than private sector workers. Mueller (1998) draws a similar conclusion from his analysis of the Canadian situation. Heitmueller (2006) discovers that women receive higher premiums from the public sector. Pedersen et al. (1990) find that people working in the public sector in Denmark receive less income than those in non-public sectors. As for transitional economies, Adamchik and Bedi (2000) reveal that the private sector in Poland enjoyed income advantages in 1996. In two surveys conducted in Vietnam, Bales and Rama (2001) find that state-owned enterprises pay employees over 20% more than private enterprises. In addition, Smith (1976), Gyourko and Tracy (1988), Birch (2006) and Cai and Liu (2011) have respectively discussed wage differentials between the public and the private sectors in the United States and Canada, adopting such methods as income decomposition, employer selectivity and quantile estimation. Generally speaking, wage premiums exist in the public sector by varying degrees worldwide, but it is uncertain whether such premiums are positive or negative.

There have also been some studies on employment income differentials between the state-owned and the private sectors in China. It is generally believed that the pay level within the establishment in China is largely affected by non-market factors, while the market is the main mechanism determining the pay level in sectors outside the establishment (Meng, 2000). With the deepening of China's economic system reform and the continuous development of the market economy, the market mechanism will play an increasingly more important role in wage-related decisions. Theoretically speaking, the ownership structure-induced segmentation of China's labour market should be weakened. This inference is true as far as the number of employees is concerned. Recent years have seen a substantial fall in the state-owned sector's share of the total employment in society. However, the pay level in the public sector is not necessarily low, because increased fiscal support may provide high pays for the relatively small number of people employed in the state-owned system. The phenomenon that the average pay level in the establishment is significantly higher than that outside the establishment has attracted the attention of the academic circles. Some scholars have carried out quantitative analysis on this phenomenon. Using the urban survey data of 1988, 1995 and 2002, Deng and Li (2009) have examined factors affecting the income gap in China and the changes in the degree of impact of each factor. They find that the type of employer ownership has a growing influence on the income gap. Adopting the survey data of Wuhan, Shanghai and Xi'an in 1999, Xie and Wu (2008) have looked at the influence of employment sectors on the income of urban residents in China, showing that employment sectors play a decisive role in determining the income of urban residents. Before the economic reform, people working in those sectors closely related to the central planning establishment could get good incomes. After the reform, however, those sectors enjoying more freedom from planning have a bigger influence on income. Using CHNS data, Yin Zhichao and Gan Li (2009) find that from 1989 to 1997 jobs outside the establishment had obvious advantages over those in the establishment, but working in the establishment started to show its advantage during the period from 2000 to 2009. In his cross-sectional quantile regression study using CHNS data, Zhang Yibo (2012) points out that before 2000, working outside the establishment had advantages in earning high incomes, but the trend was not obvious after 2000. Based on the cross-sectional data from CGSS, Sun Wenkai et al. (2016) reveal a notable fall in the premiums of working in the establishment in China, but significant premium differences remain at different quantile income levels.

There are also systematic differences in the quality of labourers between inside and outside the establishment. These are reflected in the differences in human resource endowment and personal characteristics such as gender, age, marital status, political affiliation, years of employment and level of education. When recruiting employees, different sectors show selectivity with regards to gender and level of education (Wang Meiyan, 2005a, 2005b). Labour market differences not only affect the pay level directly, but also the marginal effect of human capital factors on wages, thus indirectly leading to wage differentials. In different sectors, micro determinants of income such as returns on education are also different (Xing Chunbing, 2005). In the state-owned sector, working experience has a bigger influence on the pay level than in non-state-owned sectors. In non-state-owned sectors, education has a greater impact on pay (Zhang Chewei and Xue Xinxin, 2008). In this study, wage income is taken as the explained variable. For this reason, in addition to the factors mentioned above, other factors affecting the payment level as studied in existing literature will also be controlled as far as possible.

Compared with existing studies, this study makes two main contributions. First, most existing studies are concerned with issues of the early period. With the progress of the market economy, the continuous reform of the state-owned sector and the development of the private sector in recent years, the cross-sector flow of labourers may induce further significant changes in the level of premiums in the establishment. This study has also found a clear weakening of institutional premiums, which can reflect the evolution of labour marketization. Second, the method and data of this study both represent a significant improvement on those of existing studies. We use the large sample tracking data of China Family Panel Studies (CFPS), which can track the work situation of the same individual in different periods of time, thus making it possible to observe differences in income changes between those who join the establishment and those who remain to work outside the establishment. The problem of missing variables can be better solved by using the individual fixed effect model and the panel data quantile method. This enables better estimates of the influence of working in the establishment on pay level. In addition, we combine the matching and difference-in-differences methods to reduce the influence of individual heterogeneity and selectivity on regression results. This is also an improvement on the methods adopted in the existing literature to study this problem.

10.2 Method and Data

10.2.1 Quantitative Analysis Methods Involved in the Research

This study mainly examines the issue of wage differentials between inside and outside the establishment. What we are concerned about is whether working in the establishment in China today affects pay level. Because wages are related to not only the nature of employment, but also other observable or non-observable factors such as the economic environment and human capital elements, and wages also change over time, simply comparing the wage differentials between inside and outside the establishment, or before and after joining the establishment is not enough to unravel the influence of employer ownership type on wages. To distinguish the different factors that affect changes in pay, including changes in human capital elements, changes in time and entry into the establishment for employment, this study adopts difference in differences (DID) as the basic identification method.

In order to set up a difference-in-differences model, we firstly take the logarithm of personal income *lny* as the explanatory variable and introduce the virtual variable A_{it} to denote the nature of employment of Individual i in Period t, and the variable u_t as a virtual variable to represent the time period. To reflect personal differences between labourers, we introduce x_{it} as a vector variable that can represent the main factors such as marital status, level of education and political affiliation which affect the observable pay level, and the variable γ to represent its coefficient. In the meantime, we also introduce the variable a_i to denote all factors that can be considered as fixed effects, including observable but unchanging variables such as gender, place of birth, parents' level of education and parents' political affiliation, as well as all influencing variables that are difficult to observe. For Individual I of Period t, our quantitative model is expressed as follows:

$$lny_{it} = \beta_0 + \beta_1 A_{it} + +x_{it}\gamma + u_t + a_i + \varepsilon_{it} \tag{10.1}$$

In the regression, what we are concerned about is whether joining the establishment for employment will have an additional influence on pay level, namely the wage differential β_1 induced by the nature of employment after the exclusion of time, individual differences and other influencing factors. If $\beta_1 > 0$, it indicates that the same individual will get an increased pay after joining the establishment. Otherwise, if $\beta_1 < 0$, it means that working in the establishment will lower the pay level. If $\beta_1 = 0$, it implies that the establishment has no effect on pay, or there are no institutional premiums. The estimation method of Equation (10.1) is similar to the traditional method of difference-in-differences in the form of cross terms.

To avoid excessive dependence on the linear form of the equation and obtain more comparable internal and external samples, this study adopts a method that combines propensity score matching and difference-in-differences (PSM-DID) to re-evaluate institutional premiums.

The decomposition method is another way to reflect whether the establishment has a premium effect on income. This study adopts the Oaxaca-Blinder decomposition method and divides labourers into two groups: those inside the establishment, and those outside the establishment. Their wage differentials are also divided into two parts: the first part consists of the explainable part brought by differences in personal characteristics and endowment, including political affiliation, marital status and level of education, while the second part is the unexplainable part, which mainly reflects the influence of non-market factors on pay level and is manifested as differences in the pre-endowment coefficients of different groups. The income equations for labourers inside and outside the establishment are respectively as follows:

$$\ln \omega_u = X_u \beta_u + \mu_{ui} \tag{10.2}$$

$$\ln \omega_n = X_n\beta_n + \mu_{ni} \tag{10.3}$$

Wherein: ω_u and ω_n respectively represent the annual incomes of labourers inside the establishment and labourers outside the establishment; X_u and X_n respectively represent the human capital endowment vectors of labourers inside the establishment and labourers outside the establishment; β_u and β_n respectively represent their coefficient vectors; and μ_{ui} and μ_{ni} represent residuals.

After taking the mean value, Equation (10.2) is reduced to Equation (10.3), and the wage differentials between labourers inside and outside the establishment can be expressed as: $\ln \omega_u - \ln \omega_n = X_u\beta_u - X_n\beta_n$ To measure wage premiums, we divide the equation into three parts: $\ln \omega_u - \ln \omega_n = (X_u - X_n)\beta_n + (\beta_u - \beta_n)X_n + (\beta_u - \beta_n)(X_u - X_n)$, wherein: the first term $(X_u - X_n)\beta_n$ of the equation is the explainable part, which indicates the endowment effect and is used to represent the wage differentials resulting from differences in human capital endowment;[3] and the second and third terms of the equation represent the nonexplainable parts. The second part $(\beta_u - \beta_n)X_n$ is the coefficient effect, which can be attributed to the wage premium effect, and the third part $(\beta_u - \beta_n)(X_u - X_n)$ expresses the interaction effect. The proportion of the second part in the total wage differential reflects the income differential that can be explained by institutional premiums.

In addition, we use the quantile estimation method to estimate the degree of premiums at different income levels in the establishment. Besides the cross-sectional quantile estimation method commonly used in the existing literature, we also adopt the fixed effect quantile estimation method for panel data proposed by Canay (2011) and Powell (2016). Unlike the traditional cross-sectional quantile estimation method put forward by Koenker and Bassett (1978), the method proposed by Canay (2011) is applicable to panel data. Because non-observable fixed effects are controlled, the method can avoid coefficient estimation deviations that may be caused by missing variables in the traditional quantile estimation methods.

10.2.2 Data Source and Description of Variables

The data used in this study are from the CFPS conducted by the China Social Sciences Survey Center (ISSS) of Peking University. To reflect employment incomes more accurately, for the data of 2010, this study uses the sum of the average monthly pay of non-agricultural occupations plus the average monthly floating wage multiplied by 12 to calculate the total annual salary, and add overtime pay, various subsidies and bonuses, year-end bonuses and the cash amount in kind issued by employers to calculate employment incomes. CFPS also collects statistics on other incomes and additional economic allowances and subsidies obtained from outside labourers' main occupations. However, because these incomes are not related to the main occupations, they are not included in the employment incomes. For the data of 2012, we use the annual incomes which non-farm full-time labourers obtained from their primary occupations, and include all work-related bonuses and benefits. This treatment ensures good data comparability between 2010 and 2012.

In the empirical analysis, the main variable of concern to us is the type of ownership of organizations (employers) which labourers work for. In the CFPS survey, employers are divided into 14 major types, including government departments, party and government organs. Employers in the establishment include government departments/Party and government organs/people's organizations/the army, state-/collective-owned institutions/institutes/research institutes, as well as state-owned enterprises/state-owned holding enterprises. Employers outside the establishment include collective enterprises, joint-stock system cooperative enterprises, joint ventures, limited liability companies/joint-stock system companies, enterprises invested by Hong Kong/Macao/Taiwan residents, foreign-invested enterprises, individual businesses, private non-enterprise organizations, associations/associations/industry guilds/foundations and other social organizations, as well as community neighbourhood committees/village administrative committees and other autonomous organizations.

To eliminate the influence of other factors on pay level, it is necessary to add the time variable in order to remove the overall trend of wage changes. Besides, we also need to exclude other factors such as age, marital status, political affiliation, type of Hukou, level of education and province of residence that may cause wage changes in addition to time. For those factors like gender and parents' level of education, political affiliation and type of employer ownership that hardly change over time, we use fixed effect items to exclude the influence of these factors on pay level. The detailed variable definitions are given in Table 10.1.

We firstly screen the data and keep those samples with complete data, processed the abnormal values and removed those samples without employment and income, samples with low incomes and samples with too big income changes during the two years.[4] After screening, 14,730 qualified samples were obtained, including 6,609 samples from 2010 and 8,121 from 2012; and 4,037 samples from the establishment and 10,693 samples from outside the establishment. The descriptive statistics of the samples are shown in Tables 10.2 and 10.3.

From the descriptive statistics, we can see that for both 2010 and 2012 the pay level in the establishment was obviously higher than that outside the establishment in 2010 and 2012: 18% higher in 2010; and 20% higher in 2012. Meanwhile, from 2010 to 2012, labourers outside the establishment only had a pay rise of 4%, while those in the establishment saw their pay rising by 6%. In other words, employment income in the establishment grew faster than outside the establishment.

We can also see that labourers in the establishment have a slightly higher average age than labourers outside the establishment, but gender distribution

Table 10.1 Explanatory Notes on Variable Definitions

Main Variables	*Notes*
Logarithm of annual employment income (lny)	
Gender	1 = male; 0 = female
Age	
Type of organization ownership	1 = inside the establishment; 0 = outside the establishment
Time variable	1 = 2012; 0 = 2010
Marital status	1 = married; 0 = unmarried
Political affiliation	1 = Party member; 0 = non-party member
Type of hukou	1 = urban; 0 = rural
Level of education	Five levels are divided: no formal education, primary school, junior high school, high school and technical school, junior technical college, undergraduate and above
Province of residence	It involves a total of 25 provinces, autonomous regions and municipalities directly under the central government, including Anhui, Fujian, Gansu, Guangdong, Guizhou, Hebei, Henan, Heilongjiang, Hubei, Hunan, Jilin, Jiangsu, Jiangxi, Liaoning, Shandong, Shanxi, Shaanxi, Sichuan, Yunnan, Zhejiang, Guangxi Zhuang Autonomous Region, Beijing, Tianjin and Shanghai.

Table 10.2 Descriptive Statistics of Main Quantitative Variables

Quantitative Variable			*Sample Size*	*Mean*	*Standard Deviation*	*Max*	*Min*
Logarithm of average annual employment income	2010	Outside the Establishment	4,572	9.92	0.60	12.61	7.09
		Inside the Establishment	2,037	10.10	0.57	12.61	7.17
	2012	Outside the Establishment	6,162	9.96	0.40	12.61	6.91
		Inside the Establishment	2,000	10.16	0.36	12.47	6.91
Age	2010	Outside the Establishment	4,572	37.4	10.23	75	16
		Inside the Establishment	2,037	39.8	10.83	72	16
	2012	Outside the Establishment	6,162	37.4	11.69	78	16
		Inside the Establishment	2,000	40.1	11.03	75	17

Table 10.3 Descriptive Statistics of Main Dummy Variables

Main Variable		*2010*		*2012*	
		Outside the Establishment	*Inside the Establishment*	*Outside the Establishment*	*Inside the Establishment*
Gender		0.63(0.48)	0.64(0.48)	0.65(0.48)	0.64(0.48)
Marital status		0.81(0.39)	0.86(0.35)	0.80(0.4)	0.84(0.45)
Political affiliation		0.07(0.24)	0.28(0.45)	0.06(0.24)	0.28(0.45)
Type of Hukou		0.39(0.49)	0.82(0.38)	0.31(0.46)	0.74(0.43)
Level of education	No formal education	7.85%	2.30%	11.17%	4.99%
	Primary school	16.90%	4.55%	22.24%	7.13%
	Junior high school	40.79%	21.11%	36.29%	19.24%
	High school and technical school	20.55%	26.69%	18.53%	26.42%
	Junior technical college, undergraduate and above	13.92%	43.35%	11.66%	42.22%
Region of residence	Eastern China	62.62%	47.21%	52.02%	47.96%
	Western China	24.22%	35.50%	29.84%	32.45%
	Central	13.16%	17.29%	18.14%	19.59%
Sample size		4,572	2,037	6,121	2,000

Note: Figures in brackets are the standard deviations of data.

is similar between them, though there is a higher proportion of males than females among labourers in the establishment. In addition, there are relatively big differences between labourers inside and outside the establishment in terms of level of education, type of Hukou, and political affiliation. The labour force in the establishment has a visibly higher proportion of Party members than that outside the establishment. Less than 10% of labourers outside the establishment are Party members, compared to almost 30% in the establishment. This is consistent with China's national conditions. Besides, a higher proportion of those who work in the establishment hold an urban Hukou, which also conforms to the real situation. We can also see that labourers in the establishment have a higher level of education than those outside the establishment. In particular, there is a clear gap in the proportion of those receiving higher education between the two. Most labourers outside the establishment receive junior high school or high school education, while nearly half of the labour force in the establishment has higher education. However, from 2020 to 2012, the labour endowments of those worked inside and outside the establishment did not change much.

10.3 Estimated Results

10.3.1 Basic Results

The OLS regression results in Table 10.4 show that after the other factors are controlled, the type of employer ownership has a significant positive effect on labourers' income level. According to the regression coefficients of the other independent variables, the level of education is the primary factor affecting pay level. Marriage, political affiliation, type of Hukou and region of residence also affect pay level, and the results are significant, but their impacts are relatively small compared with that of the level of education. The coefficients of primary school education, junior high school education, high school education and junior technical college, undergraduate and education above were 0.0802, 0.145, 0.254 and 0.558, respectively, which indicates that pay level rises with the level of education.

Using the panel data method, we subsequently confirm the existence of the individual effect. Through Hausman test, we confirm that the fixed effect model should be used. Column (1) of Table 10.4 shows the basic fixed effect regression results, and Column (2) presents the regression results after the main variables affecting pay level are controlled. Because the data used in the regressions of Columns (1) and (2) are unbalanced panel data, which may affect the effectiveness of the fixed-effect model, we obtain complete tracking data for 3,094 individuals after further screening. Column (3) reports on the regression results of the samples of those tracked individuals who did not work in the establishment for the whole duration of the two years, and Column (4) reports on the regression results after the variables are controlled on the conditions of Column (3).

Table 10.4 Explained Variable: Logarithm of Annual Employment Income

		OLS Regression	*Fixed Effect Panel Model: Difference-in-Differences Estimation*			
		Results	*Results (1)*	*Results (2)*	*Results (3)*	*Results (4)*
Type of employer ownership		0.0234**	0.0181	0.0239	0.00313	0.00404
		(0.0109)	(0.0225)	(0.0224)	(0.0239)	(0.0239)
Fixed effect of time		0.115***	0.203***	0.200***	0.202***	0.349***
		(0.00854)	(0.00741)	(0.0486)	(0.00788)	(0.0329)
Age		0.0304***		0.0899***		omitted
		(0.00273)		(0.0280)		
Square of age		−0.000456***		−0.00112***		omitted
		(3.32e−05)		(0.000188)		
Gender		0.299***		0.256**		omitted
		(0.00897)		(0.125)		
Marital status		0.0735***		−0.0316		−0.00764
		(0.0133)		(0.0332)		(0.0358)
Political affiliation		0.119***		0.0167		−0.00507
		(0.0142)		(0.0389)		(0.0405)
Type of Hukou		0.0167		0.0229		0.0266
		(0.0109)		(0.0335)		(0.0453)
Level of education	Primary school Junior middle school	0.0763***		0.00599		−0.0342
		(0.0183)		(0.0457)		(0.0912)
	High school & technical school	0.138***		−0.00739		−0.00104
		(0.0171)		(0.0520)		(0.101)
	Primary school Junior middle school	0.250***		0.0612		0.111
		(0.0187)		(0.0611)		(0.111)
	High school & technical school	0.544***		0.0770		0.181

	(0.0205)		(0.0727)		(0.123)
Province of residence	Controlled		Controlled		Controlled
Sample size	14,730	14,730	14,730	6,188	6,188
R-square	0.269	0.180	0.191	0.176	0.185

Note: For the 'fixed effect model', the individual fixed effects are controlled. For regressions in Columns (2) and (4), age, gender, marital status, political affiliation, level of educational and province of residence are controlled. Figures inside and outside brackets are respectively the model regression results and their robust standard deviations. t test is adopted for the *p* value. *, ** and ***, respectively represent significance at 10%, 5% and 1% levels (the same in the tables below, and no separate notes will be given).

The regression results of the fixed effect model show that the pay level of those who joined the establishment for employment in 2012 was not significantly affected when compared with that of those working outside the establishment. Moreover, the regression results remain almost consistent after control variables are added. It shows that the fixed effect model can well eliminate the influence of non-observable personal effects on pay level, and get consistent estimates of the effect of employment type on pay level. Moreover, after we remove some non-tracked samples with unchanged jobs, the regression results remain consistent. Therefore, it can be preliminarily concluded that taking up employment in the establishment in recent years brings no significant pay premiums.

10.3.2 Heterogeneity Analysis

From the descriptive statistics above, we can find that the *Labour* force in the establishment has a higher proportion of Party members, urban residents and those with higher education than the labour force outside the establishment. In order to study whether changes in employment affect pay levels differently for different labourer groups, we further divide labourers for regression analysis. The results of classified regression are shown in Table 10.5.

From the regression results, we can easily see that while Table 10.4 shows that working in the establishment does not significantly affect pay level, it does have a certain influence on the pay level of some groups. It is worth noting that labourers with a low level of education and rural labourers are groups which can get higher pay by joining the establishment, though they only make up a small proportion of the labour force in the establishment.

Specifically, the regression results show that gender and political status generally do not affect the pay level of labourers in the establishment. In addition, as their level of education increases, there is a gradually rising proportion of people to join the establishment for employment. However, the positive impact of such employment on wages is diminishing. The wage differentials mainly exist among groups with primary school education. For labourers with a high level of education, the human capital endowment actually plays a more important role in determining their pay level. For them, working in the establishment does offer advantages in pay. Similarly, while the proportion of rural labourers in the establishment is much lower than that of urban labourers, working in the establishment nevertheless significantly affects rural labourers' pay level, bringing them a 7% increase in pay. For urban labourers, however, working in the establishment does not significantly affect their pay.

In other words, labourers with more human resource endowments have clear differentiations, which put them in a relatively favourable position in the labour market. Joining the establishment for employment cannot bring them obvious wage premiums. However, labourers with fewer human

Table 10.5 Regression Results by Type of Labourers (Only Organization Ownership Coefficients Reported)

Classification		*Proportion of Labourers Working in the Establishment*	*Explained Variable: Logarithm of Annual Employment Income Organization Ownership Type*	*Sample Size*	*R-square*
Gender	Male	27.3%	0.0134(0.0305)	9,448	0.153
	Female	27.7%	0.0283(0.0324)	5,282	0.236
Level of Education	No formal education	12.35%	−0.00990(0.0894)	1,185	0.146
	Primary school	9.92%	0.179^{*}(0.0932)	2,377	0.157
	Junior middle school	16.65%	0.0441(0.0423)	4,905	0.168
	High school & technical school	34.13%	0.0287(0.0454)	3,149	0.244
	Junior technical college, undergraduate and above	56.75%	−0.0611(0.0484)	3,114	0.157
Political Affiliation	Party member	62.71%	−0.0866(0.0570)	1,776	0.172
	Non-Party member	22.59%	0.0252(0.0251)	12,954	0.179
Type of Hukou	Urban	34.19%	0.00506(0.0275)	6,831	0.198
	Rural	15.35%	0.0662^{***}(0.00742)	7,899	0.151

Note: Figures inside and outside brackets are respectively the model regression results and their robust standard deviations. t test is adopted for the *p* value.

resource endowments are highly mobile and replaceable, and face fierce competition in the labour market. For them, working in the establishment can bring certain wage premiums. Similarly, urban labourers have a plenty of employment opportunities and big room for promotions. As a result, joining the establishment will not have a big influence on their pay level. By contrast, rural labourers face more employment difficulties, and joining the establishment for employment will give them significant wage premiums. At the same time, we can also find that the proportion of such labourers who can get wage premiums in the establishment but actually join the establishment is significantly lower than that of other labourer groups, which shows that it is more difficult for the former to enter the establishment. This is consistent with the definition of labour market segmentation on two dimensions by Fields (2007).

Region-wise, we can find that the premiums which can be brought by working in the establishment also vary slightly from region to region. From the results of the classified regression of the three major regions defined by the National Bureau of Statistics, there are relatively significant wage premiums from working in the establishment in central China, while there are no such clear premiums in eastern or western China.

In order to determine the level of wage premiums from employers of different systems, we divide employers into two categories: 'government' employers which include 'government departments/Party and government organs/people's organisations/the army', with a total of 962 samples; and 'state-owned enterprise' employers which include 'state-owned enterprises/state-owned holding enterprises' and 'state-/collectively-owned institutions/institutes/research institutes', with a total of 3,075 samples. The employer-based regression results are shown in Table 10.6. It can be seen that working in government organs or state-owned enterprises only has a very limited influence on pay level when compared with working in enterprises outside

Table 10.6 Regression Results by Type of Organization

Type	*Explained Variable: Logarithm of Annual Employment Income Type of Organization Ownership*	*Sample Size*	*R-square*
Government departments and enterprises inside the establishment	0.0284(0.0511)	11,655	0.166
State-owned enterprises and enterprises outside the establishment	0.0152(0.0255)	13,768	0.183

Note: Figures inside and outside brackets are respectively the model regression results and their robust standard deviations. t test is adopted for the *p* value.

the establishment. It shows that working in all major categories of employers in the establishment does not offer significant income advantages than working outside the establishment.

10.3.3 Robustness Analysis

We use two methods for robustness analysis: one is the now increasingly used PSM-DID method, and the other is the commonly used Oaxaca decomposition method.

The PSM-DID method requires the use of balanced panels. We use the control and treatment group generation method mentioned earlier, namely taking those who did not work in the establishment in 2020 but worked in the establishment in 2012 as the treatment group, and those who did not work in the establishment in 2020 and 2012 as the control group. The PSM-DID method can overcome the problem that some data are difficult to observe and collect data, and match and compare samples in the form of semi-parameters. To some extent, it can also solve the sample selectivity problem. Only publicly supported samples are compared and analysed.

The treatment group (i.e. labourers who joined the establishment for work from outside the establishment in 2010) analysed using the PSM-DID method has a sample size of 174, while the control group (i.e. labourers who remained outside the establishment all the time) had a sample size of 1,735. We firstly employ the logit model to estimate the propensity scores, and then use the independent variables of 2012 to analyse the probability of labourers joining the establishment in 2012. The regression results show that the main factors affecting labourers' choice whether to work in the establishment are the type of Hukou and level of education. The type-of-Hukou regression coefficient is positive and significant, which indicates that labourers with an urban Hukou are more likely to join and work in the establishment than rural Hukou holders. At the same time, low levels of education (i.e. primary school education and junior high school education), result in negative regression coefficients. Rural labourers and labourers with primary school education can significantly raise their pay level when they join and work in the establishment, but it is more difficult for them to join the establishment. Only a few of them are able to enjoy the income advantages of working in the establishment. It shows that after the reform, fewer workers can enjoy wage premiums, and it becomes more difficult to join the establishment.

To obtain reliable estimates, we test the balance of the matching covariates to see whether there are no any statistically significant differences in each explanatory variable between the treatment group and the control group. The differential incomes are estimated by applying kernel matching and other methods to the propensity results, and the results are shown in Table 10.7.

The average treatment effect (ATT) results of the matched difference-in-differences are positive, but not significant, and the results of the various

Table 10.7 Estimated Results from Combination of Propensity Score Matching and Difference-in-Differences

Matching Method	*n.Treat*	*n.Contr*	*ATT*	*Std.Err.*	*t*
Kernel matching k; norm; bw; 0.05	174	1,735	0.0126	0.0380	0.33
Minimum radius matching (0.01)	174	1,735	0.0213	0.0390	0.55
Local linear regression matching	174	1,735	0.0178	0.0472	0.38
Nearest neighbour matching	174	1,735	−0.0507	0.0472	−1.07

Table 10.8 Decomposition Results of Wage Differentials

Item	*Sample Size*	*Logarithm of Annual Income*
Labourers in the establishment	4,037	10.133***(0.009)
Labourers outside the establishment	10,693	9.945***(0.006)
Annual income logarithmic differentials	—	0.188***(0.011)
Endowment effect	—	0.192***(0.008)
Coefficient effect	—	0.011(0.013)
Cross effect	—	−0.015(0.011)

Note: Z test is adopted as the significance test for the endowment, coefficient, cross and individual variable effects. The endowment effect is the sum of the endowment effects of all individual variables, the coefficient effect is the sum of the coefficient effects of all individual variables and the cross effect is the sum of the cross effects of all individual variables.

matching methods are the same. The results confirm the conclusion of the regression analysis above: when the same individual in China joins the establishment for employment, such employment cannot, on average, bring about a significant rise in pay level. This shows that the results above are reliable.

10.3.4 Decomposition of Wage Differentials between Inside and Outside the Establishment

Another perspective is to adopt the decomposition method to analyse the respective contributions of the endowment factor and the institutional factor to wage differentials, and examine whether the establishment is an important cause of income differentials. The approach has been explained above. In the regression, we control variables such as gender, age, marital status, political affiliation, type of Hukou, level of education, province of residence and time and analyse the mixed data of 2010 and 2012. The estimated results are shown in Table 10.8.

We have already found that average pay level in the establishment is higher than that outside the establishment, the human resource endowments of those working in the establishment are also apparently higher than those of people who work outside the establishment. Through regression analysis, we have also discovered that the overall wage differentials between inside and the outside the establishment are not significant. After breaking down the wage differentials, we can further analyse their sources.

As shown in Table 10.8, the wage differentials coefficient between inside and outside the establishment is 0.188, and this result is significant, which indicates that there are indeed significant wage differentials between inside and outside the establishment. The endowment effect has an efficient of 0.192, showing that labourers' personal characteristics can explain most of the wage differentials. At the same time, the coefficient effect has a coefficient of 0.011, but it is not significant, which implies that joining the establishment cannot significantly increase labourers' pay level. The cross effect is not significant either. The regression results show that the wage differentials between inside and outside the establishment almost all come from the differences in labour structure, and working in the establishment or not does not cause pay rises. These regression results can verify the above conclusion.

10.4 Differences in Premium Effects at Different Income Levels

Through the above regression, we can find that the wage premiums brought by the establishment only exist among less competitive labour groups in the labour market, such as labourers with primary school education and rural labourers. These workers are less competitive in the labour market and generally have low incomes. We can further confirm this conclusion through quantile regression. Based on the traditional cross-sectional quantile regression, Canay (2011) has introduced a panel quantile method that accommodates the fixed effect. Powell (2016) has designed corresponding programs. We will use both the cross-sectional and panel quantile estimation methods.

Table 10.9 shows the quantiles estimated using the mixed cross-sectional data method. It is found that as income level rises, the premiums in the establishment gradually fall. When an income level is reached, negative premiums may occur in the establishment. However, when we use the panel quantile regression method to examine the effect of organization ownership type on employment income at 0.1, 0.25, 0.5, 0.75 and 0.9 quantiles, different conclusions can be reached. The results of panel data fixed effect quantile regression show that wage premiums are not significant at most quantiles after the individual fixed effect is controlled. The wage premiums only exist for labourers at the 0.25 quantile point. These labourers are mainly workers with a low level of education and rural workers. Working in the establishment can provide certain security for them, which is mutually verified by the conclusion above that working in the establishment offers high work premiums for labourers with primary school education.

For labourers at other income levels, there is no difference in pay level between working inside and outside the establishment. Labourers at the 0.75 and 0.9 quantile points are mainly urban workers, with junior technical

Table 10.9 Quantile Regression Results

	Explained Variable: Logarithm of Annual Employment Income	
	Panel Quantile Regression	*Cross-Sectional Quantile Regression*
q = 0.1	0.078(0.064)	0.052**(0.018)
q = 0.25	0.096**(0.038)	0.081***(0.016)
q = 0.5	0.074(0.079)	0.036*(0.018)
q = 0.75	0.012(0.045)	0.000(0.018)
q = 0.9	0.078(0.071)	−0.080***(0.018)
Sample size	14.730	

Note: Figures inside and outside brackets are respectively the model regression results and their robust standard deviations. t test is adopted for the *p* value.

college, undergraduate or higher education. Though working inside the establishment cannot increase their pay level, these labourers are still inclined to join the establishment. As the analysis above shows, they are much more likely to join the establishment than other labourer groups, because the establishment has a big demand for them and jobs in the establishment are more stable than those outside, with less risk of unemployment, small pressure of post competition and relatively easy work. Furthermore, working in the establishment carries more invisible welfare than working outside the establishment. Because the labour force in the establishment generally has high qualities, many labourers consider working in the establishment as conducive to developing their careers in the long term, improving their working and leadership abilities and accumulating career resources and contacts. Gould (2007) points out that job choices can be considered as part of labourers' human capital investment. For these workers, a job in the establishment can serve as a good platform for their career development and help them to accumulate human capital. Though the regression results show no existence of wage premiums from working in the establishment, it cannot deny that jobs in the establishment do appeal to labourers. In particular, the long-term impact on wages, as well as some invisible welfare associated with working in the establishment still need further exploration.

10.5 The Issue of Invisible Welfare

The above analysis shows that wage differentials between inside and outside the establishment cannot explain labourers' strong preferences for working in the establishment. It is possible that stable employment and high security in the establishment have attracted a large number of labourers. Therefore, it will be too one-sided if one confines analysis of the employment differentials between inside and outside the establishment only to the salary level. To address this problem, the current study attempts to use satisfaction with life as the explained variable. While controlling other factors that affect satisfaction with life, this study will examine how the type of employment and income affect labourers' satisfaction with life. At the same time, the regression coefficients of the two will be compared to shed light on the scale of invisible welfare associated with working in the establishment.

Again, this section will use the CFPS data of 2010 and 2012 for analysis. Besides income, type of employment, age, marital status, political affiliation, type of Hukou, level of education and other factors mentioned above, the state of health and relative income level in the local region also affect labourers' satisfaction with life. These control variables have already been mentioned in the literature (Chen Shiping and Le Guoan, 2001; Shi Yaojiang and Cui Yu, 2006).

We adopt the panel data fixed effect model for regression analysis, with the fixed effect of individuals and the fixed effect of time being controlled. The regression results are as follows (Table 10.10):

The regression results show that the type-of-employment regression coefficient is positive, which confirms the proposition above that working in the establishment offers some invisible welfare benefits, such as level of stability in life and other welfare subsidies or career development prospects. Another interesting phenomenon is that the relative income level in the local region significantly improves satisfaction with life, which is similar to the conclusions drawn by some studies on the effect of relative income on happiness. By comparing the coefficients of the two variables of working in the establishment and the relative income level in the local region, we can see that working in the establishment can generate a happiness level equivalent to raising the relative income level by 0.3% of a grade (0.0688/0.209) and the state of health by one grade (0.0688/0.0638). In other words, working in the establishment is still attractive in terms of income and some invisible welfare benefits.

Table 10.10 Explained Variable: Satisfaction with Life

Income logarithmic	0.0518	Political affiliation	0.140
	(0.0450)		(0.102)
Organization Ownership Type	0.0688*	Hukou type	0.0863
	(0.0400)		(0.0871)
Fixed effect of time	−0.267**	Level of education	−0.0310
	(0.127)		(0.0446)
Age	0.0583	Relative position in local income	0.209***
	(0.0728)		(0.0196)
Square of age	3.80e−05	State of health	0.0638***
	(0.000494)		(0.0124)
Gender	−0.301	Constant item	−0.0640
	(0.323)		(2.453)
Marital status	0.114	Sample size	14,296
	(0.0866)	R-square	0.056

Note: Figures inside and outside brackets are respectively the model regression results and their robust standard deviations. t test is adopted for the *p* value.

10.6 Summary and Recommendations

The pay gap between inside and outside the establishment affects not only the efficiency of enterprises within the establishment, but also the whole market economy. For enterprises inside the establishment, excessive labour cost and irrational resources allocation make profitability more difficult to achieve. At the same time, the wage differentials between inside and outside the establishment also cause a rent-seeking problem, which will lead to management chaos. For the whole labour market, wage premiums in the establishment will also result in inequality between labourers between inside and outside the establishment, and lead to market segmentation and inefficient social resources distribution.

China has carried out market-oriented reform for many years, and the labour market has also gradually matured. However, all early studies found a pay gap between inside and outside the establishment in the country. From the analysis of this study, we have shown that there are no significant wage premiums in the establishment, and the existing pay gap is mainly a result of the endowment effect of individuals. Labour marketization in China has already made some headways. This is also a refutation of the view that the public sector has advanced at the expense of the private sector in China.

Of course, working in the establishment still provides pay advantages for some groups. Through regression analysis, it is found that the wage differentials between inside and outside the establishment mainly exist among low-income labourers, which chiefly consist of labourers with a low level of education and labourers with a rural Hukou. At the same time, the proportion of these labourers working in the establishment is relatively low, and it is more difficult for them to enter the establishment than other groups. Only a small number of people can enjoy the dividend of working in the establishment. Different methods have all confirmed this phenomenon.

Besides, lack of significant overall wage premiums does not mean that working in the establishment has no appeals to people. In addition to pay, people working in the establishment may have other advantages, such as more stable and relaxed work, more invisible benefits or better long-term career development prospects. The data show that there are more high-quality labourers in the establishment. Various social phenomena show that working in the establishment still has high appeals. We have confirmed this through satisfaction analysis.

To sum up, we have found that the employment income premiums in the establishment have been substantially reduced in recent years, but there is still room for improvement. To improve efficiency in the labour market, we must further enhance the labour market mechanism per se, so that the market can truly play its role, reduce the impact of non-market factors on pay level and make the labour market fairer.

Notes

1 See China Youth Daily, September 14, 2015. The electronic edition can be found at the following website: http://zqb.cyol.com/html/2015-09/14/nw.D110000zgqnb_20150914_1-07.htm. Accessed in April 2016.
2 For the initial theoretical review, please refer to Chapter 9 of Sun Webkai et al., *Labour Economics*.
3 In this study, the results are not affected by the selection of any coefficient set for calculating the endowment effect coefficient.
4 Those samples with an income change of over 10 times from 2010 to 2012 and the abnormal values with an annual basic income of less than RMB1,000 or monthly basic income of less than RMB100 are screened out. Such samples are extremely small, and their removal does not affect the estimation results.

11 Gender Wage Differentials and Policy Discussion

11.1 Gender Wage Differentials and Their Traditional Explanation

In many countries in the world, women are outperformed by men in the job market. For example, men are more accomplished than women in terms of employment rate, pay and career development. Taking the income gap as an example, two American scholars Ichino and Moretti (2009) found that on average female workers in the United States get pays 20% less than their male counterparts, and the gap is about 17% in Europe. Statistical analysis of China's data shows a gender wage differential of approximately 15% in society, which is lower than that in Western countries. This is considered the result of the government's efforts to strive for equality between men and women since the founding of New China. However, gender wage differentials persistently exist and do not change much over time. This study summarizes and discusses the causes of gender income gap, and the conclusions drawn will also be applicable to the explanation of gender differentials in position, employment rate and other labour market metrics.

Most existing academic studies adopt traditional thinking and gender discrimination as the perspectives to explain gender wage differentials (Oh and Lewis, 2011). Women are supposed to pay more attention to the family, thus with less working time and lower income in the labour market. Moreover, women are discriminated against in the job market. Under the same conditions of work content, working hours and personal quality, employers pay women less. This explanation has been widely accepted and popular for a long time.

Discrimination in the job market may also have a certain amplification effect through the expectation effect. The obvious wage differentials between men and women in the job market have a great impact on family decision-making. If women earn less than men at the same level of education, families may invest less in girls' education than in boys' education. This will lead to different productivities between men and women, which further expands the gender income gap in the job market.

The above explanation is unifiedly considered as an explanation based on

DOI: 10.4324/9781003288091-14

gender discrimination in the job market. Whether gender discrimination exists or not and the degree of such discrimination have been studied in numerous academic papers. They are hot academic issues worldwide. When those parts of wage differentials that can be explained by personal characteristics are excluded, the remaining wage differential can be regarded as representing the impact of gender discrimination. Some studies on China argue that discrimination can even account for about 50% of the gender income gap. In other words, nearly half of the income gap between men and women comes from discrimination rather than from rational factors.

Is the judgment reasonable that gender wage differentials mainly derive from discrimination? The answer to this question is related to what policy the government should implement If gender discrimination indeed exists in the job market. If such discrimination is irrational, the government should certainly adopt policies to limit similar behaviours so as to reduce gender wage differentials.

11.2 Non-discrimination-Based Explanations

It is undeniable that discrimination exists in the labour market to some extent. However, the more direct question is this: is there any productivity differential between men and women even if they have similar personal characteristics, such as receiving the same education and doing the same job? If men and women with roughly the same personal characteristics have different productivities, it will not be possible to explain their wage differentials entirely by discrimination, because the pay will definitely be different if the output is different. If employees of different genders have different productivities, enterprises will certainly not give the same pay to them. If men and women have the same productivity, there will be no ground for discrimination against female workers in the job market. Instead, enterprises will proactively employ those female workers with high productivity but discriminated against in other enterprises, and benefit from their employment as a result. The balanced result of competition will be one of no discrimination and pay according to productivity.

The reason why productivity is different when people have roughly the same personal characteristics is that it is very difficult to keep 'all the other characteristics except gender completely the same'. To a great extent, productivity differentials between men and women are a result of the physiological and psychological differences between the two sexes. If there exist other income-affecting and difficult-to-observe factors that affect gender productivity and wage differentials, many of the existing studies on discrimination will be untenable.

To make up for the deficiency of existing research, it is necessary to primarily adopt the perspective of productivity differentials. However, it is difficult to measure differentials in productivity, because we analyse all men and women add with such a large size of the target samples, it is not easy to collect through experiments information on the efficiency differentials between men and women who do the same thing. There is another obvious difficulty: it is also difficult to keep the individual characteristics of men and women in the collected samples basically the same. Even so, in recent years some scholars have made preliminary attempts to solve these problems.

There is some direct medical and physiological evidence to show, for example, that males are physically stronger, with at least greater advantages in doing physical work. Therefore, men may be more productive than women in the low-end labour market, and there will be an income gap between them. This is also one of the reasons for the formation of the traditional thinking that 'The men should plough and the women weave'. Using the large sample micro database of the National Bureau of Statistics, some scholars have found a bigger gender income gap between men and women among low-income groups, and this remains the case when the controllable and observable differences in personal characteristics are controlled.

Besides certain medical evidence, some scholars have used the inherent gender differences between men and women to explain gender income differentials. For example, in a recent study on the absence rate of men and women in the job market, Ichino and Moretti (2009) found that there is a 28-day period of periodic absenteeism among women. They also used the physiological cycle of women to explain such absenteeism difference between men and women. Because of the physiological cycle, women, especially those under 45, are more likely to be absent from work than men. If women are more likely to be absent from work without good reason, employers in the job market will consider this issue beforehand, thereby reducing female employees' wages or employment rate. This will lead to a reasonable income gap between men and women. The researchers found that this physiological cycle factor accounts for one-third of the gender income differentials.

Some scholars have explained the gender income gap from the perspective of combining human capital depreciation with females' physiological characteristics. Human capital depreciation refers to the forgetting of knowledge. Because women are more likely to face employment interruptions (as a result of pregnancy, childbirth, family care, etc.), they face higher human capital depreciation than men in the course of career development. Obviously, human capital differentials can result in income differentials.

Risk tolerance also offers an explanation of gender wage differentials, because different risk tolerances require different income returns. In a recent case study of male and female high school students applying for enrollment into college majors in Turkey, Saygin (2012) found that there are significant differences in attitude towards risk between men and women. The results show that girls are more conservative about estimating their examination scores and tend to apply for majors with a better chance of admission. These majors are either less popular ones or majors with poor employment prospects. Girls also consider whether the colleges that they apply for admission into are close to their home or not, as well as factors not related or negatively related to income. By contrast, boys give more consideration to employment prospects when selecting college majors. If they fail to go to a good college or major, they would rather study for another year in order to get into a college or major with better career prospects. Obviously, risk and return are closely linked in the job market. We have seen that women are more inclined to become civil servants or teachers, while men prefer foreign enterprises or start their own business. This is bound to cause income differentials. In an analysis of survey data from China, a Chinese student reading his PhD at the University of California, Berkeley has also found that Chinese females show risk aversion when they apply for college majors.

From the perspective of family economics, the relative gender income in a family often affects family happiness. Some studies have found that women in the family are more inclined to make them earn less than their husbands. If they earn more than their husbands, women tend to quit their jobs (Bertrand et al., 2012). This phenomenon exists in many developed and developing countries (Medeiros et al., 2007). This explanation adopts the perspective of social identity cognition rather than discrimination.

Part of the gender wage differentials can also be explained by differences in specialization between men and women. A US study finds that females are more inclined to do general and less specialized jobs, while men are more likely to take up more specialized jobs. Specialization often leads to improved efficiency, which obviously helps to explain productivity differentials. All these studies indirectly demonstrate that even if other external conditions seem to be the same, the income gap between men and women may also come from the internal differences of the two genders rather than discrimination.

Recently, one of my colleagues conducted a laboratory experiment to analyse gender-related differences between men and women in their attitude to competition. He set up three experiment stages: at Stage 1, each of the male and female students was put in a cubicle to answer questions of slightly complex mathematical additions. For each correct answer, a reward of RMB5 was offered; at Stage 2, the students were asked to randomly form groups of two, but without knowing who were in their group. In each group, a 'championship type' of method was adopted for question answering. A student got all the rewards if he or she answered more answers correctly than his or her opponent in the group; at Stage 3, each person was given the choice whether to answer questions alone or participate in the 'championship type' of question answering. Each stage lasted three minutes. The results showed no significant difference between the number of correct answers given by female and male students and the average number of victories they scored under the 'championship-type' question-answering mode. In other words, there was no significant difference between male and female students in the first two stages. In the third stage, however, the female students apparently preferred to avoid the competitive championship way of question answering, and all of them basically chose to answer the questions alone, while the male students went the opposite way. This experiment proves the significant difference in attitude between men and women in the face of competition, which may lead to differences in income and position in the job market.

11.3 Research on Productivity Differentials Using Bonus Data

11.3.1 Background

This study uses the year-end bonus data of a Chinese university to study productivity differentials between male and female faculty members. Because university pay in China is relatively low, year-end bonus accounts for a large proportion of faculty members' total income. As a result, one important way for university faculty to increase income is to earn more year-end bonuses. Generally speaking, the year-end bonus consists of three main parts: research bonus, teaching bonus and administrative bonus. Because the year-end bonus is a piecework income, it can reflect the principle of more pay for more work, thus being free of discriminatory factors. The year-end bonus data can therefore well reflect the productivity of faculty members. Giving rewards for high research output is not confined to Chinese universities. In a study of the University of California, O'Keefe and Wang (2012) also discover that faculty members who publish more get higher pay. In their study on China, Heywood et al. (2011) find that research rewards have encouraged university faculty to publish more academic papers.

Apart from being a direct measure of productivity, the use of year-end bonus data for university faculty members also offers the obvious advantage of ensuring that all those faculty members of different genders participating in the study basically have the same conditions. For example, most faculty members are of similar age, basically hold a PhD degree, work in the same profession but with their own specialized research field and even have a similar family background. Another advantage of the data is that we can use specific bonus items to examine whether male and female faculty members have comparative advantages of their own.

There are already some foreign studies that focus on the differences between university faculty in teaching and research. For example, Sheehan and Welch (1996) find that female faculty members have less research output. However, Ramsden (1994) and Teodorescu (2000) find no difference in the number of publications by researchers of different genders. In their study of US university faculty performance, Link et al. (2008) discover that female faculty members devote more time to university service but relatively less time to research.

This study first uses the propensity score matching method to make maximal matching of faculty members by such factors as similar age, identical academic title, similar educational background (returnees from study abroad or home-grown ones, whether holding a PhD), whether having children, etc., and then compares differences in year-end bonus between faculty members with similar factors. In addition, the current study also adopts the Oaxaca-Blinder decomposition method to examine the effects of observable and non-observable characteristics on the time allocation, research and teaching outputs of male and female faculty members. With the use of these methods, we respectively analyse gender-related differences in terms of total bonus, teaching bonus and research bonus.

11.3.2 Data Description

Table 11.1 shows the basic statistical information of the data used in this study. It can be seen that male faculty members received more research bonus but less teaching bonus than female faculty members, and their total bonus was also slightly more than that of female faculty members. With long years of teaching and a low proportion of return from study abroad, male faculty members published more research papers than their female counterparts.

11.3.3 Statistical Analysis Results

Table 11.2 reports on the results obtained using the Oaxaca-Blinder decomposition method. Seen from the decomposition results of the three respective years, there is not much difference in total bonus between male and female faculty members, but the two genders had obvious comparative advantages in research and teaching: male faculty members got notably more research bonus, while female faculty members received apparently more teaching bonus. This is similar to the conclusion reached in the descriptive statistical analysis. The results obtained from the analysis of the mixed data of the three years are also highly consistent.

Table 11.3 shows the results of propensity score matching estimation. It can be seen that for the single yearly data and mixed data, the conclusion is consistent: there is not much difference between male and female faculty members in terms of total bonus, with male faculty members receiving more research bonus and female faculty members getting more teaching bonus. This indicates that the results obtained by the above decomposition method are relatively robust.

There is one problem not considered above: the quality of published papers. Do male faculty members get more research bonus by publishing more low-quality papers? In China, many academic journals, especially the low-quality ones, have some practice of publishing ‘relation contributions’. Because of this concern, we examine the number of papers published at different quality levels. As shown in Table 11.4, the main source of the differences in research output between male and female faculty members lies in their different publications in top-class Chinese journals. These top-class

Table 11.1 Basic Information of Faculty Members

	2010			*2011*			*2012*		
	All	*Female*	*Male*	*All*	*Female*	*Male*	*All*	*Female*	*Male*
Basic bonus	50	50	50	60	60	60	70	70	70
Research bonus	74.06	29.64	90.86	106.08	70.53	120.12	103.55	56.7	122.04
Teaching bonus	184.56	218.13	171.88	188.04	208.52	179.96	201.10	230.01	189.69
Student supervision bonus	49.02	33.21	54.97	62.45	42.53	70.31	47.81	33.33	53.53
Administrative bonus	23.18	23.88	22.92	18.58	21.67	17.36	22.84	26.28	21.48
Total bonus	380.82	354.86	390.64	435.15	403.25	447.75	445.30	416.32	456.73
Number of papers published	–	–	–	3.75	2.13	4.04	–	–	–
Teaching evaluation score	91.54	91.64	91.5	93.59	93.31	93.71	–	–	–
Whether being a teacher returning from study abroad	0.11	0.14	0.1	0.11	0.17	0.09	0.11	0.17	0.09
Years of teaching	25.99	22.64	27.26	25.22	22.1	26.45	24.72	22.10	25.75
Age	48.8	47.04	49.47	48.1	46.43	48.76	47.70	46.43	48.20

Note: The data do not contain teaching evaluation scores for 2012 or the numbers of papers published in 2010 and 2012. The unit of bonus is the number of standardized points.

Table 11.2 Oaxaca-Blinder Decomposition Results

		Male Coefficient Weight			*Female Coefficient Weight*		
		Total Bonus	*Research Bonus*	*Teaching Bonus*	*Total Bonus*	*Research Bonus*	*Teaching Bonus*
2010	Total differential	35.78	61.22***	−46.25**	35.78	61.22***	−46.25**
		(33.21)	(21.58)	(20.99)	(33.21)	(21.58)	(20.99)
	Explained	48.74	5.08	30.52	17.84	18.71	−22.31*
		(41.75)	(21.07)	(30.88)	(32.88)	(28.78)	(16.36)
	Unexplained	−12.96	56.15**	−76.77**	17.94	42.51	−23.94
		(47.26)	(27.73)	(33.39)	(41.22)	(31.01)	(25.77)
2011	Total differential	44.49	49.59	−23.70	44.49	49.59	−23.70
		(52.75)	(46.24)	(21.84)	(52.75)	(46.24)	(21.84)
	Explained	−13.48	−66.71	42.91	45.63	38.286	−12.56
		(80.64)	(67.96)	(35.55)	(46.58)	(42.79)	(15.01)
	Unexplained	57.98	116.29*	−66.61*	−1.13	11.30	−11.13
		(87.97)	(75.10)	(37.78)	(58.83)	(53.34)	(25.42)
2012	Total differential	40.41	65.33	−40.32*	40.41	65.33	−40.32*
		(54.19)	(44.58)	(21.64)	(54.19)	(44.58)	(21.64)
	Explained	−18.67	−55.77	21.51	35.31	23.81	−5.16
		(72.60)	(57.73)	(29.64)	(36.51)	(34.94)	(11.06)
	Unexplained	59.08	121.11*	−61.83*	5.09	41.53	−35.16
		(82.81)	(66.26)	(33.03)	(59.24)	(50.44)	(23.42)
Mixed Data	Total differential	18.13	58.37***	−36.72***	18.13	58.37***	−36.72***
		(23.95)	(20.04)	(10.65)	(23.95)	(20.04)	(10.65)
	Explained	−4.67	−25.52	26.82**	15.46	28.63*	−10.70*
		(29.99)	(23.85)	(14.07)	(18.38)	(16.95)	(6.33)
	Unexplained	22.81	83.90***	−63.55***	2.66	29.73	−26.02**
		(36.63)	(29.34)	(16.28)	(27.07)	(23.32)	(11.95)

Note: Significance levels: *, 10%; **, 5%; and ***, 1%.

Table 11.3 Matching Estimation Results of Propensity Scores

		Total Bonus		*Research*		*Teaching*	
		ATT	*S.E.*	*ATT*	*S.E.*	*ATT*	*S.E.*
2010	(a)	1.35	39.85	69.45**	31.9	−63.88***	24.78
	(b)	5.55	29.61	65.95***	25.31	−54.89**	24.83
	(c)	8.99	22.32	66.35***	20.38	−46.02***	17.86
2011	(a)	38.03	56.72	95.65**	42.44	−42.01	32.44
	(b)	20.6	53	83.62**	33.69	−44.15	31.34
	(c)	19.44	45.25	92.44**	40.39	−48.85**	19.13
2012	(a)	9.74	48.64	73.13**	30.91	−55.48	41.75
	(b)	16.22	43.37	80.02***	29.09	−56.37*	32.41
	(c)	24.74	33.29	75.86***	29.04	−43.05*	23.92
Mixed data	(a)	−0.13	39.63	56.76**	25.7	−52.11**	21.13
	(b)	8.7	33.79	68.35***	21.87	−57.06***	19.84
	(c)	8.87	36.1	77.56***	28.66	−63.76***	16.41

Notes: (a) nearest matching; (b) kernel matching; and (c) hierarchical matching.

Table 11.4 Matching Estimation Results of Published Papers

		ATT	*S.E.*	*t-Statistics*
Total number of papers published	(a)	0.99	1.09	0.91
	(b)	1.14	0.88	1.3
	(c)	1.04	1.08	0.97
Number of SSCI papers published	(a)	0.03	0.11	0.25
	(b)	0.04	0.11	0.34
	(c)	0.06	0.1	0.56
Number of papers published in top-class Chinese journals	(a)	0.40***	0.14	2.83
	(b)	0.38***	0.11	3.44
	(c)	0.41***	0.13	3.26
Number of papers published in other Chinese journals	(a)	0.57	0.88	0.65
	(b)	0.72	0.88	0.81
	(c)	0.58	1.11	0.52

Notes: (a) nearest matching; (b) kernel matching; and (c) hierarchical matching.
Significance levels: *, 10%; **, 5%; and ***, 1%.

journals can generally ensure better paper quality. It is clearer that the different research bonuses between male and female faculty members are a result of the significant differences in the number of papers they publish in top-class Chinese journals.

One further concern about the above analysis results is that because Chinese university teachers basically have an 'iron bow' (meaning a stable and lifelong job), they have little motivation to do research, especially after they get their professorship. At the same time, older faculty members have formed their own habit of research and teaching, which is difficult to change under the new reward system (the bonus system is a new development in recent years). In Table 11.5, we have re-estimated the results for the group with less than 20 years of teaching and the group under the age of 45. Again, we find that male faculty members have relatively more research achievements.

The final concern is whether female faculty members have more time to teach more courses at the expense of teaching quality. Table 11.6 gives the

Table 11.5 Matching Estimation Results of Different Groups

	Teachers Under 45			*Teachers with Less Than 20 Years of Teaching*		
	(a)	*(b)*	*(c)*	*(a)*	*(b)*	*(c)*
Total bonus	78.73	86.75	96.51	108.00*	109.29**	110.52*
	(60.54)	(59.55)	(66.31)	(61.20)	(55.32)	(60.57)
t-statistics	1.30	1.46	1.46	1.77	1.98	1.83
Research	66.30**	75.58**	80.83**	88.35**	88.71**	90.81*
	(32.35)	(30.46)	(39.82)	(34.51)	(36.33)	(48.40)
t-statistics	2.05	2.48	2.03	2.56	2.44	1.88
Teaching	0.09	−2.60	0.03	2.18	1.57	0.69
	(32.66)	(33.27)	(34.09)	(37.56)	(35.79)	(29.59)
t-statistics	0.00	−0.08	0.001	0.06	0.04	0.02

Notes: (a) nearest matching; (b) kernel matching; and (c) hierarchical matching.
Significance levels: *, 10%; **, 5%; and ***, 1%.

Table 11.6 Matching Estimation Results of Teaching Evaluation Scores

		2010			*2011*		
		(a)	*(b)*	*(c)*	*(a)*	*(b)*	*(c)*
	Evaluation score	−1.20*	−1.12	−1.32***	−0.53	0.14	0.15
i		(0.7)	(0.74)	(0.45)	(1.52)	(1.04)	(0.58)
	t-statistics	−1.72	−1.52	−2.93	−0.35	0.14	0.26
	Evaluation score	−1.39	−1.18*	−1.34***	−0.07	0.23	0.12
ii		(0.95)	(0.68)	(0.33)	(1.72)	(1.12)	(0.43)
	t-statistics	−1.45	−1.72	−4.08	−0.04	0.2	0.27
	Evaluation score	−1.34**	−1.14	−1.30***	0.08	0.38	0.26
iii		(0.59)	(0.7)	(0.37)	(0.85)	(1.03)	(0.59)
	t-statistics	−2.26	−1.63	−3.53	0.09	0.37	0.44

Notes: (a) nearest match; (b) kernel matching; and (c) hierarchical matching. (i), (ii) and (iii), respectively use original teaching evaluation scores (including missing values), teaching evaluation scores with average values replacing missing values and teaching evaluation scores predicted by personal characteristics.
Significance levels: *, 10%; **, 5%; and ***, 1%.

Table 11.7 Matching Estimation Results of Time Allocation

	(a)	*(b)*	*(c)*
Total time	3.14	3.52	3.00
	(5.02)	(4.38)	(4.41)
t-statistics	0.63	0.80	0.68
Time for Research	5.64*	6.70***	6.28**
	(3.93)	(2.69)	(3.67)
t-statistics	1.43	2.49	1.71
Time for teaching	−2.50	−3.19	−3.27*
	(3.46)	(3.06)	(2.14)
t-statistics	−0.72	−1.04	−1.53

Notes: (a) Nearest matching; (b) kernel matching; (c) hierarchical matching.
Significance levels: *, 10%; **, 5%; and ***, 1%.

answer to this question. In terms of teaching evaluation scores, male faculty members are even outperformed by their female counterparts. This means that female faculty members actually have more comparative advantages in teaching.

In addition, we have also conducted a survey to collect data on all faculty members' allocation of time to teaching and research. The results further confirm the comparative advantages of male and female faculty members in teaching and research. Table 11.7 shows the matching results of total working time, research time and teaching time of the surveyed male and female faculty members. We find no significant difference between them in total working hours, but male faculty members clearly spend more time on research, while their female counterparts devote more time to teaching. This confirms the comparative advantages of male faculty members in research and female faculty members in teaching.

To sum up, various methods and perspectives have repeatedly demonstrated one fact: as far as the university teaching post is concerned and in comparable terms, male and female faculty members respectively have comparative advantages in research and teaching. This is manifested in the fact that male faculty members devote more time to research, generate more research output and get more research bonus, while female faculty members give more time to teaching and get more teaching bonus and higher teaching evaluation scores. Furthermore, if research is regarded as a kind of innovative and risky work and teaching as repetitive and insurance work, the different comparative advantages between male and female faculty members do show their differences in risk aversion and relative ability.

When I presented the research findings to my students in the classroom, some students also offered other explanations. For example, a male student said that while men are generally believed to be more capable than women, women are nevertheless more patient than men and can stand loneliness, which is good for teaching and research, so it can make up for some of the inherent shortcomings of female faculty members. A female student added that the reason why women seem to be able to endure loneliness is mainly because they have too few choices. Some students questioned my selection of samples, saying that university faulty cannot reflect all men and women in society and that my research conclusion may only be limited to the academic community and cannot be extended to all sectors. These are reasonable doubts, but my statistical results do provide some new evidence for the productivity differentials between men and women and their respective comparative advantages.

11.4 Brief Discussion of Policy Implications

With the development of the market economy, there is growing doubt about the income gap that can be explained by gender discrimination - the income which different individuals get should be more based on their contribution than on gender. Existing research has attempted to explain the source of income differentials between men and women from various angles, but mainly from the perspective of productivity differentials. Due to women's special physiological characteristics, risk aversion attitude, differences in professional choices and comparative advantages, the income gap between men and women may be sustained as a result of the existence of productivity differentials between them. In fact, some scholars have analysed the data of Chinese enterprises and found bigger gender income gaps in more market-oriented private enterprises, which cannot be entirely explained by discrimination. Despite the government's decades of efforts to spread the message that 'women hold half of the sky' and advocate equality between men and women, the above study tells us that policymakers should understand the reality and formulate corresponding policies in line with the principles of productivity and comparative advantage, rather than excessively pursue equality in form and result.

12 Evaluation of Three Recent Policies

12.1 Targeted Policy to Address the Income Gap Issue

Since the reform and opening-up began, the income gap in China has been continuously widening. According to data released by the National Bureau of Statistics, China's Gini coefficient has declined slightly in recent years, indicating an improvement in the situation of income inequality. Despite this, the Gini coefficient in the country still reached 0.465 in 2016, which exceeded the international warning line of 0.4. Some researchers think that China's Gini coefficient has already topped 0.6. As an urgent issue for China to address, the high level of income inequality has received high attention from society, the academic circles and the government alike.

Apart from the normal expansion of the income gap between labourers with different abilities which arise from the development of the market economy, the irrationality of the widening income gap in China is reflected in the following aspects: (1) the income gap between urban and rural areas and between regions remains high; (2) market segmentation and income differentials exist between sectors inside and outside the establishment; (3) there are problems of equalitarianism and insufficient incentives in sectors within the establishment, which are a result of the planned economy; and (4) some monopolistic industries have incomes well above the normal level. All these problems are static short-term inequality problems. However, there are also some problems of dynamic inequality, such as high levels of opportunity inequality, and seriously unfair distribution arising from different wealth bases and contacts rather than labourer competency. In addition, there is a growing trend of wealth inequality, which is far more serious than income inequality. All these are basically related to the system – there are not only various problems of improper primary distribution, but also problems of government misplacement in the process of wealth redistribution.

To address these problems, the National Development and Reform Commission recently issued the *Key Work Arrangements for Deepening the Reform of the Income Distribution System in 2017*, which identified 19 key tasks in four aspects, calling for 'stimulating vitality, expanding scope, promoting fairness, and strengthening the foundation'. Specific opinions

DOI: 10.4324/9781003288091-15

were also put forward on improving primary distribution, intensifying redistribution, creating a favourable income distribution environment and improving the institutional basis of income distribution reform. These opinions are quite pertinent to the current problems of income distribution in China. For example, for the purpose of improving the primary distribution system, the National Development and Reform Commission outlined such measures as perfecting the incentive policy for skilled workers, implementing a distribution policy that can increase the value of knowledge, improving the incentive system for the staff of government organs and public institutions, deepening the salary system and mixed ownership reform of state-owned enterprises and striving to increase the income of farmers. All these measures are conducive to mitigating the internal and external segmentation of the establishment, reducing planning practices that lack incentives in the establishment and narrowing the gap between urban and rural areas. As for intensifying redistribution adjustment, efforts were called to expand the scope of small but low-profit enterprises entitled to preferential corporate income tax, widen the coverage of the unemployment insurance system, strengthen effective connectivity between the rural minimum living security system and poverty alleviation and development policies, promote the development of feature industries, export of labour services, education and poverty alleviation through healthcare. All these measures are helpful for directly improving the wellbeing of low-income groups and reducing the development gap between regions and the unequal development opportunities facing poor groups. As for creating a favourable environment and atmosphere, a call was made to take measures to strengthen equal opportunities for education, continue to implement the current policy of preschool education funding for young children and tuition fee waiver and government grants for high school students from poor families, ensure fair employment opportunities, strengthen public employment services, curb real estate bubbles, crackdown on excessive speculative investment in various assets. These measures are of direct significance for promoting equality of opportunity and fairness of results and reducing the wealth gap. As for strengthening the institutional basis of income distribution system reform, efforts were called to improve the statistics and accounting of income distribution, timely monitor the changes of the size of middle-income groups, establish an income distribution policy evaluation system and formulate through study a master plan for establishing a personal income and property information system. These measures will be directly helpful for furthering income distribution reform.

All the measures above also conform to the spirit of the *Opinions on Implementing Measures to Stimulating the Vitality of Key Groups and Promoting the Income Increase of Urban and Rural Residents* (hereinafter referred to as the 'Implementation Opinions') issued by the State Council. The *Implementation Opinions* called for efforts to target the seven key groups of skilled talents, new professional farmers, researchers, micro and small entrepreneurs, enterprise management personnel, grass-roots cadres and groups in difficulty but with work abilities, and implement targeted incentive schemes, help urban and rural residents to increase their overall incomes and improve income distribution. The specific measures outlined by the National Development and Reform Commission in the *Key Work Arrangements* are the corresponding plans to implement the *Implementation Opinions* of the State Council.

With the gradual implementation of the specific measures outlined in the *Key Work Arrangements*, it is believed that some problems of income distribution in China will be improved upon. The disposable income ratio between urban and rural residents in the country fell from 3.23 in 2010 to 2.73 in 2015. With the expansion of the minimum social security system and the further increase of farmers' incomes, the urban and rural income gap will be reduced further. Various measures to alleviate poverty, promote development and transfer surplus labourers are likely to reduce the income gap between regions. Improved education access and equity will also reduce opportunity inequalities and further narrow the gap between urban and rural areas. The mixed ownership system reform will help break institutional segmentation and establish an effective incentive system within the establishment.

However, some reform fields not covered in the *Key Work Arrangements* are also worth attention. For example, unfair and high profits in the monopolistic sectors need to be addressed. Currently, the high incomes in the monopolistic sectors are an important source of the low share of low-end labourers in the primary distribution of national incomes. As personal income is still highly influenced by family background and social relations, this situation also needs to be improved upon by introducing more normal institutional means to enhance fairness. Widening wealth inequalities require the rollout of a proper tax system reform to adjust wealth distribution. These complementary measures are also vitally important for improving income distribution.

12.2 Appropriate Slowdown of Minimum Wage Adjustment

In recent years, various provinces have continuously raised their minimum wages, with high wage hikes in high-income provinces. These adjustments basically comply with the *Provisions on Minimum Wage* issued as Order No. 21 of the Ministry of Labour and Social Security of the People's Republic of China in 2004. China's first minimum wage standard for enterprises was issued by the Ministry of Labour in 1993. At the time, only general principles were set forth, and even so, the general principles were not strictly implemented. The *Provisions on Minimum Wage* of 2004 are relatively specific and implemented more strictly. Article 6 of the *Provisions on Minimum Wage* stipulates that

> The monthly minimum wage standard should be set with reference to the minimum living expenses of local employees and their dependents, urban resident consumption price index, social insurance premiums and housing provident fund paid by employees, average wages of employees, local level of economic development, status of employment, and other factors.

This is in line with the characteristics of the relatively high minimum wage standards in rich provinces. For example, Shanghai implements a monthly minimum wage standard of RMB2,190, which is RMB920 higher than that in Qinghai. Meanwhile, Article 10 of the *Provisions on Minimum Wage* stipulates that 'After its release for implementation, the minimum wage standard shall be duly adjusted if the relevant factors specified in Article 6 of these Provisions have changed. The minimum wage standard shall be adjusted at least once every 2 years'. The requirement of at least one adjustment every two years has led to frequent adjustment of the minimum wage standard in various provinces. For example, 28 regions in China raised their minimum wages in 2015.

There are many academic studies on the impact of minimum wage on the labour market. Most studies have found a negative impact on employment because enterprises will reduce the demand for low-productive workers who otherwise must be paid no less than the minimum wage. Such reduced demand is especially obvious for the 'risk groups (i.e. women, young workers and old-age workers)'. If there exist irregular labour markets, those labourers squeezed out of the regular market will enter the irregular labour markets, which may further reduce wages. In addition, the minimum wage is divided into two types: minimum monthly wage and minimum hourly wage. For people who do flexible jobs, raising the minimum hourly wage standard will also reduce the number of their working hours. In some cases, an increase in minimum wage may have little impact on employment. For example, when the minimum wage is much lower than the wage level in the labour market, it will not affect employment or actual wages in the market. Besides, some measures taken by enterprises to cope with the raised minimum wage also reduce the impact of minimum wage sometimes. For example, when the minimum wage is raised, enterprises do not have to dismiss employees. Instead, they can use their power in the market to adjust product price and shift the pressure of rising cost to others; adjust wage distribution by reducing the magnitude and speed of pay rises for high-income employees; offset rising wages by encouraging employees to work harder and more efficiently; increase wages and reduce welfare benefits to offset increased cost due to rising minimum wage or reduce overtime hours and overtime pay. To a certain extent, these flexible adjustment mechanisms enable enterprises to cope with changes in the minimum wage standard.

Raising the minimum wage standard can have a positive impact only in a few situations, such as when enterprises have the power of monopoly in the job market and workers' bargaining power is too weak. In these circumstances, minimum wage can prevent excessive exploitation and even increase employment, because existing enterprises will reduce pay by threatening workers with reduced employment and increased unemployment.

Currently, the labour supply in China remains big. In relative terms, the buyer's force is strong in the labour market. Consequently, there is certain rationality for setting a minimum wage standard and implementing it. Moreover, the ratio between the minimum wage and local average wage in China is still fairly low when compared with that in developed countries. So, the groups affected by the minimum wage system will be limited, and its negative impact on the labour market will not be very significant. However, as the labour market is well regulated and the minimum wage system is better implemented, the adjustment of minimum wage should slow down in the long run. The reasons are mainly as follows:

First, the decline of economic growth rate. Forcing localities to frequently adjust their minimum wage standard will bring more burdens to enterprises, further dragging down their investment and causing economic slowdown. Past experience shows that local governments seldom adjust their minimum wage standard by less than 10% each time. There is even an average adjustment of nearly 20%. If wage adjustment continues at this rate at least once every two years, the minimum wage will soon exceed enterprises' affordability to pay minimum-income groups.

Second, the trend of population ageing in China. Currently, the Chinese labour force is ageing fast, and the government is also formulating an age table for postponed retirement, which means that more elderly people will remain in or return to the labour market and the supply of labour will be rising. This naturally requires the labour market to reduce wages in a balanced way. However, the minimum wage may be an obstacle to this spontaneous adjustment process of the market.

Third, the present situation of urbanization in China. There is now a drastic fall in the speed at which migrant workers enter cities and the proportion of young and middle-aged migrant workers is also declining. Against the background of a low urbanization ratio and the need for higher urbanization, a large number of elderly or female migrant workers will continue to enter towns and cities, which will increase the size of 'risk groups'. Slowing down the adjustment of the minimum wage standard will help to increase the demand for these groups and better coordinate the future urbanization process.

There is a relatively big income gap in China's labour market, and the number of low-income people who may be affected by the minimum wage can be quite considerable. When all these factors are considered, it will be wise to appropriately slow down the adjustment of minimum wage.

To slow down the adjustment of the minimum wage, the first step is to change the regulations. The requirement of adjusting the minimum wage at least once every two years as set forth in the *Provisions on Minimum Wage* should be changed to allow a longer time span of adjustment or free and flexible adjustment by localities. Most fundamentally, the government should improve the employment ability and skills of low-end labourers and provide training to enhance their ability to get income in the market through training. By all analyses, the minimum wage is not the best way to raise the income of low-income groups or compensate for low-income people.

Postscript

This book has summarized the progress and issues of China's Hukou system reform, family planning policy and their impacts, as well as several issues related to the labour market. Presented under similar topics, these contents bring together the research results that the author has obtained over the years. Due to limited publication space, I have deleted more than one-third of the content. These deleted contents cover studies on the impact of the Hukou system on labour mobility and employment of university graduates and discussions of specific policies. Also due to limited space, I have not included in this book the Hukou liberalization panel data, which we have compiled for more than 200 prefecture-level cities in China. In recent years, the issue of urban Hukou liberalization has become less and less important, and the most important issue is how to overcome the difficulty of gradually opening up rural resources to the outside. It is regrettable that no discussion of these issues has been included in this book.

Currently, large cities are the key field of Hukou system reform in China. The task of Hukou system reform at the next step is to relax Hukou restrictions in large cities and decouple Hukou status from basic social welfare. Similarly, the current adoption of a universal second-child policy is a move to cope with the growing pressure of population ageing and the declining fertility rate in the country. However, due to a huge population base, family planning will remain a long-term national policy for China. As a result, more careful consideration is needed for rolling out more radical policies, such as subsidies for the second child, so as to avoid things from going to the other extreme. As reform gradually deepens, the income premiums arising from gender, the establishment and other factors have decreased significantly. It is very important to understand the causes of the income gap, such as getting to know the rational elements of gender wage differentials. Otherwise, a good intention may result in a bad outcome.

I personally believe that there are still many issues calling for reform in China's labour market. Currently, there is still room for further studies on these issues. I also very much hope that the Chinese government will take academic research findings more into account when it formulates policies.

References

Chinese literature

Cai Fang, Citizenisation of Rural Migrant Workers and Development of New Consumers, *Journal of Graduate School of Chinese Academy of Social Sciences*, 2: 5–11, 2011. (in Chinese).

Chen Binkai, Lu Ming and Zhong Ninghua, Household Consumption under Hukou Restriction, *Economic Research Journal*, (supplement): 62–71, 2010. (in Chinese).

Chen Shiping and Le guo'an, A Research on Urban Residents' Life Satisfaction and Its Related Factors, *Journal of Psychological Science*, Issue 6: 664–666, 765, 2001. (in Chinese).

Chen Zhao and Lu Ming, From Segmentation to Integration: The Political Economy of Urban-Rural Economic Growth and Social Harmony, *Economic Research Journal*, Issue 1: 21–32, 2008. (in Chinese).

Deng Kebin and Ding Juhong, Household Registration, Economy Growth and Income Disparity, *ZHIDU JINGJIXUE YAN JIU*, Issue 1: 44–67, 2010. (in Chinese).

Dong Wei, Blue Book on Chinese Society: New Trends of Difficult Employment for University Graduates, *Employment and Security*, Issue 1 (supplement 1): 19–20, 2013. (in Chinese).

Feng Xiaotian, The Socialisation Process of Only Children and Its Outcome, *Social Sciences in China*, Issue 6: 118–131, 208, 2000. (in Chinese).

Feng Xiaotian, A Study of China's Only Child: Retrospect and Prediction, *Jianghai Academic Journal*, Issue 5: 90–99, 207, 2002. (in Chinese).

Feng Xiaotian, The Construction and Demonstration of the Only Child's Negative Image in Media, *Sociological Studies*, Issue 3: 177–198, 24–246, 2010. (in Chinese).

Gao Wenli, A Survey on the Health, Learning and Living Situations of Only Children, *Population Journal*, Issue 6: 40–44, 1992. (in Chinese).

Hou Li, Breakthrough and New Projects for Reform of Household Registration System, *Population Journal*, Issue 6: 22–29, 2014. (in Chinese).

Lai Desheng, Why Is It Difficult for University Graduates to Get Jobs? *QIUSHI*, Issue 20: 22–24, 2013. (in Chinese).

Li Honbin, Meng Lingsheng, Shi Xinzheng and Wu Binzhen, How Does Parents' Political Capital Affect University Graduates' Performance in the Labour Market? Empirical Research Based on an Employment Survey of Chinese University Graduates, *China Economic Quarterly*, Issue 3: 1011–1026, 2012. (in Chinese).

Li Shi, The Status of the Floating Population in China's Labour Market, *Studies in Labour Economics*, Issue 1: 51–68, 2013. (in Chinese).

Liu Jinwei, The Level of Urban Hukou Liberalisation in China and Its Influencing Factors – An Evaluation of 63 Sample Cities, *Journal of Chinese Academy of Governance*, Issue 5: 91–95, 143–144, 2016. (in Chinese).

Liu Xiaofeng, Xhen Zhao and Lu Ming, Social Integration and Economic Growth: Endogenous Policy Transition in Urbanisation and Urban Development, *Journal of World Economy*, Issue 6: 60–80, 2010. (in Chinese).

Lu Yilong, Structure and Change: The Household Registration System in China after 1949, *Journal of Peking University (Humanities and Social Sciences)*, Issue 3: 123–130, 2002. (in Chinese).

Ma Guangrong and Zhou Guangsu, The Impacts of New Rural Pension Program on Household Saving: Evidence from CFPS, *Economic Research Journal*, Issue 11: 116–129, 2014. (in Chinese).

Qu Xiaobo and Cheng Jie, Association of Regional Differences, the Advance of Urbanisation and Household Registration Reform Cost, *Reform*, Issue 3: 37–44, 2013. (in Chinese).

Research Team of the State Council Development Research Center, The Impact of Citizenisation of the Floating Population on Stimulating Domestic Demand and Economic Growth, *Economic Research Journal*, Issue 6: 4–16, 41, 2010. (in Chinese).

Shi Yaojiang and Cui Yu, Citizens's View on Fairness and Its Influence on Assessment to Social Fairness and Living Satisfaction, *Management World,* Issue 10: 39–49, 2006. (in Chinese).

Sun Wenkai and Bai Chongen, Income Fluctuation and Influential Factors on Farmer' Consumption, *Journal of Tsinghua University (Philosophy and Social Sciences)*, Issue 6: 133–138, 158, 2008. (in Chinese).

Sun Wenkai, Bai Chongen and Xie Peichu, The Effect on Rural *Labour* Mobility from Registration System Reform in China. *Economic Research Journal*, Issue 1: 28–41, 2011. (in Chinese).

Sun Wenkai, Lu Jiangyong and Bai Chongen, An Analysis of Income Mobility in Rural China, *Economic Research Journal*, Issue 8: 43–57, 2007. (in Chinese).

Sun Wenkai, Song Yang and Wang Xianghong, *Labour Economics*, Beijing: Tsinghua University Press, 2015. (in Chinese).

Sun Wenkai, Sun Ang and Wang Yijie, Does Family Planning Harm Entrepreneurship in China? *Journal of Economic Literature*, Issue 2: 138–160, 2016.

Sun Wenkai, Wang Jing and Li Hong, Wage Premiums in the Establishment and the Development of Market Economy – An Empirical Analysis Based on CGSS Data, *Studies in Labour Economics*, Issue 4: 73–97, 2016. (in Chinese).

Sun Wenkai and Wang Yijie, Re-examining the Effect of Hukou Change on Migration Household Consumption – Evidence from Micro Tracking Data, *Economic Research Journal*: 68–100, 2016. Working Paper WP1131. (in Chinese).

Tan Qinggang, Institutional Unemployment and the Difficulties in the Employment of Chinese College Graduates, *Population & Economics*, Issue 1: 22–26, 2011. (in Chinese).

Wan Haiyuan and Li Shi, The Effects of Household Registration System Discrimination on Urban-Rural Income Inequality in China, *Economic Research Journal*, Issue 9: 43–55, 2013. (in Chinese).

Wang Dewen, Cai Fang and Zhang Guoqing, Employment and Wage Determinants of Rural Migrant Workers: Importance of Education and Training, *China Economic Quarterly*, 7(4), 1131–1148, 2008. (in Chinese).

Wang Meiyan, Employment Opportunities and Wage Gaps in the Urban *Labour* Market: A Study of the Employment and Wages of Migrant *Labour*ers, *Social Sciences in China*, Issue 5: 36–46, 205, 2005a. (in Chinese).

Wang Meiyan, Gender Wage Differentials in China's Urban *Labour* Market, *Economic Research Journal*, Issue 12: 35–44, 2005b. (in Chinese).

Wang Meiyan and Cai Fang, The Experiences and Perspectives of China's Household Registration System, *Social Sciences in Guangdong*, Issue 6: 19–26, 2008. (in Chinese).

Wang Tingli, Liu Yanxi and Rao Yu, A Brief Analysis of Influencing Factors on Difficult Employment of Female Graduates of Independent Colleges, *Theory Research*, Issue 35: 65–66, 2012. (in Chinese).

Wang Xiaolu, Urbanisation and Economic Growth, *Comparative Economic & Social Systems*, 2002, Issue 1: 23–32. (in Chinese).

Wu Kaiya and Zhang Li, Developmentalist Government and Urban Hukou Threshold: Rethinking Hukou System Reform, *Sociological Studies*, 2010, Issue 6: 58–85, 243. (in Chinese).

Xia Jijun, Population Mobility, Public Revenue and Expenditure--Analysis of the Evolution of Huji System, *Economic Research Journal*, 2004, Issue 10: 56–65. (in Chinese).

Xing Chunbing, On the Wage Determination System in State Owned–, Collective Owned, and Private Sectors: 1989–1997, *Economic Research Journal*, 2005, Issue 6: 16–26. (in Chinese).

Yao Yuqun and Peng Sizhou, An Overview on Chinese College Students' Difficult Employment, *Population & Economics*, 2008, Issue 3: 36–40. (in Chinese).

Yin Zhichao and Gan Li, Wage Differentials between Public and Nonpublic Sector in China, *Economic Research Journal*, 2009, Issue 4: 129–140. (in Chinese).

Yuan Gang, Nature, History of Household Registration and Reform of System of Household Registration in Our Country, *Tribune of Study*, 2008, Issue 5: 71–75. (in Chinese).

Zhang Juwei and Xue Xinxin, State and Non-state Sector Wage Differentials and Human Capital Contribution, *Economic Research Journal*, 2008, Issue 4: 15–25, 65. (in Chinese).

Zhang Li and Wu Kaiya, An Analysis of Local Public Fiscal Pressure of Free Hukou Settlement in Cities, *Chinese Journal of Population Science*, 2013, Issue 12: 17–26, 126. (in Chinese).

Zhang Xun, Liu Xiaoguang and Fan Gang, Rural *Labour* Migration and Household Saving Rate: The Perspective of Discrepancy in Income and Social Security, *Economic Research Journal*, 2014, Issue 4:130–142. (in Chinese).

Zhang Yibo, The Change of Income Differentials between Public and Nonpublic Sector in China, *Economic Research Journal*, 2012, Issue 4: 77–88. (in Chinese).

Zheng Gongcheng, Employment Difficulties of University Graduates and Policy Options of the Government, *China Labour*, 2006, Issue 4: 17–19. (in Chinese).

Zhou Delu, The Influence of the Property of Single Child on the Growth and Future Development of University Students, *Dongyue Tribune*, 2009, Issue 9: 128–132. (in Chinese).

Zhu Tian and Zhang Jun, How Much Is China's Consumption Rate Underestimated? *China Journal of Economics*, 2014, Issue 2: 42–67. (in Chinese).
Zou Yinan, The Endogenous Logic and Policy Options of Hukou System Reform, *Economist*, 2015, Issue 4: 48–53. (in Chinese).

English literature

Adamchik, V. A. and A. S. Bedi, Wage Differentials between the Public and the Private Sectors: Evidence from An Economy in Transition, *Labour Economics*, 2000, 7(2): 203–224.
Andreoni, J., Impure Altruism and Donations to Public Goods: A Theory of Warm-Glow Giving, *Economic Journal*, 1990, 100(401): 464–477.
Antman, F. M. G., *Migration and the Mexican Family: Exploring the Consequences for Those Left Behind*, Palo Alto, California: Stanford University, 2007.
Au, Chun-Chung and J. Vernon Henderson, Are Chinese Cities Too Small? *Review of Economic Studies*, 2006, 73(3): 549–576.
Audretsch, D. B., and Keilbach, M., Entrepreneurship Capital and Economic Performance, *Regional Studies*, 2004, 38:949–959.
Baker, M., Emily, H., and Jasmin, K., The Married Widow: Marriage Penalties Matter! *Journal of the European Economic Association*, 2004, 2(4): 634–664.
Bales, S. and M. Rama, Are Public Sector Workers Underpaid? Appropriate Comparators in A Developing Country, *World Bank Policy Research Working Paper*, 2001, 2747, 39.
Barro, R. J., Are Government Bonds Net Wealth? *Journal of Political Economy*, 1974, 82(6): 1095–1117.
Becker, Gary S., A Theory of Marriage: Part I, *The Journal of Political Economy*, 1973, 81(4): 813–846.
Becker, Gary S., A Theory of Marriage: Part II, *The Journal of Political Economy*, 1974a, 82(2): 11–26.
Becker, Gary S., A Theory of Social Interactions, *Journal of Political Economy*, 1974b, 82:1063–1093.
Becker, Gary S., *A Treatise on the Family*, Cambridge, MA: Harvard University Press, 1981.
Becker, Gary S., and Nigel Tomes, Child Endowments and the Quantity and Quality of Children, *Journal of Political Economy*, 1976, 84(4): 143–162.
Becker, S. O., and Ichino, A., Estimation of Average Treatment Effects Based on Propensity Scores, *Stata Journal*, 2002, 2(4): 358–377.
Behrman, J. R., Pollak, R. A., and Taubman, P., Parental Preferences and Provision for Progeny, *Journal of Political Economy*, 1982, 90: 52–73.
Bergstrom, T., Blume, L., and Varian, H., On the Private Provision of Public Goods, *Journal of Public Economics*, 1986, 29(1): 25–49.
Bernheim, B. D., Shleifer, A., and Summers, L. H., The Strategic Bequest Motive, *Journal of Political Economy*, 1985, 93(6): 151–182.
Bertrand, M., Kamenica, E., and Pan, J., *Gender Identity and Relative Income Within Households* [R/OL], Retrieved December 2012 from http://faculty.chicagobooth.edu/emir.kamenica/documents/identity.pdf
Birch, E. R., The Public-Private Sector Earnings Gap in Australia: A Quantile Regression Approach, *Australian Journal of Labour Economics*, 2006, 9(2): 99–123.

Bitler, Marianne P., et al., The Impact of Welfare Reform on Marriage and Divorce. *Demography*, 2004, 41(2): 213–236.

Blinder, A. S., Wage Discrimination: Reduced form and Structural Variables, *Journal of Human Resources*, 1973, 8(4): 436–455.

Bogue, D. J., *Internal Migration*, Chicago: University of Chicago Press, 1959.

Bohannon, E. W., A Study of Peculiar and Exceptional Children, *The Pedagogical Seminary*, 1896, 4(1): 3–60.

Bongaarts, John, and Susan Greenhalgh. An Alternative to the One-Child Policy in China, *Population and Development Review*, 1985, 11(4): 585–617.

Borenstein, S. and Courant, P.N., How to Carve A Medical Degree: Human Capital Assets in Divorce Settlements, *American Economic Review*, 1989, 79: 992–1009.

Cai, Linxin and Amy Y. C. Liu, Public-Private Sector Wage Gap in Australia: Variation along the Distribution, *British Journal of Industrial Relations*, 2011, 49(2): 362–390.

Cameron, L., Erkal, N., Gangadharan, L., and Meng, X. Little Emperors: Behavioral Impacts of China's One-Child Policy, *Science*, 2013, 339(6122): 953–957.

Canay, I. A., A Simple Approach to Quantile Regression for Panel Data, *Econometrics Journal*, 2011, 14(3): 368–386.

Chen, B., Lu, M. and Zhong, N., How Urban Segregation Distorts Chinese Migrants' Consumption? *World Development*, 2015, 70: 133–146.

Chen, F., and Short, S. E., Household Context and Subjective Well-being among the Oldest Old in China, *Journal of Family Issues*, 2008, 29: 1379–1403.

Chiappori, Pierre-André, Sonia Oreffice, and Climent Quintana-Domeque, *Match with a Handicap: The Case of Smoking in the Marriage Market*, No. 5392. Discussion paper series//Forschungsinstitut zur Zukunft der Arbeit, 2010.

Choukhmane, T., Coeurdacier, N., and Jin, K., The One-Child Policy and Household Savings. London School of Economics, *Working Paper*, 2013, 59.

Chyi, H., and Mao, S., The Determinants of Happiness of China's Elderly Population, *Journal of Happiness Studies*, 2012, 13: 167–185.

Dehejia, R., Practical Propensity Score Match: A Reply to Smith and Todd, *Journal of Econometrics*, 2005, 125(1): 355–364.

Deng, Q. and Li, S., What Lies Behind Rising Earnings Inequality in Urban China? Regression-based decompositions, *CESifo Economic Studies*, 2009, 55(3): 598–623.

Djankov, S., Qian, Y., Roland, G. and Zhuravskaya, E., Who are China's Entrepreneurs? *American Economic Review*, 2006, 96(2): 348–352

Duflo, Esther, Grandmothers and Granddaughters: Old-Age Pensions and Intrahousehold Allocation in South Africa, *The World Bank Economic Review*, 2003, 17(1): 1–25.

Dutton, M., *Policing and Punishment in China: From Patriarchy to the People*, Cambridge: Cambridge University Press, 1992.

Dyer, D. T., Are Only Children Different? *Journal of Educational Psychology*, 1945, 36(5): 297–302.

Ebenstein, A., The Missing Girls of China and the Unintended Consequences of the One-Child Policy, *Journal of Human Resources*, 2010, 45(1): 87–115.

Edlund, L., Li, H., Yi, J. and Zhang J., Sex Ratios and Crime: Evidence from China, *Review of Economics and Statistics*, 2013, 95(5): 1520–1543.

Eeckhout, J., R. Pinheiro, and K. Schmidheiny, Spatial Sorting, *Journal of Political Economy*, 2014, 122(3): 554–620.

Emsley, R., Lunt, M., Pickles, A. and Dunn, G., Implementing Double-robust Estimators of Causal Effects, *Stata Journal*, 2008, 8(3): 334–353.

Falbo, T., *The Single-Child Family*, New York: Guilford Press, 1984.

Falbo, T. and Polit, D. F., Quantitative Review of the Only Child Literature: Research Evidence and Theory Development, *Psychological Bulletin*, 1986, 100(2): 176–189.

Feldstein, M., Social Security Induced Retirement and Aggregate Capital Accumulation, *Journal of Political Economy*, 1974, 82(5): 905–926.

Fenton, N., The Only Child, *The Pedagogical Seminary and Journal of Genetic Psychology*, 1928, 35(4): 546–556.

Fields, G. S., Labour Market Policy in Developing Countries: A Selective Review of the Literature and Needs for the Future, *International Policy Center Working Paper Series*, 2007, 32, 79.

Fleisher, Belton M. and Dennis T. Yang, Labour Laws and Regulations in China, *China Economic Review*, 2003, 14: 426–433.

Giles, J., Park, A. and Zhang, J., What is China's True Unemployment Rate? *China Economic Review*, 2005, 16(2): 149–170.

Gould, E. D., Cities, Workers and Wages: A Structural Analysis of the Urban Wage Premium, *Review of Economic Studies*, 2007, 74(2): 477–506.

Greenhalgh, Susan, Shifts in China's Population Policy, 1984–86: Views from the Central, Provincial, and Local Levels. *Population and Development Review*, 1986, 12(3): 491–515.

Greenhalgh, Susan, Zhu Chuzhu, and Li Nan, Restraining Population Growth in Three Chinese Villages, 1988–93, *Population and Development Review*, 1994, 20(2): 365–395.

Gu, B., Wang, F., Guo, Z. and Zhang, E., China's Local and National Fertility Policies at the End of the Twentieth Century, *Population and Development Review*, 2007, 3(1): 129–148.

Gyourko, J. and J. Tracy, An Analysis of Public- and Private-Sector Wages Allowing for Endogenous Choices of Both Government and Union Status, *Journal of Labour Economics*, 1988, 6(2): 229–253.

Heckman, J. J., Sample Selection Bias as a Specification Error. *Econometrica*, 1979, 47(1): 153–162.

Heinrich, Carolyn, A. Maffioli and G. Vazquez, A Primer for Applying Propensity-Score Match, *Technical Notes*, Inter-American Development Bank, 2010, No. IDB-TN-161, 59.

Heitmueller, A., Public-Private Sector Pay Differentials in a Devolved Scotland, *Journal of Applied Economics*, 2006, 9(2): 295–323.

Heywood, J. S., Wei, X., and Ye, G., Piece Rates for Professors, *Economics Letters*, 2011, 113:285–287.

Hooker, H. F., A Study of the Only Child at School, *The Pedagogical Seminary and Journal of Genetic Psychology*, 1931, 39(1): 122–126

Horioka, C. Y., Fujisaki, H., Watanabe, W., and Kouno, T., Are Americans More Altruistic Than the Japanese? A US-Japan Comparison of Saving and Bequest Motives, *International Economic Journal*, 2000, 14(1): 1–31.

Ichino, A., and Moretti, E., Biological Gender Differences, Absenteeism, and the Earnings Gap. *American Economics Journal: Applied Economics*, 2009, 1(1): 183–218.

Jacobs, J., *The Economy of Cities*, New York: Vintage Books, 1969.

Koenker, R. and G. Bassett, Regression Quantiles, *Econometrica*, 1978, 46(1): 33–50.

Krueger, A. B. Are Public Sector Workers Paid More Than Their Alternative Wage? Evidence from Longitudinal Data and Job Queues, *NBER Working Paper*, 1988, 2500, 27.

Lam, David, Marriage Markets and Assortative Mating with Household Public Goods: Theoretical Results and Empirical Implications. *Journal of Human Resources*, 1988, 23(4): 462–487.

Lee, S. Y., Florida, R., and Acs, Z. J., Creativity and Entrepreneurship: A Regional Analysis of New Firm Formation, *Regional Studies*, 2004, 38(8): 879–891.

Li, H., Liu, P. W., Zhang, J., and Ma, N., Economic Returns to Communist Party Membership: Evidence from Urban Chinese Twins. *The Economic Journal*, 2007, 117:1504–1520.

Li, L., and Wu, X., Housing Price and Entrepreneurship in China, *Journal of Comparative Economics*, 2014, 42(2): 436–449.

Li, H., Yang, Z., Yao, X., Zhang, H. and Zhang, J., Entrepreneurship, Private Economy and Growth: Evidence from China, *China Economic Review*, 2012, 23(4): 948–961.

Link, A. N., Swann, C. A., and Bozeman, B., A Time Allocation Study of University Faculty, *Economics of Education Review*, 2008, 27(4): 363–374.

Lucas, R. E., and Stark, O., Motivations to Remit: Evidence from Botswana. *The Journal of Political Economy*, 1985, 93(5): 901–918.

Martin, L. G., and Tsuya, N. O., Interactions of Middle-Aged Japanese with Their Parents, *Population Studies*, 1991, 45:299–311.

Medeiros, M., Osório, R. G., and Costa, J. Gender Inequalities in Allocating Time to Paid and Unpaid Work: Evidence from Bolivia. Bard College, *Working Paper*, 2007, No. 495, 17.

Meng X., *Labour Market Reform in China*, Cambridge: Cambridge University Press, 2000.

Modigliani, F., and Brumberg, R., Utility Analysis and the Consumption Function: An Interpretation of Cross-section Data, In: Kurihara, K. K., Ed., *Post-Keynesian Economics*, New Brunswick: Rutgers University Press, 1954, 388–436.

Mueller, R. E., Public-Private Sector Wage Differentials in Canada: Evidence from Quantile Regression, *Economics Letters*, 1998, 60(2): 229–235.

Oaxaca, R., Male-Female Wage Differentials in Urban Labour Markets, *International Economic Review*, 1973, 14:693–709.

Oh, S. S., and Lewis, G. B., Stemming Inequality? Employment and Pay of Female and Minority Scientists and Engineers, *Social Science Journal*, 2011, 48(2): 397–403.

O'Keefe, S., and Wang, T-C., Publishing Pays: Economists' Salaries Reflect Productivity, *Social Science Journal*, 2012, 50(1): 45–54.

Pedersen, P. J. et al., Wage Differentials between the Public and Private Sectors, *Journal of Public Economics*, 1990, 41:125–145.

Polit, D. F. and Falbo, T., Only Children and Personality Development: A Quantitative Review, *Journal of Marriage and Family*, 1987, 49(2): 309–325.

Powell, D., *Quantile Regression with Non-additive Fixed Effects* [R/OL], 2016. http://works.bepress.com/david_powell/1/.

Ramsden, P., Describing and Explaining Research Productivity, *Higher Education*, 1994, 28(2): 207–226.

Roberts, Kenneth D., The Determinants of Job Choice by Rural Labour Migrants in Shanghai, *China Economic Review*, 2001, 12: 15–39.

Rosenzweig, Mark R. and Oded Stark, Consumption Smoothing, Migration, and Marriage: Evidence from Rural India, *Journal of Political Economy*, 1989, 97(4): 905–926.

Sakudo, M., *Strategic Interactions between Parents and Daughters: Co-residence, Marriage, and Intergenerational Transfers in Japan* [D], Chicago: Department of Economics, University of Chicago, 2007.

Saygin, P. O., *Gender Differences in College Applications: Evidence from the Centralized System in Turkey* [R/OL]. Retrieved December 2012 from https://ub-madoc.bib.uni-mannheim.de/32599/1/Saygin_12-21.pdf.

Scharping, *Thomas. Birth Control in China 1949–2000*, New York: Routledge, 2003.

Schumpeter, Curzon, *The Theory of Economic Development*, Cambridge, MA: Harvard University Press, 1934.

Sheehan, B. A., and Welch, A. R. The Australian Academic Profession, In: P. G. Altbach (Ed.), *The International Academic Profession: Portraits from Fourteen Countries*, Princeton: Carnegie Foundation for the Advancement of Teaching. 1996, 51–94.

Smith, Sharon P., Pay Differentials between Federal Government and Private Sector Workers, *Industrial and Labour Relations Review*, 1976, 29(2): 179–197.

Song, L., Wu, J. and Zhang, Y., Urbanization of Migrant Workers and Expansion of Domestic Demand, *Social Sciences in China*, 2010, 31(3): 194–216.

Sun, W. and Wang, X., Do Relative Income and Income Inequality Affect Consumption? Evidence from the Villages of Rural China, *The Journal of Development Studies*, 2013, 49(4): 533–546.

Teodorescu, D., Correlates of Faculty Publication Productivity: A Cross-National Analysis, *Higher Education*, 2000, 39(2): 201–222.

Thomas, Duncan, Intra-household Resource Allocation: An Inferential Approach, *Journal of Human Resources*, 1990, 25(4): 635–664.

Tsuya, N. O., and Martin, L. G., Living Arrangements of Elderly Japanese and Attitudes toward Inheritance, *Journal of Gerontology*, 1992, 47(2): 45–54.

Wakabayashi, M., and Horioka, C. Y., Is the Eldest Son Different? The Residential Choice of Siblings in Japan, *Japan and the World Economy*, 2006, 21(4): 337–348.

Wei, S. and Zhang, X., The Competitive Saving Motive: Evidence from Rising Sex Ratios and Savings Rates in China, *Journal of Political Economy*, 2011a, 119(3): 511–564.

Wei, S., and Zhang, X., Sex Ratios, Entrepreneurship, and Economic Growth in the People's Republic of China, *NBER Working Paper*, 2011b, 16800.

Xie, Y and Wu, X., Danwei Profitability and Earnings Inequality in Urban China, *The China Quarterly*, 2008, 195(1): 558–581.

Yelowitz, Aaron, Will Extending Medicaid to Two Parent Families Encourage Marriage? *The Journal of Human Resources*, 1998, 33(4): 833–865.

Ziegler, Regina G., William F. Anderson, and Mitchell H. Gail, Increasing Breast Cancer Incidence in China: The Numbers Add Up, *Journal of the National Cancer Institute*, 2008, 100(19): 1339–1341.

Index

H

I

J

K

L

For Product Safety Concerns and Information please contact our EU representative GPSR@taylorandfrancis.com
Taylor & Francis Verlag GmbH, Kaufingerstraße 24, 80331 München, Germany

www.ingramcontent.com/pod-product-compliance
Lightning Source LLC
LaVergne TN
LVHW021125300926
849160LV00010B/871

* 9 7 8 1 0 3 2 2 6 3 9 1 5 *